REVIEWS FOR

Making of a Godly Warrior:

Scott focuses on his real-life experiences and how God uses those day-to-day life moments to teach him profound spiritual lessons. There is something in this book for all believers who know there is something missing in their relationship with God; but cannot put their finger on it. The author has a real knack for fleshing out the non-essentials and bringing laser focus on the things that really matter in our walk with God.

~ **Randy J. Harris**, Assistant Vice President/Treasury.

***

Scott's spiritual journey and the building of his relationship with the one true God is one that any man or woman can relate to. This book is a compelling revelation of what God can do to transform our human and sinful nature into a life that is spiritually deep, rich, and abundant through obedience to God's Word. Scott provides a practical approach on how to execute that obedience and thus have a deeper and more meaningful relationship with our Lord and Savior – Jesus Christ. The personal examples and revelations that the Lord imparted to Scott through people, places and circumstances shows us that our Lord meets us right where we are, and teaches us what we can do to follow him and have a more intimate relationship with him. I pray the Lord will use this book to lead many souls to Christ and I thank God for Scott's perseverance and discipline in completing this work.

~ **Nancy A. Cline**, Senior Human Resources Leader.

***

Many books teach the reader what must be done (devotions, etc.) but this is a life changing book which teaches the reader **how to engage the heart** through proof of God performing specific verses in His Word when the author obeys His commands. This is the story of a quest to know God and how He engages those who pursue Him. True personal stories reveal the truth of God's Word, the importance of understanding it, and the spiritual progress accomplished by *actually doing it*. This is no ordinary book; it proves through direct interaction with God *how* sanctification is accomplished.

~ **Pastor David Mcintosh,** Christian Assembly Berkshires, MA.

***

The *Making of Godly Warrior* highlights the daily lessons learned in God's "spiritual boot camp". In an otherwise non-transparent world, Harris takes off his mask and reveals the good, the bad, and the ugly associated with walking in obedience to the word of God. He gains spiritual understanding while being misunderstood. He willingly embraces the seeming restrictive commands of God and experiences the liberation that only obedience provides. On the Potter's wheel he remains, being shaped, and fashioned into the man he is called to be. In these pages, an effective, transformative tension is introduced. Allow yourself to be wooed into a deeper affection for, and obedience to, the word of God. Experientially know, that faith and wisdom travel the same road together as do love, grace and obedience. Take from these pages that which will further shape you into the warrior God is calling you to be and shore up those pillars of truth keeping you victorious in Christ.

~ **Dr. Gary Hewins, Pastor**, *Community Bible Church. Highlands, NC.*

***

On a group tour in Israel, my husband and I, attached ourselves to Scott and his wife Gigi. We liked them! I got to get to know this friendly man's intense Bostonian personality. I could see how God has gentled him. In his first book, Scott tells how God was willing to hear his bold challenge to "Show me what to do and I'll do it."

Scott Harris is evidence that God will take an honest challenge! Proving change in life is possible no matter how late we ask, Scott was willing to do whatever He said. Scott precisely records each step of what he heard from the Lord on disciplines to practice, confirmed in the living Word and by his response of obedience. He wants others to be able to discover God is faithful to change and use us if we are serious to follow His ways. I found his testimony easy to read; it piqued my curiosity and stimulated questions from within. This book is just the beginning for Scott; I am counting on more discoveries by this warrior.

~ **Christia Ashmore**, *Global Media Outreach Missionary*

***

I had a vision of Scott waking up from a deep, deep sleep. I saw my husband stretch his left arm, then his right, take a long deep breath as he rubbed his eyes, and, in a flash, he took off like a bullet.

A man on a mission, he was running hard after the truth of who God is and asked Him, "Tell me what to do and I'll do it." He had found what he had been missing all his life. Scott scheduled his priorities as one who searches and chases God with all his might. I watched the death of the man I had married and saw a Christ like man unfold in front of my eyes.

I witnessed the transformation of the man Scott was in the past to the man he is today. I am the primary beneficiary of the results of his relentless obedience and devotions to God the Father, Jesus Christ His Son, and the guidance of the Holy Spirit. We are now reaping the rewards and favor of God available to those who diligently seek Him.

~ **Gigi Harris**, Intercessory Prayer Warrior. Scott's wife.

The Making of a Godly Warrior:

Through Relentless Obedience

SCOTT A. HARRIS

Published by KHARIS PUBLISHING, imprint of KHARIS MEDIA LLC.

Copyright © 2020 Scott A. Harris

ISBN-13: 978-1-946277-74-9
ISBN-10: 1-946277-74-6

Library of Congress Control Number: 2020943748

All KHARIS PUBLISHING products are available at special quantity discounts for bulk purchase for sales promotions, premiums, fund-raising, and educational needs. For details, contact:

Kharis Media LLC
Tel: 1-479-599-8657
support@kharispublishing.com
www.kharispublishing.com

KHARIS
PUBLISHING

v

Dedication

I dedicate this book to God the Father, Jesus Christ, and the Holy Spirit, who directed every step of this journey of transformation. Eternally grateful, all I can offer is a life of relentless obedience.

> **Ecclesiastes 12:13** *Let us hear the conclusion of the whole matter: Fear God, and keep his commandments: for this is the whole duty of man.*

Thank you to my wonderful wife, who prayed endlessly for the hope of God to be manifested in me. Gigi, you are my best friend and confidant; I would not be the person I am if it were not for you. Thank you for the countless hours you spent editing and praying over this, my first book. I love you!

Many thanks to my parents Jerry and Priscilla Harris who faithfully prayed for many years that I would become who God called me to be. I love you, Mom and Dad.

My brothers Brian, Chris, Randy, and John.

May you live the dream God has placed in your hearts.

Dave Erickson

For accountability, may God bless you, mightily.

CONTENTS

References

This book is a culmination of ten years of experience corresponding to the Word of God; it is a detailed progression of a journey to know the One True Living God. Several methods have been used to interpret the scriptures to provide meaning that is not readily understood. This is otherwise known as hermeneutics: the interpretation of the Bible and the following resources were employed:

King James Bible: 1611

Strong's Exhaustive Concordance for Hebrew and Greek by James Strong S.T.D. LL.D: 1890

Webster's 1828 Dictionary of American English: 1828

Ancient Hebrew Lexicon of the Bible: Ancient Hebrew Research Center, Jeff A. Benner: 2005

Septuagint (Greek Translation of Hebrew scriptures) 3rd Century BCE

Revelation knowledge:[1,2] Scripture interpreting Scripture, authentic life experiences aligned with scripture, allegories, dreams, and visions all linked directly to God's Word.

As time progressed, the etymological meaning of words morphed and became different meanings today than originally intended when the King James Version of 1611 was translated. Therefore, Webster's 1828 version and Strong's Exhaustive Concordance from 1890 were used to define words in order to maintain the integrity of the meaning as closely as possible to the original meaning of the King James Bible.

---

[1] Ephesians 1:17.
[2] Galatians 1:12.

For the Reader

I pray that through this book, the Spirit of God will open the eyes of you, the reader, to understand that there is a true meaning and purpose of life, and God sent His son Jesus Christ to die for you that you might find it. It is my sincere hope as you read this account, you will realize that the relationship with God described in this book is available to anyone who chooses to prioritize God in his or her life. This book is a testament to **how** to know God, the one thing that eluded me. Speakers often relayed the "**what**" to do to know God, but the "**how**" was much more difficult to ascertain. The following is a roadmap of how I came to know the Ruler of the Universe and how He showed me how to love Him. Because I loved Him, I knew Him, and He transformed me into a Godly Warrior. May the Spirit provide the understanding and true transformation in your life…

Preface

The Making of a Godly Warrior

The *Making of a Godly Warrior* is unique in that the Lord teaches lessons directly through experiences and *communicates His assessments concerning the outcomes* so the reader can get a rarely seen, powerful understanding of God's perspective on His Word. Frequently throughout the book, the Lord uses situations to impart *characteristics of His heart as well as His emotions.* The most important aspect of this book is the main theme: a personal journey of an ordinary man observing remarkable results through diligently seeking God. Thus, anyone who reads it will identify with the journey because there is nothing special about the author, yet the responses from God are extraordinary, in both direct communication as well as the performance of His Word.

Many books teach the reader what must be done (devotions, reading God's Word, etc.) but this is a life changing book which teaches the reader (through engaging real-life stories), **how to engage the heart** through proof of *God performing specific verses in His Word* when the author obeys His commands. This is the story of a quest to know God, and how He engages those who pursue Him. True personal stories reveal the truth of God's Word, the importance of understanding it, and the spiritual progress accomplished *by actually doing it.* This is no ordinary book; it proves through direct interaction with God *how* sanctification is accomplished. It entertains while teaching, touches the heart while convicting, transforms while provoking, and incites the reader to engage the heart.

Additional insight is provided as the author discusses each chapter in corresponding videos (available for download on **navigatingthelighted-path.com**). These videos reveal the power of transformation through compelling testimonies not found in "The Making of a Godly Warrior" nor the Field Notes.

The following are all available at: www.navigatingthelightedpath.com

- *The Making of a Godly Warrior*

- *Field Notes from the Making of a Godly Warrior – A Comprehensive Study Guide*

- *Corresponding Videos* are all available at the following website: navi-gatingthelightedpath.com

Corresponding Videos

Additional insight is provided as the author discusses each chapter in 15 cor-responding videos (available for download on ***navigatingthelighted-path.com***). These videos reveal the power of transformation through com-pelling testimonies not found in *The Making of a Godly Warrior* nor the *Field Notes from The Making of a Godly Warrior – A Comprehensive Study Guide.*

The author speaks about each chapter of "The Making of a Godly Warrior" as well as the Field Notes while hiking in the beauty of the Great Smoky Mountains, showcasing waterfalls and mountain views while drawing corre-lations between the physical journey and our spiritual path.

The following are all available at: www.navigatingthelightedpath.com

- *The Making of a Godly Warrior*

- *Field Notes from the Making of a Godly Warrior – A Comprehensive Study Guide*

- *Corresponding Videos* are all available at the following website: navi-gatingthelightedpath.com

Foreword

Jesus said something that has changed my life, made it so simple, not easy, just simple; He is very deep and yet very simple. He said, "I will show you what it is like when someone comes to Me, listens to My teaching, and then follows it." (Luke 6:47) Come, listen, and follow! Simple, yet rare to find even in churches. It looks like, to me, that's what your book is about.
~ **Pastor David McIntosh**

Luke 6:47 *Whosoever cometh to me, and heareth my sayings, and doeth them, I will show you to whom He is like:*

Luke 6:48 *He is like a man who built a house, and dug deep, and laid the foundation on a rock: and when the flood arose, the stream beat vehemently upon that house, and could not shake it: for it was founded upon a rock.*

Introduction

The Role of Grace in Salvation, Repentance, Obedience, Sanctification, and Transformation

I accepted the Lord at just seven years of age, and after 38 years in the church, I knew I was saved by grace,[3] but somehow, I knew there had to be more to it. After all, it was many years earlier. I had "accepted Jesus into my heart." I had spent most of those years doing my best to do right, but sometimes failing. Nevertheless, something was different now, and I *knew it*. I would eventually come to understand what that difference was exactly. When I first made the decision to give my life to the Lord, I asked the Lord to forgive my sins, and I wanted Him to come into my heart and take over my life. That was truly Biblical:

> **Romans 10:13** *For whosoever shall call upon the name of the Lord shall be saved.*

> **Romans 10:9** *That if thou shalt confess with thy mouth the Lord Jesus, and shalt believe in thine heart that God hath raised him from the dead, thou shalt be saved.*

According to those two verses, there is no doubt I was saved without prejudice because Jesus saved the thief on the cross next to Him according to the gospel of Luke.

> **Luke 23:42-43** *And he said unto Jesus, Lord, remember me when thou comest into thy kingdom. And Jesus said unto him, Verily I say unto thee, To day shalt thou be with me in paradise.*

Over the next ten years, I attended church with my family three times a week: twice on Sunday and once on Wednesday. This routine would last until I turned 18 and moved out of my parents' house. I spent the next 20 years in and out of churches, but never completely committed to a life of truly chasing after God. I had been married and divorced during that time, and although I was aware of God, I had not made Him Lord of my life. I read the Bible only occasionally, and when I did, I followed a "read the Bible through in a year" prescription to "get through it." I did not see the Bible from God's perspective but rather as a task to be completed. I had no knowledge of God, even though I repeatedly read His Word. This was a result of doing the task,

---

[3] Ephesians 2:8.

but not engaging the heart. God's Word says a lack of knowledge will destroy His people, and *it almost destroyed me:*

> **Hosea 4:6** *My people are destroyed for lack of knowledge: because thou hast rejected knowledge, I will also reject thee, that thou shalt be no priest to me: seeing thou hast forgotten the law of thy God, I will also forget thy children.*

I had come to understand that choosing God enacted a war over my soul between God and the evil one. At the time, the enemy of my soul was so deceptive; I did not even know he was working against me. The enemy convinced me that I was doing all I could; however, I had not drawn near toward God[4] , as His Word stated. Engaging the heart *takes a conscious decision and is necessary to know Him;* knowing God is of the utmost importance because it is why He created us: to have a personal relationship with Him.

> **Revelation 3:20** *Behold, I stand at the door, and knock: if any man hear my voice, and open the door, I will come in to him, and will sup with him, and he with me.*

The thief on the cross died within a few hours, so his salvation did not require anything more than calling on Jesus' name. However, I would soon learn salvation has conditions for those of us who live long enough to encounter multifaceted grace:

> **Ephesians 2:8** *For by grace are ye saved through faith; and that not of yourselves: it is the gift of God.*

Grace is largely misunderstood. It is truly the favor of God as many profess; however, grace is *manifold,* which means *multifaceted:*

> **1 Peter 4:10** *As every man hath received the gift, even so, minister the same one to another, as good stewards of the manifold grace of God.*

Webster's 1828 Dictionary defines **manifold** as *of divers kinds; many in number; numerous, multiplied. Exhibited or appearing in diver's times or in various ways.*

That means grace has depth, and favor is just one of its many manifestations. Strong's concordance defines the word for **grace (charis** in Greek) as **especially the divine influence upon the heart, and its reflection in the life.**

Strong's Concordance defines the word *faith* in the same verse, Ephesians 2:8, as (**pistis** in Greek), **especially reliance upon Christ for salvation, believe.** The root word for **pistis** is **peithō,** and it means to **have confidence, obey, trust, and yield.** This means the definition of **faith is "trust**

---

[4] James 4:8.

displayed through obedience," which means the first part of **Ephesians 2:8** says:

"For by the divine influence on the heart and its reflection in the life are you saved by trust displayed through obedience."

In the second part of Ephesians 2:8, *"... and that not of yourselves: it is the gift of God,"* the word *gift* refers to the grace He has imparted. This means the gift received is the divine influence on the heart and how it is reflected in our lives, and it is dependent upon obedience. *The divine influence on the heart is the gift of God; it is an opportunity for obedience unto salvation.* The following two verses affirm:

> **Hebrews 5:9** *And being made perfect, he became the author of eternal salvation unto all them that obey him;*

> **Matthew 19:17** *And he said unto him, Why callest thou me good? there is none good but one, that is, God: but if thou wilt enter into life, keep the commandments.*

Understanding that made all the difference, I now comprehended the key to salvation was obedience reflected in my life based upon the divine influence I allowed God to communicate to my heart.

Salvation is God's gift to all through Jesus,[5] however, like any gift, salvation must be received, and in order to understand, action is required, not merely acknowledgement of Jesus, as some believe. *Salvation is through sanctification of the Spirit and belief of the truth*:

> **2 Thessalonians 2:13-14** *But we are bound to give thanks alway to God for you, brethren beloved of the Lord, because God hath from the beginning chosen you to salvation through sanctification of the Spirit and belief of the truth: Whereunto he called you by our gospel, to the obtaining of the glory of our Lord Jesus Christ.*

The word belief in this verse is the same Greek word **(*pistis*)** as the word faith in Ephesians 2:8, and its root word **peithō** means *obey*. The cross below depicts how the blood of the Lamb, faith, and grace comes from above and are naturally reflected in the lives of those who believe.

> **Revelation 12:11** *And they overcame him by the blood of the Lamb, and by the word of their testimony; and they loved not their lives unto the death.*

> **Hebrews 11:1** *Now faith is the substance of things hoped for, the evidence of things*

---

[5] Romans 6:23

not seen.

Ephesians 2:8 *For by grace are ye saved through faith; and that not of yourselves: it is the gift of God:*

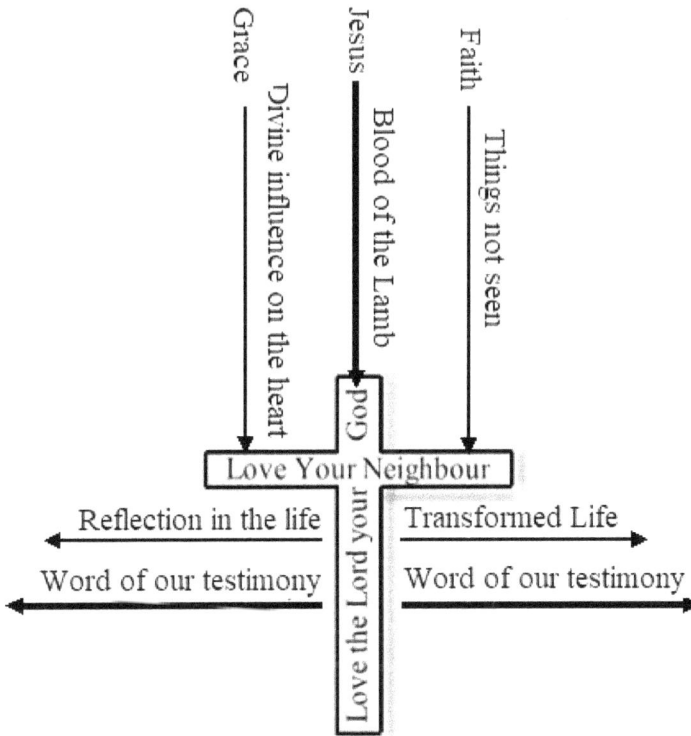

This book is about the journey of sanctification; after all, salvation requires *repentance and transformation:*

Luke 13:3 *I tell you, Nay: but, except ye repent, ye shall all likewise perish.*

Acts 3:19 *Repent ye therefore, and be converted, that your sins may be blotted out,* *when the times of refreshing shall come from the presence of the Lord;*

Strong's concordance defines **repent** in both verses as *to think differently or afterwards, i.e., reconsider (morally, feel compunction): —repent.* This means salvation requires a transformation of our previous life to a new one:

> **Romans 12:2** *And be not conformed to this world: but be ye transformed by the renewing of your mind, that ye may prove what is that good, and acceptable, and perfect, will of God.*

This story is about the earthly blessings and eternal rewards of spiritual transformation through relentless obedience. I would find grace is much more than I originally believed; *we receive grace for obedience unto faith and righteousness:*

> **Romans 1:5** *By whom we have received grace and apostleship, for obedience to the faith among all nations, for his name:*

> **Romans 6:16** *Know ye not, that to whom ye yield yourselves servants to obey, his servants ye are to whom ye obey; whether of sin unto death, or of obedience unto righteousness?*

Webster's 1828 dictionary defines **righteousness** as *true religion*:

RIGHTEOUSNESS, *noun* ri'chusness.

1. Purity of heart and rectitude of life; conformity of heart and life to the divine law. *Righteousness*, as used in Scripture and theology, in which it is chiefly used, is nearly equivalent to holiness, comprehending holy principles and affections of heart, and conformity of life to the divine law. It includes all we call justice, honesty, and virtue, with holy affections; ***in short, it is true religion***.

Obedience is *how* the Holy Spirit can guide us to righteousness and holiness, which *is required to see the Lord*:

> **Hebrews 12:14** *Follow peace with all men, and holiness, without which no man shall see the Lord:*

It is through this journey I would discover *obedience is the key to all spiritual growth and true engagement of the heart.*

Acknowledgement

Thanks to Paul Losapio for previewing this book and providing feedback.

Thanks to Richard Sayball for previewing this book and providing feedback.

Thanks to Pastor David McIntosh for previewing this book and providing feedback.

Thanks to my brother Randy Harris for all you have done in this endeavor.

CHAPTER 1

Old Things are Passed Away; Behold All Things are Become New

Ephesians 4:22 *That ye put off concerning the former conversation the old man, which is corrupt according to the deceitful lusts;*

The Old Man

I accepted the Lord at just seven years of age, but in truth, it did not "take." Somehow, I continued in life without giving it a second thought. I grew up in a Christian household, attended church three times a week, and even read my Bible through in a year a couple of times. Through the years, there was something wrong with my relationship with the Lord, but I was unable to detect that there was even a problem.

I got married at eighteen because there was a baby on the way, but that was the least of my problems. Looking back, there was no doubt I was a father and a husband much too early. I had no concept of fatherhood and felt as though I had sold my future for the present.[6] The result was that I shortchanged my wife and two kids as well. I dropped out of college and got a factory job to support my new family. I received considerable support from my in-laws, who were also Christians, but for some reason, although I was *technically* a Christian by man's standards, I really did not know what that meant. Eventually, I got a job at a high-tech company and began working endlessly to climb the ladder of what I thought was success. The unintended consequence was a stunted relationship with my wife and children as I spent countless hours at work, all in the name of making their lives better with "things." Thus, my title as a husband and father was all but nonexistent, and my relationship with my family suffered. Sometime over the next few years, pornography became a problem, and eventually, an addiction. I never had a problem with drugs or alcohol, but the lust of the flesh was my downfall. It

---

[6] Hebrews 12:15-16.

would take about fifteen years before my marriage ended from philandering, among other things. It was those "other things" which would haunt me for most of my life; personality flaws I did not recognize because of pride was outwardly visible to others, but was hidden from me and eventually became my primary undoing. Unfortunately, my wife and I divorced after seventeen years of marriage, further damaging my relationship with my kids.

After my marriage ended, I went back to church; I knew the answers were there as I had learned during the many years that I attended as a child. Many memories of hearing God's Word would flood my mind while in that familiar environment. However, no sooner had I stepped out of the church, I became concerned "with all things, not God," and went about life, as I knew it.

I had succumbed to the deception of the enemy for many years. The end of my marriage shocked me into attending church again because I had been taught about the Lord, and that teaching had never left me,[7] it had just been "pushed aside" until that moment. Unfortunately, I still did not engage my heart toward God even after reacquainting myself with the church. I had gotten a more secure job as a software engineer and attended college in that field before I got married for the second time two years later. I met a woman in church and, determined to seek the Lord's guidance; I told the Lord He would have to make it abundantly clear if I was to get married again. She, being a woman of God, also asked the Lord if she should marry me. She said His reply was: "It is up to you. He is a diamond in the rough."

Soon after, the Lord provided an encounter that would reveal His counsel. My wife Gigi and I were on a date in Government Center in Boston before we were married. Strangely, the crowd cleared, and suddenly it seemed as though we were walking alone, except for one homeless man, just ahead sitting on the ground with a hood pulled over his head. As we approached, we could not see his face; but just as we passed by, without even looking up, he said: "If you don't marry her, I will."

We were shocked and kept walking. Moments later, we turned around...

But he was gone.
Thankfully, she decided to go ahead and take the chance, and as I would soon learn, God not only sees the future; in His wisdom, **He creates it.**[8]

---

[7] Proverbs 22:6.
[8] Proverbs 8:20-21.

Proverbs 8:20-21 *I lead in the way of righteousness, in the midst of the paths of judgment: That I may cause those that love me to inherit substance; and I will fill their treasures.*

Years later, the Lord revisited this expression of being a diamond in the rough; but at this point, although I *thought* I knew Him, I was nowhere near the expectations He had for me.[9] I had become a board member of the church where I met my wife, although I did not entirely understand what it was to know God in a personal way. Back then, I thought knowing God was attending church and reading the Bible. However, this was the church where God made a strong push at developing an intimate relationship with me. I cannot remember the entire phrase He spoke, but at the end of the service, someone addressed the entire church and said: "I see you through My Son's blood…I have pulled you from the muck and mire"[10]

Those words echoed in my head as I stood at my seat shaking and sweating. I knew God was speaking directly into my life, but I would soon shake it off as I left the service and entered the "reality" of life, as I knew it. The enemy had succeeded in deceiving me into believing what I was doing was "good enough," and although I believed I was engaging my heart, I could not have been more wrong.

My wife was a solid believer in Christ, and of course, I was on my best be-havior. My philandering days were over, and I was now back attending church. She did insist, however, that I take a personality test with a Christian psychotherapist to determine if we were compatible for marriage. Looking back, this is where those "other things" first surfaced. They did not seem to be deep flaws, but I would find out later that they were truly impactful.

"The results reveal you are able to make decisions without conscience, but you must decide to use that for good and not evil," the psychotherapist an-nounced. At the time, I saw it as an advantage that my decisions were not all tied up in emotions. But I had come to understand later; this was the root of many other problems; without a proper conscience toward others, I would become undone in all things concerning relationships. Nonetheless, it took a few years before I discovered these flaws would be my undoing. It was at work where they first surfaced. I had received a rating from my manager that I disputed concerning my yearly accomplishments; I demanded to see the director of our department. My boss complied, so the next morning, I

---

[9] Jeremiah 29:11.
[10] Psalm 40:2.

scheduled a flight to company headquarters; I had faxed the 19 pages of accomplishments the night before. The meeting lasted about 30 seconds; after I asked the director if he got my fax, he replied, "It is not what you did; it is how you did it." Then I flew back home. I had not seen it was through manipulation, intimidation, conniving, and overall lack of integrity I had amassed such an impressive list of accomplishments. It was not long after I was having some words with my manager when he exclaimed, "You have had problems with every boss you ever encountered." I thought about that for a long time and knew there was something wrong with me, but I could not put my finger on it. The truth was, I would discover later, I was riddled with pride, a nasty characteristic because it cannot be seen by its host;[11] it conspires with deception, and the host is most always in denial. I would come to understand submission overcomes pride and deception, but it would take years before I came to that conclusion. I had put all trust in myself; I attended night school for many years to protect my job status by acquiring the necessary degrees in my field. That only bolstered the pride as I was now "educated" and believed I was above others.[12]

Meanwhile, at home, I had married the sweetest person alive and she had just thrown a chair across the kitchen in frustration. That got my attention and I realized I was changing her into someone more like me, but I did not know how to stop it. It was not long after that she was contemplating the financial ramifications of divorce. I had just begun to reflect on my inner flaws, but it seemed as though I might have been too late.

We started attending a new Messianic church, primarily attended by Jewish believers in Christ. And (although neither my wife nor I am Jewish) we decided to take part in this church, as we found this group was more relaxed than what we had been accustomed to in the past. Still ensnared by pornography, I got involved with a female parishioner through internet messaging. It started out innocent enough, but I had soon developed an unhealthy attachment to this woman, and the emotional soul tie was a connection not easily broken. The relationship surfaced and was dealt with swiftly as my wife, the woman, and I all had a conversation about how it needed to immediately end. At just about the same time, the church leader had a personal meltdown. I had developed my relationship with the Lord *through* him, so when he faltered, my faith was shaken. That caused my cavalier relationship with the Lord to collapse, and I began to question the core of my faith and its *very existence*; I began to question what exactly it was I believed and why I believed

---

[11] Obadiah 1:3.
[12] Romans 12:3.

it.

Hence, the perfect storm; my second marriage was on the rocks, and I was hooked on pornography. I had multiple character flaws and a completely failed faith. I had grown up knowing *about* God, but I had never actually engaged my heart; I just did not know how. This state of events forced me to deep reflection on my life. Then I made a decision that changed my life forever. I looked at the sky and asked, "Who are you? Tell me what to do, and I will do it; because when I stand before you, I am going to say I did everything you told me, but nothing happened." I had set out to prove God did not perform His Word.

> *What I had misunderstood in my quest was this: He had not performed His Word for me, because I had not performed it for Him.*[13]

At the time, I did not know I had stumbled upon the key to the kingdom of God: *Relentless Obedience*. This is the extraordinary story of how God taught me how to know Him and love Him. In the process, He redeemed my soul, cleared my character flaws, and freed me from pornography. Through my relentless obedience, the Creator would eventually call me by name:

> **Isaiah 45:3** *And I will give thee the treasures of darkness, and hidden riches of secret places, that thou mayest know that I, the LORD, which call thee by thy name, am the God of Israel.*

A New Foundation

"Tell me what to do, and I will do it" was my invitation to the Creator to change my life, but in order to do that, He needed to break down my faulty foundation and replace it with a sturdy new one based upon the fear of the Lord. He used a vivid dream,[14] which was frankly disturbing. As the dream began, I was carrying a large clay pot down a stone walkway. As I entered a doorway on my left, a red flag would leave the pot, circle the ceiling of the stone room, and enter back into the clay pot; I would perform this ritual daily along with another individual. As I left the room, suddenly, God appeared; He was so immense, only his foot was visible, which caused me to fall face down on the ground immediately.[15] The dream continued as I was suddenly at the other end of the stone path and sitting next to Jesus. He wrapped chains around my wrists and punctured my left ear with an awl by nailing it

---

[13] James 1:22
[14] Psalm 16:7
[15] Psalm 65:8

to a door.[16] No sooner had Jesus finished than I found myself seated at a table, and Jesus was teaching at a blackboard. It was then I saw where I was; Jesus had come down a trap door with a set of stairs to commune with me. I had seen my future of life after death. I certainly was not in hell, but the Savior had to come down a staircase to visit me as I was not actually living *with* Him, but rather *near* Him (just downstairs). He would venture to my dwelling place to meet me once weekly; it seemed He was visiting me as often as I visited Him when I was on earth. The strange part about it was I did not feel slighted in any way while it was happening; I simply knew this was my lot, and I was content. I do not know if that is what heaven will be like for some, but it certainly made an impression on me. To intensify the reality of the dream, God completely removed Himself from my spirit. I woke up from the dream with the most horrible feeling I have ever felt, and I imme-diately knew what it was: I was separated from God, one of the attributes of hell itself.[17] The feeling was indescribable; it was a total loss of hope, pres-ently as well as eternally. I felt as though my heart was blackened[18] , and my very soul was lost with no remedy.[19] Thus, I was able to understand, on an exceedingly small scale, Jesus' emotions when He uttered the words:

Mark 15:34 *And at the ninth hour Jesus cried with a loud voice, saying, Eloi, Eloi, lama sabachthani? Which is, being interpreted, My God, my God, why hast thou forsaken me?*

It did not stop there. The Lord said to me: "This is the best you will ever be no matter what you do, and you will never reach beyond what you have seen."

I knew the Creator could not lie,[20] so I became more depressed and distraught as the days passed. I attempted to sleep as much as possible to alleviate the hollow feeling of emptiness. It was on the third day of hopelessness that the Lord sent someone to my door; a friend of my wife, she said she had a word for me sent directly from God. She had no idea the plight I was under, so I told her if it were disparaging, I did not want to hear it; I was already about as low as I could get. She told me it was from the book of Zechariah:

Zechariah 3:3-4 *Now Joshua was clothed in filthy garments and stood before the angel. And he answered and spake unto those that stood before him saying 'Take*

---

[16] Deuteronomy 15:17
[17] Isaiah 59:2
[18] Jeremiah 8:21
[19] Hebrews 12:17
[20] Titus 1:2

away the filthy garments from him.' And unto him, he said 'Behold, I have caused thy iniquity to pass from thee, and I will clothe thee with change of raiment.'

The word brought hope that slowly lifted the depression, but what about what the Lord had said? If I could never be any better than what I had seen, what was the point in trying? I would come to understand He intended to encourage me to join my spirit[21] with His:

Mark 10:26-27 *And they were astonished out of measure, saying among themselves, Who then can be saved? And Jesus looking upon them saith, With men, it is impossible, but not with God: for with God, all things are possible.*

The Journey Begins
The Bible recorded a story in the book of Acts when Saul met Jesus on the road to Damascus:

Acts 9:3-4 *And as he journeyed, he came near Damascus: and suddenly there shined round about him a light from heaven: And he fell to the earth and heard a voice saying unto him, Saul, Saul, why persecutest thou me?*

Immediately, Saul asked, "who are you?" and then said, "what will you have me to do?"

Acts 9:5-6 *And he said, Who art thou, Lord? And the Lord said, I am Jesus whom thou persecutest: it is hard for thee to kick against the pricks. And he trembling and astonished, said, Lord, what wilt thou have me to do? And the Lord said unto him, Arise, and go into the city, and it shall be told thee what thou must do.*

This was the beginning of an extraordinary journey throughout the remainder of Saul's (also known as Paul) life. Jesus visited Paul suddenly when his journey began. The extraordinary journey you are about to read was commenced by using those same words Paul used almost 2,000 years ago; in desperate pursuit of the Lord, I uttered the same words which caused Him to draw near.

The story began long before; I accepted the Lord when I was just seven years old. I would later discover the Bible is an endless deep source of God's character and **knowing Him from His perspective** is the **one true purpose** of our entire lives:

Jeremiah 9:23-24 *Thus saith the LORD, Let not the wise man glory in his*

---
[21] 1 Corinthians 6:17

wisdom, neither let the mighty man glory in his might, let not the rich man glory in his riches: But let him that glorieth glory in this, that he understandeth and knoweth me, that I am the LORD which exercise lovingkindness, judgment, and righteousness, in the earth: for in these things I delight, saith the LORD.

It was two years before I had made the declaration: "*Who are You, tell me what to do and I will do it,*" that the Lord began illuminating the path. My wife and I had become good friends with a very spiritual woman at the Messianic church we were attending. One evening I was at the altar with her praying for others' needs. The tradition in this church was to remove one's shoes at the altar to reverence its holiness, so I adhered to the custom. When we had finished praying for everyone, she looked down at my feet and said: "You have the feet of a priest."

An obscure phrase, to be sure, and since she was a friend, and this was my local church, I disregarded the words and subsequently forgot them. At the time, I did not understand the power of God's Word. When He speaks, He releases power into the universe He created.[22] He calls things that are not as though they are,[23] in effect, ***making things that are not as He calls them to be***. I would come to understand when God uses obscure phrases such as this, complete comprehension is not immediately required. He reveals the meaning at the perfect time. I only had a rough estimate of when He first spoke this phrase but soon afterward, I began to record all communication with Him so I would not forget as time passed. Then God intervened the second time. An evangelist from Africa had come to our church and was praying for people at the altar. He walked over to me as I was praying, placed his hand on my head, and shouted: "**Revelation! Revelation! Revelation!**"

He walked away as if to pray for someone else; then stopped, turned, then came back and placed his hand on my head and shouted it again: "**Revelation! Revelation! Revelation!**"

That generated strong emotions. I would eventually come to understand the power of revelation knowledge; however, it would be a long journey, and I had just begun…

---

[22] Genesis 1:31
[23] Romans 4:17

CHAPTER 2

Obedience: the key to true transformation; the requirement for genuine salvation

Romans 1:5 *By whom we have received grace and apostleship, for obedience to the faith among all nations, for his name:*

Grace (*charis* in Greek) is defined as **especially the divine influence upon the heart, and its reflection in the life.**

Thus, the journey began. For 45 years, I had learned through life experience that very few things turned out as expected, regardless of how much I tried. However, the Bible said God holds His Word above His name; [24]His Word is truth;[25] and He performs His Word;[26] all I had to do was believe it.[27] Therefore, I resolved deep in my soul that I would believe *and behave* as if it were true; I would do everything He instructed, so one day when I stood before Him, I could say, "I did everything you told me, but nothing happened." Through life experience, I had come to believe that dashed expectations were the norm. In life, I was often misunderstood, and because I was misjudged, I was often mistreated. Circumstances where I had performed "by the rules," were disappointing because I never achieved the expected results. Since that is all I had experienced in life, I expected God's "rules" to generate a similar outcome. Over the next ten years, I would come to understand His Word; as the heavens are higher than the earth, so are His ways higher than our ways, and His thoughts higher than our thoughts.[28] God is faithful and performs[29] all He declares in His Word.[30] Draw near to

---

[24] Psalm 138:2
[25] Psalm 33:4, John 17:17
[26] Jeremiah 1:12
[27] Mark 11:23
[28] Isaiah 55:9
[29] Luke 1:45
[30] Psalm 138:2

Him, and He will draw near to you,[31] His Word declares, and through experiences over the next ten years, I found through *relentless obedience*, His response was always magnificent, splendid, and intensely personal. There is no end to knowing Him; the more I pursued Him, the deeper our relationship became, which caused me to pursue even further. It was an endless spiral of love and connection with the King of the Universe.

Obedience: Building on The Foundation

To begin the journey, I took the few verses I did understand and put them into action. Strangely, although I had attended churches for most of my life, *I did not know how to carry on a conversation with the King of the Universe.* I had never really taken the time to invest in a relationship with God, so I did not know how to begin. However, I did know two things from His Word caught His attention: humility[32] and praying for leaders.[33] Therefore, I began reading the Bible *to discover God's character* rather than reading it as a requirement. Each day, I prayed for my leaders, starting with the President of the United States and ending with my boss at work. I prayed daily in my basement because it was the lowest part of my house – the only way I knew how to show humility to the Creator. It would take five years of building a relationship with Him before He would teach me true humility, the power of it, and how to receive it. I quickly understood obedience was the very foundation of the path the Lord had set for each of us. His Word says He has a plan to prosper and not to harm us.[34] Why would He feel it necessary to emphasize that His plan is not to *harm* us? The answer is in His Word:

> **Hebrews 5:8** *Though he were a Son, yet learned he obedience by the things which he suffered.*

We learn obedience through suffering, and knowing obedience is the foundation of a right relationship with Him, God graciously told us all things would work together for good to those who love Him,[35] and His plan is not to harm, but prosper us. He knew sometimes it would feel as though He was harming us, but true spiritual growth requires adversity. James asserted:

> **James 1:2-4** *My brethren, count it all joy when ye fall into divers temptations; Knowing this, that the trying of your faith worketh patience. But let patience have her perfect*

---

[31] James 4:8
[32] Isaiah 57:15
[33] 1 Timothy 2:1-3
[34] Jeremiah 29:11
[35] Romans 8:28

work, that ye may be perfect and entire, wanting nothing.

God calls us to be perfect,[36] but we cannot be perfect in and of ourselves. We must be *perfected by Him* according to Hebrews as well as 2 Samuel:

> **Hebrews 13:20-21** *Now the God of peace, that brought again from the dead our Lord Jesus, that great shepherd of the sheep, through the blood of the everlasting covenant, Make you perfect in every good work to do his will, working in you that which is wellpleasing in his sight, through Jesus Christ; to whom be glory for ever and ever. Amen.*

> **2 Samuel 22:33** *God is my strength and power: and he maketh my way perfect.*

God perfects those who know Him, and we know Him by drawing near to Him.[37] This was the key to the beginning of my journey. Choosing to draw near is a *conscious choice from within that changes behavior without.* In this case, the decision caused a prioritization change; seeking God became most important and everything else secondary.

> *Many know about God and love Him for what He can do; true followers know Him for who He is and love Him for what He did.*

This "prioritization" was the catalyst in my relationship with Him because it incorporated obedience into the very foundation of the relationship. I would eventually understand obedience is the key to all prosperity, both spiritual and physical. However, one more verse intrigued me:

> **Hebrews 11:6** *But without faith it is impossible to please him: for he that cometh to God must believe that he is, and that he is a rewarder of them that diligently seek him.*

What exactly were these rewards? I believed they were real; all I had to do was determine the definition of "diligently seeking Him" and understand the definition of faith because I needed faith to please Him. I figured that would somehow work itself out, so I began by just seeking after God. Eventually, I found seeking God with all my heart and soul caused me to love Him, and loving Him generated obedience to His Word because seeking God with all my heart and soul *is* obedience. It is the first commandment:

---

[36] Matthew 5:48
[37] James 4:8

Matthew 22:37-40 *Jesus said unto him, Thou shalt love the Lord thy God with all thy heart, and with all thy soul, and with all thy mind. This is the first and great commandment. And the second is like unto it, Thou shalt love thy neighbour as thyself. On these two commandments hang all the law and the prophets.*

All I had to do was obey the *first* commandment because the second commandment is subject to the first:

1 John 2:5 *But whoso keepeth his word, in him verily is the love of God perfected: hereby know we that we are in him.*

To know God is to love Him and to love Him is to want to please Him. We please Him by surrendering our free will to His commands, which is accomplished by believing He will perform his Word.[38] We believe His Word **through** actions of obedience; *faith is executed by believing those actions will generate spiritual results.* Actions of obedience to God's Word are often directly opposed to conventional wisdom and experience; that is because they directly conflict with the understanding of our sinful nature. We must implement faith that will generate a spiritual result, and God often uses situations that require actions of obedience to break pride. The difference between pride and humility is simply where we place trust. Pride is trust in oneself; humility is trust in God.

God's gift is our free will; our gift is surrendering it to Him.

We trust and love God by surrendering our free will; doing His Word is how we know we know God:

1 John 2:3 *And hereby we do know that we know him, if we keep his commandments.*

John 15:10 *If ye keep my commandments, ye shall abide in my love; even as I have kept my Father's commandments, and abide in his love.*

1 Corinthians 8:3 *But if any man love God, the same is known of him.*

This is why submission is the essence of a deep relationship with the Lord;[39] knowing Him requires deference to His first commandment, and once we know Him, all things are possible.[40] I would find, however, obedience

---

[38] Luke 1:45
[39] Romans 6:16
[40] Matthew 19:26

understood is simple, while obedience applied is the most difficult of tasks. God would teach me how to perform the first commandment over the next ten years. Those actions would cause me to perceive my life spiritually, in effect, seeing life from an eternal perspective while simultaneously leaving behind the earthly frame of reference. This is the beginning of *abundant life*. Having attended church most of my life, I heard many sermons covering a range of subjects. However, one thing kept nagging at me; *God's Word gives all kinds of promises, but they never seemed to work for me; why was that?* It was just a confirmation of what I had already experienced in life: *the results never measure up to playing by the rules.* Therefore, I contemplated; I would obey *every one* of God's commands to determine if He would really do what His Word says. I had no idea what I was about to experience as I approached the path the Creator of the Universe had set for me to follow. For me to comply, He decided I first needed to understand the definition of obedience from *His perspective.* Obedience is the foundation of a relationship with God, so He presented me with a series of tests that required obedience through experience. These tests reinforced *His definition of obedience in my spirit,* so there was no ambiguity in my understanding as to precisely what He expected in our relationship.

Obedience: No Statute of Limitations

One of the many tests I faced early on was simply to keep quiet concerning a matter; I found this to be one of the most difficult tests of all; I was a "talker," and God's Word depicts the tongue as an unruly evil:

> **James 3:8** *But the tongue can no man tame; it is an unruly evil, full of deadly poison.*

God designed these tests to overcome my "natural state" of gossiping, which would prove I was "walking in the spirit" rather than the flesh. Unfortunately, I failed. As a software engineer in a large company, I encountered all kinds of coworkers. One person would tend to take credit for others' work. She had the ear of the upper managers and intimidated others into getting on projects for which she would report progress as if she were doing the work. The adage "it is not *what* you know; it is *who* you know" certainly applied; everyone was exasperated, including me. The fact that this person could not do her job was blatantly apparent one day as I was working with her; she could not perform the most basic job function. After that experience, my first inclination was to tell others indeed, we were right all along: she was truly incompetent. Immediately the Lord said: "**Do not tell anyone of this**"[41]

---

[41] Proverbs 11:13

I kept this to myself for over two months, which I considered quite an accomplishment, and one day this person's name came up in a conversation with my boss. I figured the statute of limitations must have run out on this "keep quiet" policy from God, so I told my boss what had happened. Two days later, I was working on a software program and having difficulty – I could not figure out how to solve a particular issue. I called my boss for help and found the answer was simple. This repeatedly happened over the next few days and was frankly embarrassing. I asked the Lord, "Why is this happening? You are supposed to take care of me." He replied: **"You uncovered her nakedness, so I uncovered yours."**[42]

I realized two things from this encounter with God. First, God says what He means, and He expects complete, not partial, obedience. Second, I realized everything I knew, and all I was, I received from God.[43] He blocks knowledge and hides things as He chooses. However, I would realize later, and He also reveals secrets, wisdom, understanding, and knowledge to those who fear Him.[44]

Obeying Benefits Us

The next lesson I learned was the value of hearing and obeying the Lord's voice, especially when my thoughts were the opposite of His.[45] Distinguishing His voice is the crux of a relationship with Him. It is required for growth because He only shares secrets with those who fear Him:

> **Psalm 25:14** *The secret of the LORD is with them that fear him; and he will shew them his covenant.*

This would prove true as I continued to obey His voice, but for now, I was just in the beginning stages, and He was using His voice to reshape my character to His. While we were at the Messianic Church, my wife received a word from the Lord to buy me a tallit,[46] a prayer shawl Jewish people wear in prayer or in church service. Webster's Definition of a *tallit* is *a shawl with fringed corners worn over the head or shoulders by Jewish men, especially during morning prayers.* My wife bought me an authentic tallit from a Jewish convention she attended. We were not Jewish, so it seemed unusual that the Lord would tell her this,

---

[42] Isaiah 47:3
[43] Psalm 24:1
[44] Psalm 25:14; Psalm 111:10; Proverbs 9:10
[45] Isaiah 55:8
[46] Numbers 15:38

but when I received it, I immediately began to wear it when we attended church. Unfortunately, the Messianic leader faltered spiritually, and we left that church to attend a conventional Pentecostal church. I put the tallit away and told my wife I wanted nothing to do with it. I felt it represented a leader who had perverted the Word of God, so I packed the tallit away. I always prayed in the basement, and it would get somewhat chilly in the winter months, so I would wrap myself in a blanket while praying. One morning, my wife walked by and said, "It looks like you are wearing a tallit"; "It is not a tallit!" I snapped, irritated to be associated with the leader who had shipwrecked my fragile faith. Immediately, referring to the tallit, the Lord said: **"That is me, you know."**

From that day on, I completely changed my perspective and have worn it every day for prayer since. It is a special bond between the Lord and me because it represents Him *as well as my submission to Him*. This was a test of quick and complete obedience contrary to my own thinking, and I passed, but the next test was much more difficult.

Obedience: Doing to Completion

The next part of the journey was to repair relationships from the past as the Word says we must pursue peace with all men.

> **Romans 12:18** *If it be possible, as much as lieth in you, live peaceably with all men.*

> **Hebrews 12:14** *Follow peace with all men, and holiness, without which no man shall see the Lord:*

The Holy Spirit revealed to me a list of past relationships that needed reconciliation, most importantly, the one with my father. The Lord brought to my attention two incidents for which I had not forgiven my father: one from 25 and the other from 35 years prior. Compared to atrocities others have suffered, these incidents were negligible and amounted to simple unfairness from my perspective as a child. However, they were of monumental importance in the spiritual world because they involved unforgiveness.[47] When I pondered the two occurrences, I immediately winced and thought, "*I don't know if I can do this.*" Immediately I heard the Lord's voice:

"So, you want to be like the servant who walked away sad because he had great possessions?"[48]

---

[47] Matthew 6:15
[48] Matthew 19:22

He impatiently added: **"Do you want to be like him?"**

I quickly repented and got up the next morning to make the call. "Well,"I thought, *"I will just call my father and forgive him for the past, and that will be the end of it."* Knowing that thought,[49] God said: **"You must name each incident."**

That was almost overwhelming to imagine, but as I picked up the phone, I reached my Dad and told him I had to forgive him for two incidents, and I had to name them. He got quiet and said he was ready, so I went on to explain - he was so broken - I had never seen him so subdued and quiet. He did not try to defend himself, and I told him I forgave him and needed him to forgive me for holding on to them for so long. *I would understand later that the problem was mine alone; I needed forgiveness from my father for harboring these incidents.* Nonetheless, as I broached the subject, the Lord covered me[50] by preparing my father before the call. We talked for an hour, and before we got off the phone, he said, "I just want you to know you just made my year. Thank you so much for calling. I love you." God used these tests of obedience to clear the way for traveling on the spiritual path. In this instance, I had unforgiveness, which would not allow progression on the journey. I had convinced myself I was over these past offenses, but the Lord searches the heart.[51] That is why knowing Him is essential; He knows every facet of our being and the precise circumstances for growth we require to succeed on the spiritual journey to live His plan for our lives.

Precise Obedience
After completing the list of those I needed to contact, I reasoned there was perhaps one more person I should call because of the contentious relationship we had in the past. One day as I was driving, I decided to head over to this person's house to make amends, but the Lord directed: **"I did not give you that name"**

I was surprised, but also came to understand obeying the Lord is following His commands and *not doing what He does not command.*[52] He had prepared each person for my call as I followed His lead. However, for some reason unknown to me, He did not want me to contact this person. The Lord wants to maintain a tight-knit relationship with us. When He gives a command, He

---

[49] Psalm 139:2
[50] Psalm 1:1-3
[51] Psalm 44:21
[52] Deuteronomy 12:32

16

expects *precise obedience*. I was attempting to obey this *detailed command* in *a general manner*; I was going to call anyone I may have offended and apologize to them. Instead of obedience, I was attempting to change my overall behavior – an enormous task that would most definitely fail under my own power. That is the Holy Spirit's work; He gently guides us one step at a time. I was jumping off the cliff rather than taking the stairs, and He gently guided me back to the staircase before I harmed myself. I had attempted to "over obey" this command; the upside has I now had a much clearer understanding of obedience than I had previously. Obeying to completion was exactly that; not coming up short, but also not overreaching the goal of what I now understood to be *precise obedience*.

Obeying Requires Inquiring [53,54]

The tests advanced to deeper levels that would encompass the first inklings of loving my neighbor; in this case, literally next door. This test would teach me how to avoid offense altogether rather than short-circuiting my progress by holding unforgiveness. I was having difficulty with my new neighbor, who was continually borrowing tools. I knew I was required to let him borrow:

> **Proverbs 3:28** *Say not unto thy neighbour, Go, and come again, and tomorrow I will give; when thou hast it by thee.*

The problem was at the time, I was not sure where kindness ended, and weakness began. My neighbor continually borrowed one of my tools (it was brand new!) and kept it for months on end. I finally asked for its return. When I got it back, I said to the Lord, "This isn't right. He uses that tool more than I do. I know you see this." He said: **"I give you all of this, and you can't share it?"**

Just a few days later, he asked to *borrow it again,* and I gladly handed it over in obedience to the Lord. I was not sure, however, what to do afterwards. Should I just let him keep it? Should I ask for it back? The Lord told me it was mine, and I certainly should ask for it back; this was kind, yet firm. Letting him keep it would be a weakness. When returned, it was not working properly, and I was livid. Should I use this infraction to prevent him from borrowing anything again? Should I confront him or wait until he asked to borrow it again? I decided to confront him, so my anger would not fester.[55] I was on my way out of the house and decided to call him while on the road.

---

[53] 1 Chronicles 14:10
[54] 1 Chronicles 14:14
[55] Ephesians 4:26

As I was driving, I inquired of the Lord, "*What should I do?*" I knew I should probably wait to call him, as "cooler heads would prevail." I said to the Lord, "*I want to please you, but I can't do the right thing if I don't know what it is.*" He immediately showed me a vision of the parable in the Bible where one man (forgiven of a huge debt) choked another[56] who owed him a small debt. I quickly understood I was the unforgiving man choking my neighbor in the vision; Jesus forgave me and expected me to forgive others. I never called the neighbor; I just forgave the infraction and let it go.

Relentless Obedience: The Fear of the Lord

I responded to every situation with quick, complete, radical obedience regardless of the repercussions. Often, obeying God's command did not look like it would produce the desired result, but rather be detrimental to me personally; *I obeyed anyway.* Often, obeying the Lord made me look small in men's eyes; it hurt my pride; *I obeyed anyway.* Frequently, I would decide to do God's commands while afraid, because I had not yet learned to trust Him; *I obeyed anyway.* I had decided to obey *no matter how I felt or looked like to others*; my only concern was what God would think about how I had acted according to His commands. I would receive direction and encouragement from Him through sermons, reading His Word, reading devotionals, prayer, and even secular movies and songs. Then one day, I received a reward because of all that spiritual growth through adversity; the Lord notified me I had acquired the Fear of the Lord by learning to obey through suffering.[57]

It was a cold day in October, and a freak snowstorm dropped about a foot of snow. Reluctantly, I pulled out the snowblower and began clearing the driveway. I had almost all of it completed, but not the dreaded end by the road – the heavy stuff. Suddenly, the situation took a turn for the worse: the snowblower simply stopped working. It was still running all right, but the transmission had suddenly malfunctioned, so the driveshaft could no longer push it along. *Well*, I thought, *after seventeen years, I guess it has had enough.* I trudged back to the garage to get the plastic snow shovel I had – probably not much younger than the snowblower, but at least it worked. I looked at the end of the driveway and slowly started toward the daunting task ahead. Strangely, I was not angry, which surprised me.[58] Nonetheless, I arrived at the end of the driveway just in time to see a city snowplow approaching from up the hill. Anyone who has shoveled snow knows a city snowplow is an unwelcome sight; as it clears snow from the street, the snow inevitably ends up in each driveway along the road. I waited, fully expecting my burden to

---

[56] Matthew 18:28
[57] Hebrews 5:8
[58] James 1:20

increase tenfold. Then it happened. I stood there in awe as the city snow-plow slowed and stopped at my driveway, gently tipped the plow and cleared all of the snow out of the end of my driveway, and simply continued down the road as if nothing unusual had happened. *I had never experienced that before, and never since.* As I stood there in amazement, the Lord said: **"I think about you all the time."**[59]

The next morning, I was reading the Bible and the Lord interjected: **"Look up scriptures that have eagles in them."**

I had a Bible with a limited concordance, but I found one in Psalm 103:5:
Psalm 103:5 *Who satisfieth thy mouth with good things; so that thy youth is renewed like the eagles.*

Then He instructed: **"Read the rest of the chapter."**

When I read the thirteenth verse, I understood why:

Psalm 103:13 *Like as a father pitieth his children, so the LORD pitieth them that fear him.*

The God of Israel had just pitied (had compassion on) me in my driveway, and He used that experience to confirm His Word. He directed me to Psalm 103:13 to reveal, *according to Him,* I now possessed the fear of the Lord. I immediately searched for all scriptures related to the fear of the Lord. There are many, but the few that caught my attention were:

Psalm 34:7 *The angel of the LORD encampeth round about them that fear him, and delivereth them.*

Psalm 25:12 *What man is he that feareth the LORD? him shall he teach in the way that he shall choose.*

Proverbs 22:4 *By humility and the fear of the LORD are riches, and honour, and life.*

What exactly is the fear of the Lord? It is doing absolutely anything necessary not to disappoint God. It is immediate, complete obedience, regardless of understanding or discomfort to us. We all have people in our lives that have notions of who we should be, what we should do, and how we should do it.

---

[59] Psalm 139:17-18

However, our Creator is the only person who really matters; often, pleasing God disappoints others, and sometimes even ourselves. Jesus said we love Him if we keep his commandments[60] , and we have no idea of the things He has in store for those who love Him.[61] We must believe His word, and *we prove it by the trust displayed when obeying His commands*, sometimes to the detriment of our own plans.[62] This is what He meant when He said we must lose our life in order to find it.[63] God is never in a rush; He is looking for soldiers who will execute heavenly commands regardless of earthly consequences. When God determines we have acquired the fear of the Lord, He enacts His promise of fulfillment.[64] The fear of the Lord does not need the "why" beforehand; it will perform the act of obedience simply due to the confidence that the Lord has issued the command. *Why* He issued the command is of no consequence. When the reason is known beforehand, the spiritual growth is "used up" on the actual act of obedience in order to instill confidence for further acts of submission—*receiving the "why" after the act is much more powerful than beforehand.* Since we perform the act of obedience no matter the earthly consequence, God can provide spiritual growth in much more critical areas than if He reveals the benefit prior to the act when we perform an act of obedience without knowing why all the growth comes after the fact. We have already built the courage supported by confidence through previous acts of submission. God provides the "why" after the act to promote deep spiritual growth, which cultivates the fruit of the spirit. These fruits (love, joy, peace, patience, gentleness, kindness, faith, humility, and temperance[65]) require the fear of the Lord to develop to perfection. Fear of the Lord comes only through continued actions that require progressively increasing trust. Disobedience, on the other hand, is evidence of a character not yet fully formed. Acquiring the fear of the Lord takes time; each small victory predicates the next. As the tests progress, the stakes become higher, and the progress of the spiritual journey more prominent. Eventually, the fear of the Lord is established, and once prioritized, advancement on the spiritual journey progresses at an increasingly rapid rate, and only then can the fruit of the spirit develop to the level God originally intended. The Holy Spirit always has our best interest at heart: to deepen our relationship with God in every facet of our life, to instill relentless obedience in every situation, and to accomplish the total loss of our own life so He might replace it with the more abundant life He

---

[60] John 14:15
[61] 1 Corinthians 2:9
[62] Psalm 15:4
[63] Matthew 10:39
[64] Psalm 37:4
[65] Galatians 5:22-23

originally purposed us to live. Immediately upon learning that I had acquired the fear of the Lord, I found the verse in Proverbs:

Proverbs 22:4 *By humility and the fear of the LORD are riches, and honour, and life.*

I had not even understood the meaning of the fear of the Lord, and now according to the Creator of the Universe, I had acquired it!

Fear of God's judgment is immature; fear of disappointing Him is perfect love.

That is why it is so important to forge an intimate relationship with Him. Once the Lord knows us, the Holy Spirit guides us to the individual path He set for each of us to follow. I now needed the first half of that verse to receive riches and honor and life. Humility, as I discovered, would take considerable time to understand, and even more to install as a character trait. I had just finished 20 years of night school and received two master's degrees from a prestigious school. That is where I had placed my trust and priority; I really believed in it – so much so that I arrogantly declared to the Lord, "There is no way a bag lady can be ahead of me in the Kingdom of God." He patiently replied, **"You better believe it."**

That is when I knew I did not know Him or what He valued. *All I had devoted myself to was worth nothing in His Kingdom.* I had acquired the fear of the Lord all right, but I had a long way to go to *understand* humility. Thankfully, the King of the Universe is patient and never appalled. He has seen it all and lovingly corrects; in order to grow, all we need is to hearken to His voice and *obey it.* Progression on the path of life *is not possible* without knowing Him. By building a relationship with Him, we hear His commands; and when heard, if we obey, He reveals the perfection of His plan. Humans, the most intelligent species on the earth, are the only ones who do not *get it.* Frogs jump, deer run, dogs bark, and lions roar. They all do exactly what God created them to do. A frog never tries to roar; it simply does what God created it to do. Humans, however, attempt to do anything and everything other than formulating an intimate relationship with God, the very purpose for which He created us. Humans, though, do have an adversary, a crafty enemy who has deceived them into chasing temporal things designed to distract them from God's one true purpose for creating man: to have a personal relationship with Him. Once our spirit is joined with God's, He provides direction to perform what He anointed us to accomplish; it is then that we walk in the

Spirit[66] on the path He *created for each person individually*. It is by finding this unique path through knowing Him we experience the abundant life Jesus came to give.[67]

It was at this time in my quest I began to pray for humility. The Lord had affirmed with me I had acquired the fear of the Lord, and according to Proverbs 22:4, in order for God to reward me with riches and honor and life, somehow, I needed to acquire humility.

I had heard from many leaders that praying for humility can bring about painful consequences; that was an accurate assessment. I suffered humiliation in many ways because when praying for humility, the only way to understand it is to experience *humiliation*. However, it would be another four years before the Lord would teach me the genuine path to receive true humility.

Meanwhile, God continued to bring tests to strengthen our relationship through obedience to His Word, much like an underlying current dictating the flow of water in the ocean; and that current brought increasingly difficult situations as time passed. However, I was learning to inquire of the Lord, and He was always there with encouragement to be sure I did not falter. He had assured me He would always be there to encourage me; one day as a church leader yet again disappointed me, He said: **"No man will encourage you; I am your Encourager."**[68]

Not long after, the Lord reassured me through multiple visions and allegories that would forever transform my relationship with Him. I was about to learn of the depth of His love, the power of His instruction, and the magnitude of His Word:

> **Ephesians 3:16-21** *That he would grant you, according to the riches of his glory, to be strengthened with might by his Spirit in the inner man; That Christ may dwell in your hearts by faith; that ye, being rooted and grounded in love, May be able to comprehend with all saints what is the breadth, and length, and depth, and height; And to know the love of Christ, which passeth knowledge, that ye might be filled with all the fulness of God. Now unto him that is able to do exceeding abundantly above all that we ask or think, according to the power that worketh in us, Unto him be glory in the church by Christ Jesus throughout all ages, world without end. Amen.*

---

[66] Galatians 5:25
[67] John 10:10
[68] Joshua 1:9

A Vision: The Christmas Party

The Lord gave me a vision one day of a Christmas party for seven-year-olds. The Christmas tree in the living room had shiny presents with bright bows waiting for the eager children. The woman who owned the house had placed a sign at the door "please take off your shoes," and she was in the kitchen preparing the snacks for the party. One by one, the kids arrived, and soon the living room was alive with laughter and screams of excitement. As the woman entered the living room from the kitchen, she glanced across the room; one pair of shoes was neatly placed by the door. Her eyes immediately darted toward the children to find the one child who was without shoes, undoubtedly looking to praise that child for his/her obedience. God is the same way; He searches for those who have complete, whole, friendly, perfect hearts.[69] We make our hearts ready by *doing* God's Word. At the beginning of this journey, I asked the Lord to "tell me what to do, and I will do it." He used that relentless obedience to teach me how to know Him by imparting precise physical actions from His Word that generate spiritual results. God performs His Word for those who believe;[70] we need only to know Him intimately. He provides the instructions that guide us on the perfect path He created for each of us. Without that intimate relationship, we are hopelessly adrift, never able to access our path because He is the only one who can reveal it.[71,72,73]

---

[69] 2 Chronicles 16:9
[70] Luke 1:45
[71] Psalm 23:3
[72] Proverbs 2:6-9
[73] Proverbs 8:20

23

CHAPTER 3

Discerning and Recognizing the Still Small Voice

1 Kings 19:11-12 *And he said, Go forth, and stand upon the mount before the LORD. And, behold, the LORD passed by, and a great and strong wind rent the mountains, and brake in pieces the rocks before the LORD; but the LORD was not in the wind: and after the wind an earthquake; but the LORD was not in the earthquake: And after the earthquake a fire; but the LORD was not in the fire: and after the fire a still small voice.*

One morning I received a vision, which taught me the high value of hearing God's voice.

A Vision: The Test

I was sitting at a long white table, and the Master and Creator of the universe was standing on the other side facing me; I could only see Him from the shoulders down. He handed me a piece of paper: it was a test. The questions included quantum physics, calculus, and some mathematics I had never seen before. Looking at it, I said, "I can't do this." Then I heard a voice: it was Jesus sitting next to me, and He prompted: **"Let me see it."**

I passed the paper to Him, and He proceeded to fill out the answers and hand it back. The Father gently retrieved it from my hands and exclaimed: **"You got a 100!"**

"But I didn't do anything," I said. Jesus, knowing my thoughts, looked me in the eye and said: **"Your only responsibility is always just to give it to Me"**[74,75]

That was a true inspiration, and it was quite sometime later, I realized in order to give the test to Jesus; *I had to hear his voice.*[76] I had been hearing His voice

---

[74] 1 Peter 5:7
[75] Psalm 55:22
[76] Revelation 3:20

ever since I had decided to engage in a relationship with Him. God highly values those who engage their heart, according to Jeremiah:

Jeremiah 30:21-22 *And their nobles shall be of themselves, and their governor shall proceed from the midst of them; and I will cause him to draw near, and he shall approach unto me: for who is this that engaged his heart to approach unto me? saith the LORD. And ye shall be my people, and I will be your God.*

Hearing His voice is a *required attribute* of those who know Him:

John 10:27 *My sheep hear my voice, and I know them, and they follow me:*

John 8:47 *He that is of God heareth God's words: ye therefore hear them not, because ye are not of God.*

Ears to hear are critical; we must hear His commands in order to obey them. In fact, the Ancient Hebrew Lexicon of the Bible defines the word obey as *A careful hearing of someone or something as well as responding appropriately in obedience or action.*[77] Obedience is critical to hearing God's voice:

Psalm 66:18 *If I regard iniquity in my heart, the Lord will not hear me:*

Understanding this scripture is vital to hearkening to God's voice. Strong's defines **regard** (**rââh** in Hebrew) as *approve, or consider* and **iniquity** (**'âven** in Hebrew) as *wickedness, specifically an idol.* An **idol** is defined by Webster's 1828 Dictionary as *anything on which we set our affections, that to which we indulge an excessive and sinful attachment.* Therefore, anytime worldly affections are set above the desire to love God, those worldly affections will hinder our spiritual ears from hearing God's voice. Paul also instructs those who "name the name of Christ" to depart from iniquity:

2 Timothy 2:19 *Nevertheless the foundation of God standeth sure, having this seal, The Lord knoweth them that are his. And, Let everyone that nameth the name of Christ depart from iniquity.*

Strong's defines iniquity in this verse as *unrighteousness.* Webster's 1828 dictionary defines **unrighteousness** as *a single unjust act, but more generally,* **when applied to persons, it denotes a habitual course of wickedness.** Those who continue in habitual sin actually "regard iniquity in the heart" and cannot

---

[77] Job 36:11 obey, AHLB

hear God's voice, forfeiting His guidance and intimacy. However, we can unblock any **hindrance** by asking the Lord Himself:

> **Psalm 51:10-12** *Create in me a clean heart, O God; and renew a right spirit within me. Cast me not away from thy presence; and take not thy holy spirit from me. Restore unto me the joy of thy salvation; and uphold me with thy free spirit.*

Hearing instruction from man may help us, but instruction from the Spirit is always profitable.[78] Only the Spirit knows the "what and when" for each of us; that is wisdom which comes straight from God. The Lord gave me an allegory about hearing God's voice called *"The Chasm."*

An Allegory: The Chasm

One morning as I was worshipping the Lord, I saw a vision.[79] I was standing on the edge of a chasm, with a cable, secured behind me, stretching out into nothingness. The cable was taut but disappeared into the fog; I could not see the other side of the chasm. As I was pondering the situation, a man came up from the woods below to my right, yelling, "hello! hello!" As he approached, I could see he was carrying some equipment; he was obviously the rugged wilderness type. When he finally got close enough so we could speak without shouting, he said, "I oversee the zip line. I hike to this location and bring zip line equipment when the Lord prompts me. Often, I get here, and no one is here, but it is all worthwhile when someone has waited[80] long enough, so my hike up here was not in vain." Somewhat concerned, I looked out over the chasm and asked, "This is a zip line? How far does it go?" "Don't know," he said, "I've never been across. The Lord charged me with helping others cross when they arrive here. Many times, they turn around and leave before I get here because they perceive this to be an impossible situation, or they are outright afraid of what is in front of them. Either way, they cannot proceed on the path, all because they would not wait. I have gotten here a few times," he explained, "and the person is on their way across without any equipment. They start crawling out over the line because they believe they know the Lord's will without hearing His voice. But you know what? That is exactly what they miss; the lesson here is to wait to hear[81] His voice. Those who do not wait are never successful.[82] I have heard their screams as they fall to the chasm floor." "How far down is it?" I asked. "It

---

[78] 1 Corinthians 12:7
[79] Acts 2:17
[80] Psalm 59:9
[81] John 10:27
[82] 1 Samuel 13:8-13

is about 2,000 feet from here to the bottom," he replied, "And of course, you cannot see the other side. Add to that the unpredictable weather, and you can see why many turn back. In fact, there is an entire village of people living comfortably right down in the valley near me. They have decided to stop the journey for fear of the unknown. They just do not have the courage to continue. As he handed me a trolley wheel, a carabiner, and a harness, he said, "You can hear the wind, but you cannot predict the weather because, at this altitude, the fog is present virtually all the time. Here is a piece of advice: wait until you hear the wind go silent – you will feel a prompting from your spirit to go. That is God's voice– do not hesitate. There is a very small window where you will be successful, and the only way to proceed is with patience and trust."[83]

As he turned to go, I thanked him for the advice and the much-needed equipment. He stopped and said, "Remember, there is only one way across the chasm, be still[84] and wait[85] for the perfect timing of the stillness of the wind and His command; be sure to seek His voice, for only then will you hear it.[86] The stillness and the voice; one without the other will not do – the stillness and the voice, in harmony." With that, he turned and smiled as he made his way back down through the trees…

The Lord showed me this vision for encouragement. Analogous to "The Test" vision at the long white table, I was now able to *hear His voice clearly*. The past, as I now knew it, had placed me in the valley in the allegory because I based my relationship with the Lord on some shallow assessment of the perception of men. I could not hear the voice of the Lord *because I did not even know Him*. Thus, I had no desire to cross the chasm; my comfort was more of a priority than pleasing God. However, I was now ready for the challenge because my priorities had changed; that was the primary reason for the spiritual progress I had experienced in the past year. I had made more progress in my relationship with the Almighty God in one year than I had in the previous forty-five. Only one explanation exists for this extraordinary progression: I had made an *active choice to know Him* because knowing God does not happen by default; it entails *a particular action from the heart* we must perform. The initial action I had made was a *deliberate decision to prioritize Him in my life, and it was that commitment from within that made all the difference*. I did not do it for a man to see, or for some other reason, a man told me about. I think this is

---

[83] 1 Kings 19:11-13
[84] Psalm 46:10
[85] Isaiah 40:31
[86] John 10:27

the most difficult, yet the most important part of the journey, the commencement. How does one begin? I had come to a point where I needed to self-assess what exactly I had been doing all those years in the church, and the answer came down to this: I had always assessed my value as a Christian according to the yardstick of men. I had been a board member in the church yet was spiritually deficient. I was deceived into believing I was doing what was necessary to know God. Although men believed I was a devoted Christian because I attended church every week, but, deep down where no man could see, I was secretly bound by pornography and lust; nothing I ever wanted anyone to know, so I kept it hidden. However, by hiding the ugly truth, I had made it more powerful.

It is important to note here that the *spiritual level of destruction* from addictions is entirely dependent upon the heart. Many struggle with addictions of many kinds and are held captive by the enemy. The struggle is important because it incorporates conviction as well as ongoing attempts to be free. Those struggling with bondage are ineffective and not overcomers. Hence, they are not living according to God's Plan for their lives.

> *Many attempt to break addiction and bondage through strength of will; but willful submission to God breaks all oppression of the enemy.*[87]

Others, who do not struggle but rather attempt to have a relationship with God but continue in disobedient behavior, are in rebellion and deceived. Rebellion prohibits the transformation required for salvation. Two men can exhibit the exact same disobedient behavior, and while one is saved but in bondage but the other unsaved and in rebellion, it is a matter of the heart. God can verify the motives of the heart, and therefore He is the perfect judge:

Jeremiah 17:10 *I the LORD search the heart, I try the reins, even to give every man according to his ways, and according to the fruit of his doings.*

Romans 2:16 *In the day when God shall judge the secrets of men by Jesus Christ according to my gospel.*

In my case, I was in rebellion, not willing to give up pornography but deceived into believing my relationship with God was still intact. I did not have a true relationship with God because I truly did not value what God valued; that was the crux of the problem. In fact, I did not even know what God valued; only the values determined by the perception of men. I had been ensnared by what Jesus had warned about:

---

[87] James 4:7

Luke 16:15 *And he said unto them, Ye are they which justify yourselves before men; but God knoweth your hearts: for that which is highly esteemed among men is abomination in the sight of God.*

I was not transformed, or even in the sanctification process; I was simply "doing good works" and assessing my value based on what I had constructed others to perceive of me. I had engineered a perception to verify my salvation based upon what *I believed* they saw. The worst part is *I believed it myself*; that only the outside appearance mattered, when the inside is all that matters; God sees all things. In fact, He sees and knows the heart; and He understands *all the imaginations of the thoughts:*

Hebrews 4:13 *Neither is there any creature that is not manifest in his sight: but all things are naked and opened unto the eyes of him with whom we have to do.*

Job 34:21 *For his eyes are upon the ways of man, and he seeth all his goings.*

1 Chronicles 28:9 *And thou, Solomon my son, know thou the God of thy father, and serve him with a perfect heart and with a willing mind: for the LORD searcheth all hearts, and understandeth all the imaginations of the thoughts: if thou seek him, he will be found of thee; but if thou forsake him, he will cast thee off for ever.*

1 Samuel 16:7 *But the LORD said unto Samuel, Look not on his countenance, or on the height of his stature; because I have refused him: for the LORD seeth not as man seeth; for man looketh on the outward appearance, but the LORD looketh on the heart.*

I had to know God first, *and then* obey what I heard in order to find the perfect path God had set for me. This is the most critical concept many miss. The first commandment is crucial to this concept:

Matthew 22:37-38 *Jesus said unto him, Thou shalt love the Lord thy God with all thy heart, and with all thy soul, and with all thy mind. This is the first and great commandment.*

Many misconstrue the sequence in which Jesus commanded us to obey Him; they read the scriptures much like the Pharisees and believe they receive everlasting life by doing the good works Jesus described. The Pharisees believed they could do the Word of God and reject Jesus, but He told them *eternal life is through Him:*

John 5:39-40 *Search the scriptures; for in them ye think ye have eternal life: and they are they which testify of me. And ye will not come to me, that ye might have life.*

Knowing Jesus is the only way to eternal life:

John 14:6 *Jesus saith unto him, I am the way, the truth, and the life: no man cometh unto the Father, but by me.*

When one attempts to achieve eternal life by doing good works, it is a deception, which will result in death. Jesus must be the primary force in our lives, not the secondary; we do the works not because they are in the scriptures; rather, *we do the works commanded by Him.* This is what Jesus was saying to the Pharisees in John 5:39-40 because they were doing the works in the scriptures, but they did not *know* Him. Without knowing Jesus, performing *the works through reading the scriptures is futile.* Jesus is the way, the truth, and the life; so, knowing Him is required to receive eternal life. This requires hearing His voice,[88] and that only comes with an intimate relationship with Him. It is not **what** is accomplished that matters; it is **how** it is accomplished. We must establish a relationship with God to be successful with a ministry, not IN a ministry, but WITH a ministry. God determines success to be that the ministry comes from Him to cause us to grow. It does not come from us to cause Him to grow.

A relationship with God always causes a ministry to develop. A ministry will not always cause a relationship with God to develop.

Many are lost because they get this backwards. They believe doing "good works" for God will get them into heaven or generate rewards. However, rewards only come to those who diligently seek Him,[89] and no one will enter heaven without an intimate relationship with God.[90] Knowing God, I would find, is the very purpose for which He created us because *everything comes from Him.* Therefore, perfection and completion come through knowing Him. Knowing Him caused me to give Him my heart; when He got a hold of my heart, He transformed my ideas, thoughts, beliefs, behaviors, and priorities to His perspective. He gave me another vision to instill the importance of this *giving of the heart.*

---

[88] John 10:27
[89] Hebrews 11:6
[90] Luke 13:27

A Vision: The Trade

I was holding up a bucket toward heaven – it was comprised of my heart, my will, and all the other junk of my life mixed in.[91] He reached down, took it from me, and said: **"That is a good trade."**[92]

One morning as I was praying, the Lord gave me an allegory about the importance of *hearing His voice and obeying it:*

An Allegory: The Travelers

There was a time when the requirement to be a Christian was *"to travel";* that was the only instruction given. Two men, Smith and Jones, had become Christians and had been reading their Bibles to know God as their local church had instructed. Each man had a car parked in front of his house, and the custom was to get in, drive it to the next intersection, and take right-hand turns at each subsequent intersection to come back to his starting place. They did this daily as they had heard this was the behavior of a traveler. Smith read the Bible through every year and had the notebook with each year checked off to prove it. He also logged the miles he traveled each year as he drove around the block each day.

Jones began on the same path as Smith, as per the instructions they had received when they first became Christians. Jones began to invest more time with the Lord than was necessary to read his Bible every day. In fact, Jones began to ask the Lord questions as to what the Bible meant and listen to others teach. He still traveled the same as Smith – he took three rights each day and ended up back at his house, just as instructed. Time passed, and one day Jones drove to the first intersection and he was about to take a right when he heard: "Take a left"

He had never experienced the voice, but he obeyed and took a left. As he drove, he continued receiving instructions that eventually put him on a highway. He had never driven on such a busy road with signs and rules and other cars driving fast – it was somewhat dangerous.

Meanwhile, Smith was now watching traveling shows on television to add to his Bible reading and traveling around the block. He had timed his traveling so he could complete it in a specific amount of time so he could fit it between other activities whenever he had an opening.

---

[91] Psalm 143:8
[92] Matthew 10:39

As Jones was driving on the highway, he obeyed the next command: "Take the next exit."

Soon he was in New York City. This was crazy! Pedestrians everywhere, traffic congestion, and kamikaze cabs. He spent a few years living and driving in the city before he received directions to head back out on a different highway, which now seemed like a country drive after driving in the city.
By now, Smith had downloaded some audio files of the Bible, so he could listen to the Bible while he was driving around the block. That way, he could multitask and cut down on the time spent following the rules to be a Christian and live life!

Jones, on the other hand, heard the next command to leave the highway and God told him to stop in front of a camping store; then he heard: "**Trade the car for a backpack, tent, and camping gear.**"

He gathered all the necessary camping gear with the help of the storeowner and departed out the rear door on a path to the backcountry. He was now reliant upon the Lord for deeper instructions on how and where to hunt for food and the habits of wild animals. He learned he must put his food high in the trees to avoid attracting predators. He spent several years in the forest but continued to follow the path that led to the mountain in the distance.

Smith had learned how to drive with one hand so he could listen to the Bible, travel, and eat all at the same time. Thus, he could now maximize time for recreation and other distractions, all while still conforming to the rules.

Jones reached the mountain and pulled out his climbing gear as the Lord directed him to scale a cliff to continue on the path. It was a whole new set of skills he needed to learn, and it took some time to figure it all out; while there were no wild animals to contend with, gravity was the new safety concern.

Smith had decided he could still read the Bible through in a year if he listened to twice as much every other day as he drove around the block twice every other day. This way, he still followed the traveler rules but was able to have every other day for recreation.

Meanwhile, Jones had reached the top of the mountain and the path that led the way down the other side. *Now, this is easy*, he thought, *walking downhill – it does not get any easier than this*. When he reached the bottom, he came to the beach, and the Lord said: "**Trade your camping gear for a boat ride out**

to the island."

As he heard the Lord's voice, Jones turned to see a man in a boat waiting to give him a ride five miles out to the island.

At this point, Smith began worrying about Jones. He had not seen him on the travel route and at the local church either. He asked others at the church if they had seen him, but they had not. They surmised he had probably backslidden, so they began praying the Lord would convict him and bring him back to the church.

Jones waved and thanked the man in the boat as he sped away and left Jones on the beach. "**Follow the path to a cave entrance in the center of the island.**"

Jones began walking and found the path was not difficult to follow and found his way to the cave entrance before nightfall. He communed with the Lord that evening and slept at the cave entrance for the night.

Smith had given up on Jones and redoubled his efforts to follow the rules he received when he became a Christian. He was sure to attend church every week now (he had skipped a few times in the summer and was reprimanded by others). He traveled around the block – even in the rain because he did not want to end up lost like Jones. He was glad to have known Jones because Jones' backsliding was a guiding post that kept him on the "straight and narrow."

Jones awoke the next morning and followed the path into the cave. This was a little more challenging than the path that led him here, but from the hiking and cliff climbing experience in the past, he had no problem navigating the rocky cave. At some points, he was chest-deep in fast-moving water as he strove against the current. At last, he arrived at the destination; the path had opened to a large cave with a high ceiling. In the center was a pool of dimly lit water, and he waited for further instructions. He admired the structure as best he could see in the dimly filtered light through the rocky ceiling forty feet above. Then the instructions came: "**Dive into the water.**"

Jones took a deep breath and dove in. He had trusted the Lord through this entire journey, and the Lord was always faithful in making it an amazing, joyous adventure. What awaited him beneath the water could only make him stronger, because he had learned to rely on the Lord completely. There was no place he would rather be. Further instructions followed "just in time" as he continued to rely on the Lord for each new path[93] of the adventure. Time

---

[93] Proverbs 12:28

passed, and both travelers eventually died and faced God in the judgment hall.

Smith had his notebooks of all he had done and gave them to the angel assigned to handle his case. The Lord sat on the throne, and as he looked at Smith, the Lord said: **"Depart from…"**
Smith quickly interrupted – he was sure the Lord had missed all his service, and he mentioned the notebooks and that he had read the Bible through every year for 35 years. The Lord said: "**That just makes you 35 times worse off than the person who read it once and didn't do it**"

Smith was flabbergasted. How could this be? He did all they told him; he followed the instructions exactly as he had been told. "**My Word is not something to be read only; it is to be done; I told you that. If you were reading to understand how to know me, you would have known. Instead, you read My Word to appease a man.**"
"**Depart from me, I never knew you.**"

As Jones entered the room, the Lord smiled and said:
"**Remember the command to dive into the water? Not many people who reached that point were able to do it, but you did. You reached a level of trust beyond most; and so, you will be trusted here more than most.**"

"**Well done, good and faithful servant; enter into the joy of the Lord.**"

CHAPTER 4

Diligently Seeking God: Are You Willing to Go A Little Further?

Hebrews 11:6 *But without faith it is impossible to please him: for he that cometh to God must believe that he is, and that he is a rewarder of them that diligently seek him.*

The Lord Rejoices Too

One afternoon, I happened to catch the end of the movie *"The Legend of Bagger Vance"* on television, and the Lord said: **"Be sure to see the rest; I will reveal to you more about who I am."**

I quickly rented the movie and eventually bought it. The story is about a golfer invited to a premier tournament, who struggles with pride and self-confidence. His more spiritual caddy helps the golfer conquer his inner demons and succeed both physically and spiritually. This was not a movie associated with the Bible, yet God used it to reveal Himself. He revealed His perspective – how He desires to have a close relationship and befriend us but will only fully engage when we turn toward Him.[94] He has already chosen us;[95] we just need to reciprocate by choosing Him. As I watched each scene, and He revealed His character, I associated His character traits from the movie to Bible verses in His Word. It was in the very last scene I encountered a problem. The caddy (who God revealed was Himself) departed and left the golfer to his own devices on the last hole. This represented when Jesus left the world, and He imparted the Holy Spirit to humanity. The golfer had learned all the essential skills and no longer needed his caddy at his side. The caddy was long gone by the time the golfer took the final shot – it was a difficult shot no one expected him to make. However, as the intricate training he had grasped kicked in, he was able to strike the ball perfectly, and success was all but assured. The ball tumbled into the hole, and the crowd erupted in

---

[94] Exodus 3:4
[95] John 15:16

35

applause. The caddy, on the beach far below, heard the cheers and stopped, cocked his head, and then spun around in a dance as if to release the joy inside at the feat his student had accomplished. It was then I set down my pencil and uttered, "God, I can't write that. I don't know of anywhere in your Word; you do that."

As the next week or so went by, I left the analysis of the movie unfinished, all complete except the ending. It seemed God had not accounted for the last scene, and I considered forgetting about it, but I knew God is perfect,[96] so there had to be a reason why He chose this movie to reveal Himself. A week passed, and I received a birthday card, which referenced a verse in Zephaniah chapter 3.

> **Zephaniah 3:17** *The LORD thy God in the midst of thee is mighty; he will save, he will rejoice over thee with joy; he will rest in his love, he will joy over thee with singing.*

I had gotten into the habit of searching the meanings of words used in the Bible in the original Hebrew and Greek languages to understand the deeper meaning before they were translated to the English words I was reading. I found the original words often have many English meanings in the original languages, so to understand the verse itself; it is important to know all the English words interpreters could have used. Therefore, I looked up each word of Zephaniah 3:17 and found the two words "*joy*" in that verse are from two different Hebrew words. The first one (**simchah** in Hebrew) meant *joy*, however, I almost fell out of my chair when I saw the meaning of the second word. Strong's concordance defines the Hebrew word for *joy* (**giyl** in Hebrew) **as to spin around (under the influence of violent emotion).** *The Creator of the Universe, the One True Living God, had answered my question, and my life would never be the same.* It was then I knew I would spend the remainder of my life on a quest to know and understand Him as Lord, King, Savior, and friend. He would use this encounter, years later, to remind me of His joy when I obeyed His commands – even to my own hurt.[97] I found God often referred back to past interactions such as this in order to emphasize His hand-iwork in the Plan He had so masterfully designed for me to follow.

Knowing God: From His Perspective
I had decided to take two of my granddaughters and my stepson to an amuse-ment park that included a waterpark. The youngest was four years old, so I was determined to keep a close eye on her for the duration of the trip. We

---

[96] Matthew 5:48
[97] Psalm 15:4

spent the morning enjoying the rides; after lunch, we changed our clothes and headed to the waterpark. This was a busy place, so I was sure to keep the four-year-old close; at one point, I was trying to get her to go down a slide, so I sat on the slide next to her to alleviate her fears. However, the water was spraying in her face, so she was apprehensive about moving forward. I knew we were holding up the line, but I really wanted her to have a positive experience. It was about that time I heard a voice behind me:

"I'm waiting."
"I'm waiting."
"I'm waiting."
"I'm waiting."
"I'm waiting."
"I'm waiting."

Finally, I turned around to see a seven-year-old just as the words were coming out of his mouth. I looked at him and said, "You can wait all day." *Well, that shut him up*, I thought; I turned my attention back to my granddaughter, who finally conquered the spray of water across her face, and we careened down the slide much to her delight. Later, as I was backing the car out of the parking lot, I said to the Lord, "Was that wrong? Should I have not said that to the little boy?"
The Lord declared: "**I say the same thing.**"

Then He inquired: "**How many people were in that water park?**"

I figured there were about two hundred fifty.
He asked: "**How many of them did you know?**"

Well, I thought, *I only knew my two grandchildren and stepson, for a total of three.* Then the Lord revealed the entire park represented the world, and the water park within the amusement park symbolized His church. The people in the water park were people in His church, and *He only truly knows about three out of 250 of them (just over one percent).* Just one year earlier, I was one of the people He did not know, and now God was telling me *He does not know the vast majority of His church*; those He does not know continually say, "I'm waiting" for an answer to their prayers, or for Him to act in their lives; but because He does not know them, He refutes them:[98] "**You can wait all day.**"

---

[98] Matthew 13:15

37

As I drove away from the park, I realized a day is as a thousand years to the Lord,[99] so in effect, He is saying **He will not hear those who He does not know; just as those He does not know cannot hear Him.** Jesus affirms it:

> **John 10:27-28** *My sheep hear my voice, and I know them, and they follow me: And I give unto them eternal life; and they shall never perish, neither shall any man pluck them out of my hand.*

Whether or not Jesus truly knows us will determine our final condition on judgment day; Jesus revealed exactly what He would say to those He does not know:

> **Matthew 7:21-23** *Not ever one that saith unto me, Lord, Lord, shall enter into the kingdom of heaven; but he that doeth the will of my Father which is in heaven. Many will say to me in that day, Lord, Lord, have we not prophesied in thy name? and in thy name have cast out devils? and in thy name done many wonderful works? And then will I profess unto them, I never knew you: depart from me, ye that work iniquity.*

Whether Jesus knows us is *determined by Him*,[100,101] not us, or by any other person. That is the deception; I believed I knew God because of the perception of men. They determined I knew God from looking at the outside, but God looks on the heart, and He determines our relationship with Him based upon *His evaluation* of our internal spirit. He says He "tries" the reins.

> **Jeremiah 17:10** *I the LORD search the heart, I try the reins, even to give every man according to his ways, and according to the fruit of his doings.*

Prepare for Rain

I was praying one morning, and the Lord instructed: "**Prepare for Rain**"

I knew rain in the Bible represented blessing, so I was excited even though I did not know what it meant. I did recognize the Lord was already blessing me in many ways: I had relatives coming to remodel my kitchen, and people delivering wood to my house at no cost, among other things, so I replied: "Lord, it's already raining" to which He replied: "**That is just a sprinkle; Prepare for Rain.**"

That was from His Word:

---

[99] 2 Peter 3:8
[100] 1 Corinthians 8:3
[101] Galatians 4:9

Deuteronomy 11:14 *That I will give you the rain of your land in his due season, the first rain and the latter rain, that thou mayest gather in thy corn, and thy wine, and thine oil.*

The definitions of these words would shape the very core of my walk with the Lord. He spoke into my life what He called me to do; I just did not know it yet. Strong's defines the words ***first rain (yôreh*** in Hebrew) as ***sprinkling,*** and the Ancient Hebrew Lexicon of the Bible defines ***first rain*** as ***a throwing of the finger to show a direction to walk or live. The throwing of an arrow. The throwing down of water in the rain.*** Strong's defines the latter words ***rain (malqowsh*** in Hebrew) as ***figuratively, eloquence,*** and the Ancient Hebrew Lexicon of the Bible defines ***latter rain*** as ***a late rain that causes a latter growth of crops.*** The meaning of the phrase "***Prepare for Rain***" meant He would teach me which way to walk His predetermined path for my life, and through obedience, I would receive eloquence. The Lord would support this original phrase through visions and circumstances revealed in upcoming chapters. For that reason, the word ***eloquence*** is defined here; Webster's 1828 Dictionary defines *eloquence as* ***the art of speaking well, or with fluency and elegance, appropriate and rich expressions, with fluency, animation, and suitable action. Hence, eloquence is adapted to please, affect, and persuade—*the power of speaking with fluency and elegance. Elegant language is uttered with fluency and animation. It is sometimes applied to written language.***

Howbeit, at this time, I did not yet fully understand the meaning of the phrase, so I continued diligently with my daily devotions. A week or so later, I was praying, and the Holy Spirit was nudging me to do something about my conversation – to stop negative things from coming out of my mouth.[102] A few days later, I got a call from my elderly friend who told me she had some books for me to read – *they were all about my mouth.* One of these books was entitled *God's Creative Power ® Gift Collection by Charles Capps.* I opened this book, and it had three subjects: Wisdom, Healing, and Finances. In each of those subjects were numerous verses in italics; the reader was to read aloud. This took about 20 minutes and seemed very ritualistic, so I asked the Lord why He wanted me to do this. He asked: "**How do you prepare for rain?**"

I said, "By planting seeds."[103] He affirmed: "**That's right; that is what you**

---

[102] Ephesians 4:29
[103] Hosea 10:12

are doing."

Then I found it in His Word:

> **Hosea 10:12** *Sow to yourselves in righteousness, reap in mercy; break up your fallow ground: for it is time to seek the LORD*, till he come and rain righteousness upon you.

It was then I knew reading this book aloud directly connected me to the rain of the future; I have been reading it daily ever since. Then I decided to look up the author who wrote it. *"Of course,"* I thought, as I read Charles Capps, now with the Lord, *was a farmer for 30 years before he wrote "God's Creative Power ® Gift Collection by Charles Capps."* That is how God is: incredibly detailed in how He guides and directs. Sometime later, I would receive a vision of a little white house further confirming the original phrase, *Prepare for rain.*

A Vision: The House and the Cornfield

I saw, in a vision, a little white house in the middle of a cornfield; the corn was so numerous it was right up against the house; there was no yard, and it extended as far as I could see. At the time, there was a drought where I was living, and the words came out of my mouth "But Lord, it is not raining." He said: **"It is raining *inside* the house."**

This was from the verse concerning the fear of the Lord.

> **Psalm 25:12** *What man is he that feareth the LORD? him shall he teach in the way that he shall choose.*

I would later understand the meaning of that vision; Strong's defines the word ***teach* (yarah** in Hebrew) as **properly, to flow as water (i.e., to rain).** *The rain was teaching,* and the corn stalks were others blessed through what the Lord had taught me.

I would often ask the Lord in prayer to search my heart and if there was anything in me not of Him, to root it up and burn it. I would see a vision of a hand coming down and pulling up small weeds; my viewpoint was from about two feet off the ground, looking down on a small plot of land. After about a month or so of praying this way, I asked Him to *plant anything in Him that was not in me.* One day, my viewpoint in the vision changed from looking down on a small patch of land to looking forward. It was then I could see the small white house in the distance; *the immense cornfield was in my heart.* This

40

was the desire He had placed within me:[104] that He would bless me that I may bless others.

That was a powerful revelation; the words "Prepare for rain" could be translated as "Prepare for teaching," and I was about to receive an understanding of the Lord's delight when He finds one who delights in Him.

The Perfect Stone

I was working on a project in my back yard, and the Lord used it to reveal what *He feels* when He finds someone with a perfect heart. My wife loved the sound of streams so much we would sit by them for hours so she could hear the sound of the gurgling water flowing through the moss-covered rocks. This gave her so much joy I decided to build a waterfall and stream in our back yard so we would not have to drive to hear the water; instead, we could enjoy the sound of the stream right in our back yard. I was in the process of digging out from underneath a crawl space under our house to increase the size of our basement when I encountered a number of boulders I had to leave in place as I removed the loose dirt. Once finished, I jackhammered the rocks into pieces and piled them in the backyard; I used the pieces of rock to build the waterfall and stream. This was a three-foot-high waterfall atop a hill with a 22-foot stream and a powerful pump at the bottom, which kept the waterfall constantly running. I began placing the rocks together to form the streambed; they were pieces of boulders (this was not a kit), building it was like a 22-foot 3D jigsaw puzzle with no picture to reference. I pieced together broken fragments of boulders in order to build the waterfall spillway and streambed. Often, as the stones were not seamless, I filled in the gaps between the rocks with waterfall foam. After I had placed over 100 stones, I came across a stone that fits perfectly with the stones around it. I was so excited. I said aloud, "That's *perfect!*" Immediately the Holy Spirit said: **"That's how it is."**

As soon as I heard the words, the Lord imparted the meaning: He is building a spiritual house;[105] we are the living stones,[106] and ***He gets excited[107]*** when he finds a perfect (complete) stone -- *a stone that has allowed itself to be shaped through suffering* -- for the exact purpose He created it. He says this in His Word:

---

[104] Psalm 37:4
[105] Ephesians 2:19-22
[106] 1 Peter 2:5
[107] Zephaniah 3:17

Proverbs 11:1 *A false balance is abomination to the LORD: but a just weight is his delight.*

The Strong's definitions for three words in that verse:
> *just* (**shâlêm** *in Hebrew*) means **complete, perfect**
> *weight* (**'eben** *in Hebrew*) means **a stone**
> *delight* (**ratsown** *in Hebrew*) means **(good) pleasure**

Proverbs 11:1 can be understood as: "**but a perfect stone is his good pleasure.**"

The Lord is looking for perfect stones to build His house:

> **1 Peter 2:5** *Ye also, as lively stones, are built up a spiritual house, an holy priesthood, to offer up spiritual sacrifices, acceptable to God by Jesus Christ.*

In order to become a perfect stone for His house, we must build our house within;[108] this is completed with wisdom and understanding, and furnished by knowledge:

> **Proverbs 24:3-4** *Through wisdom is an house builded; and by understanding it is established: And by knowledge shall the chambers be filled with all precious and pleasant riches.*

Strong's definition of **wisdom** (**chokmah** in Hebrew) means **wisdom (in a good sense): —skilful, wisdom, wisely, wit;** and Webster's 1828 definition is, in Scripture theology, **wisdom** is true religion; godliness; piety; **the knowledge and fear of God, and sincere and uniform obedience to his commands. This is *wisdom*, which is from above.**
The Heart of God

The Lord decided it was time for me to understand His *feelings*; how He truly felt when humans rejected Him. I was running a Bible study for about ten people in our home when one of the group members began receiving words from the Lord and posting them on the Bible study website. At first, I was excited the Lord was moving in our group. Then slowly, week after week, the posts continued, and the group members began responding to the posts. In the beginning, I felt it was necessary to keep involved on the website to maintain some control of the group. Eventually, though, the posts came every morning, and I found I was losing control – it seemed as though the

---

[108] Luke 17:21

group was following this one member. I complained to the Lord, to no avail. I found I was getting jealous, but I did not attempt to stop it because the posts were indeed Biblical; it was clear to me the Lord was speaking to this person. As time passed, I found there was nothing I could do – God was not responding to my complaints, and I was completely at a loss for how to handle the "takeover," as I called it. I spoke with my accountability partner (who was not attending this Bible study), explained the situation to him, and confessed I was jealous. Once spoken aloud, the confession opened the path for me the next morning to repeat those words to the Lord in prayer. I spoke to God about the jealousy – could I have a jealous spirit that must be cast out? Could I be jealous without a spirit of jealousy? I said, "Lord, I am jealous about this – I am losing my people." Immediately He replied: "**Yes, I am a Jealous God.**[109] **You lost your people just like I lost mine; now you know what it feels like**"

Immediately upon finishing prayer, God released me from this jealous feeling. That was true intimacy – experiencing the heart of God. The next day, the posts stopped. The following Sunday, I approached the person who had been posting on the website and told him the story. He responded by telling me the day of my prayer; the Lord told him to stop posting on the website. Sometimes God does not answer prayer because we are in spiritual training, and an answer to our prayer will interrupt the lesson. The Lord is always more interested in our spiritual growth than our personal comfort. If we do not respond correctly during the lesson, we will likely never understand what happened or why. As spiritual growth goes, it is usually uncomfortable as God replaces our nature with His; He does not provide growth so we can abide at the mountaintop around His feet admiring His teachings. The Lord is a man of war, and He has a "book of wars:"

Exodus 15:3 *The LORD is a man of war: the LORD is his name.*

Numbers 21:14 *Wherefore it is said in the book of the wars of the Lord, What he did in the Red sea, and in the brooks of Arnon,*

We receive spiritual growth by investing time with Him for one reason: to acquire the skill and art of advanced weaponry. These skills are required to defeat the enemy – whose desire is to steal, kill, and destroy.[110] The more advanced these skills become, the more difficult the attacks will be to overcome. God allows this because He knows our capabilities; He is looking for

---

[109] Deuteronomy 4:24
[110] John 10:10

continual spiritual growth to create Godly Warriors who will become an integral part of His arsenal against the enemy. He uses circumstances to teach success in spiritual warfare; these tests are not to determine overall success or failure, but rather to teach us to grow in the Spirit:

2 Samuel 22:35, Psalm 18:34 *He teacheth my hands to war; so that a bow of steel is broken by mine arms.*

Psalm 144:1 A Psalm of David. Blessed be the LORD my strength, which teacheth my hands to war, and my fingers to fight:

I now had a small understanding of *how God felt*, and it was heartbreaking, but He was about to instruct me on **how** to have a closer relationship with Him.

Going a Little Further
It was now about two years after I had begun to pray in earnest to build a relationship with the Lord. One day, He guided me regarding the act of praying itself: **"If you really want to know me, you are going to have to pray in tongues."**[111]

Many are skeptical about tongues, but that is because tongues are so powerful the enemy introduced confusion into the subject. Satan does not mind if you believe in tongues if you never use them; or if you believe tongues are only for some people. After all, that is in direct conflict with God's Word:

James 1:17 *Every good gift and every perfect gift is from above, and cometh down from the Father of lights, with whom is no variableness, neither shadow of turning.*

That means God does not exclude anyone from His gifts; He is no respecter of persons:

Ephesians 6:9 *And, ye masters, do the same things unto them, forbearing threatening: knowing that your Master also is in heaven; neither is there respect of persons with him.*

That means He sees everyone the same; God holds no one higher in respect than any other. All His promises are yes and amen;[112] He excludes no one from any promises:

---

[111] 1 Corinthians 14:2
[112] 2 Corinthians 1:20

2 Corinthians 1:19-20 *For the Son of God, Jesus Christ, who was preached among you by us, even by me and Silvanus and Timotheus, was not yea and nay, but in him was yea. For all the promises of God in him are yea, and in him Amen, unto the glory of God by us.*

Some believe tongues are no longer valid today – they were only for Biblical times; others believe they are only for "special people" and not for everyone. This is deception, pure and simple.[113] Those who believe tongues are not for everyone simply cannot be convinced otherwise; they are deceived. Praying in tongues *requires* faith but also *builds* faith. These are individual tongues, also known as *praying in the Spirit*, as one would pray in private devotions. There are other tongues for public use; only some people have that gift. This is where the enemy introduced confusion because he would have you believe not everyone can speak in tongues; this could not be further from the truth. Private tongues are available to everyone, and they promote obedience through edification:

1 Corinthians 14:4 *He that speaketh in an unknown tongue edifieth himself; but he that prophesieth edifieth the church.*

Webster's 1828 dictionary defines **edification** as *a building up, in a moral and religious sense, instruction,* **improvement and progress of the mind,** *in knowledge, in morals, or in faith and holiness.* Thus, privately praying in tongues, *also known as praying in the Spirit,* renews the mind as commanded in the following two verses:

Romans 12:2 *And be not conformed to this world: but be ye transformed by the renewing of your mind, that ye may prove what is that good, and acceptable, and perfect, will of God.*

Ephesians 4:23 *And be renewed in the spirit of your mind;*

The Greek word for edify (**oikodomeō**) means **to be a house-builder, i.e., construct or (figuratively) confirm, embolden.** So, praying in the Spirit also builds God's house:

Ephesians 2:22 *In whom ye also are builded together for an habitation of God through the Spirit.*

1 Peter 2:5 *Ye also, as lively stones, are built up a spiritual house, an holy priesthood,*

---

[113] Acts 2:4

to offer up spiritual sacrifices, acceptable to God by Jesus Christ.

Speaking in tongues is a powerful part of a relationship with God, but we must believe it in order to experience it. As with all spiritual things, a small bit of faith is required to overcome inertia.[114] Once results are experienced, there is confidence all things are possible.[115] Some have questioned the importance of tongues; after all, if we can pray in our native language, why do we need to pray in tongues?

Suppose we are like snails on the side of train tracks. A locomotive comes along, and in order to communicate with us, it must slow down to our pace. That is what it is like praying in our native language. We think it is efficient; however, we are communicating with the Creator of the Universe, whose thoughts and ways are higher than ours.[116] On the other hand, if we speak in tongues, we, as snails, are able to jump onto the train and travel at speeds we never thought could exist. We travel more in one minute on the train than we could ever travel as a snail in a lifetime. Intimacy with the Lord intensifies our ability to journey in the spiritual realm. He is always available to communicate with us. However, using our language, the exchange of information is extremely slow. When we communicate in *His heavenly language*, although the information imparted to us is beyond our natural understanding, our *spirit* is edified.[117] Praying in tongues edifies the spirit to promote obedience of the flesh; our spirit becomes joined with God's spirit. His Word says God is a Spirit and those who worship Him in spirit and in truth are *true worshippers*:

> **John 4:23** *But the hour cometh, and now is, when the true worshippers shall worship the Father in spirit and in truth: for the Father seeketh such to worship him.*

> **John 4:24** *God is a Spirit: and they that worship him must worship him in spirit and in truth.*

Those who worship Him in spirit become more intimate with Him, which reinforces *relentless obedience*, also known as the fear of the Lord. The fear of the Lord is the catalyst to our progress in the spiritual realm, namely

---

[114] Matthew 17:20
[115] Mark 9:23
[116] Isaiah 55:9
[117] 1 Corinthians 14:4

wisdom,[118] knowledge[119] , and understanding[120] from God's perspective. I had received the baptism of the Holy Spirit with the evidence of speaking in tongues[121,122] years before, but I had shelved it. I never practiced, so although I had the ability to speak in tongues, I had no idea of the power associated with doing it. Although I was uncomfortable with praying in tongues, He had told me it is one of the aspects of *how to know Him*, so I began. I prayed in tongues for the first time for about three minutes; then I pushed to five, then fifteen. I had decided when I reached 30 minutes daily; I would continue that as part of my devotions. I found praying in tongues was extremely difficult primarily because my mind would wander as I performed what *seemed to be* an unproductive task, which is exactly what God said it would seem to be:

1 Corinthians 14:14 *For if I pray in an unknown tongue, my spirit prayeth, but my understanding is unfruitful.*

I did not understand what I was saying; I just spoke in faith, believing what the Lord had said; speaking in tongues would make my relationship with Him more intimate. No sooner had I reached my goal of speaking in tongues for 30 minutes, when I received a book in the mail from my elder, mentoring friend: *"The Walk of the Spirit – The Walk of Power: The Vital Role of Praying in Tongues."*[123] A man who dedicated himself to praying in tongues eight hours a day wrote this book. He found praying in tongues to be extremely boring, and I was interested in how he overcame that obstacle. As I read, I eventually arrived at what the Lord wanted me to understand: the author noted the Holy Spirit is not "hard of hearing" and so one could pray in tongues under their breath while simultaneously praying silently in their native language. Well, *that revelation set me free.* I was able to pray in tongues while simultaneously praying for leaders, family, and others, so I decided to increase praying in tongues to one hour per day. I accomplished this by praying in tongues *almost as a whisper* while praying in my native language silently. The first day, I easily reached one hour and decided this would become the timeframe for the praying part of my devotions. However, God had other plans. The next morning, in prayer, as I reached the 55-minute mark, I saw a vision of a man sitting by a stone wall in a field. I pushed the scene out of my head (realizing

---

[118] Psalm 111:10
[119] Proverbs 1:7
[120] Proverbs 9:10
[121] Luke 3:16
[122] Acts 2:4
[123] Roberson, Dave

it was from the movie "Shawshank Redemption"). No sooner had I dismissed it, the scene reappeared, the man sitting at the wall opened a note, and it read: **"If you've come this far, maybe you're willing to come a little further."**

The Lord had used a scene from "The Shawshank Redemption" to encourage me. The actual letter in the movie said:

"Dear Red, if you're reading this, you've gotten out. And if you have come this far, maybe you are willing to come a little further. You remember the name of the town, don't you? I could use a good man to help me get my project on wheels. I will keep an eye out for you and the chessboard ready. Remember, Red, hope is a good thing, maybe the best of things, and no good thing ever dies. I will be hoping that this letter finds you and finds you well. Your friend, Andy."

A few days later, the Lord further revealed the connection to the Shawshank Redemption:

Andy was falsely accused and sent to prison; My Son was falsely accused and died on the cross. Andy escaped from prison; My Son escaped death. Andy went to an island to get a place ready; My Son has gone to prepare a place for you. You are at the wall; Are you willing to come a little further?

The next line in the movie is, "Get busy living, or get busy dying." I decided to waste no time and get busy dying, losing my life in order to find it.[124] The Creator of the Universe was actually encouraging me to push further in my quest to know Him,[125] so the next day I began praying in tongues for 90 minutes a day. I kept this up for a while, and I had been reading the Bible for 30 minutes a day, so I was investing about two hours a day in devotions with the Lord the first thing in the morning. This went on for a week or so until I realized I was 24 minutes short of spending the first 10 percent of the day with the Lord. God's Word speaks of giving the first 10 percent of our increase to the Lord,[126] so I decided to do that with my *time*. I slowly added time to the two hours until I reached two hours and 24 minutes (10 percent of 24 hours). I would read the Bible for 30 minutes, pray in tongues (and silently in English) for 90 minutes, and lay face down on the floor, worshipping the Lord for 24 minutes. I wondered, was this the Lord's plan, or was I just guessing? Something felt right about it, and I decided to continue hoping

---

[124] Matthew 10:39
[125] James 4:8
[126] Malachi 3:10

He would eventually confirm it or direct me toward a different path. Early in this pursuit, the Lord told me to rest on Sundays, the days I attended church,[127] and allow the church experience to be my devotions for that day, making my devotions six days per week. It *was eight months later;* I got a call from my elder friend who sent me the book on tongues; as always, we discussed how the Lord was performing His Word in our lives. She asked me how I was doing, and I replied, "I have been giving the first 10 percent of my time to the Lord." She told me the Lord had directed her to do exactly that five years earlier, but she had not been able to do it. Two weeks later, I was in a store parking lot where I happened upon an older couple I knew from church 20 years before. The wife asked me how I was doing, and I answered I was dedicating the first 10 percent of my day to the Lord. She revealed the Lord had told her to do exactly that 20 years before, but she had not been able to do it. As I was driving home, the Lord displayed these words on my windshield: **"That's what I meant"**

That was a direct reference to His original statement: *If you have come this far, maybe you want to come a little further.* Giving the first 10 percent of my day to the Lord was "going a little further," and God had confirmed it. *I had found my path to know Him.*[128] This was an *extremely important milestone* because finding the path to know Him is personal for everyone. That is the one major task to accomplish in life; once we discover our specific path, travel on that path toward the promise of abundant life begins.[129] That is exactly what happened next, and it was an experience I would not soon forget.

Ask Me for Something

The Old Testament story of Solomon is well known and intriguing. The King of the Universe told Solomon to ask Him for anything he wanted:

> **1 Kings 3:5** *In Gibeon the LORD appeared to Solomon in a dream by night: and God said, Ask what I shall give thee.*

Solomon asked for wisdom, and it pleased the Lord:

> **1 Kings 3:9-10** *Give therefore thy servant an understanding heart to judge thy people, that I may discern between good and bad: for who is able to judge this thy so great a people? And the speech pleased the Lord, that Solomon had asked this thing.*

---

[127] Exodus 34:21
[128] Jeremiah 29:11-13
[129] John 10:10

Therefore, the Lord granted Solomon's request, then blessed him with things he had not asked for:

1 Kings 3:11-14 *And God said unto him, Because thou hast asked this thing, and hast not asked for thyself long life; neither hast asked riches for thyself, nor hast asked the life of thine enemies; but hast asked for thyself understanding to discern judgment; Behold, I have done according to thy words: lo, I have given thee a wise and an understanding heart; so that there was none like thee before thee, neither after thee shall any arise like unto thee. And I have also given thee that which thou hast not asked, both riches, and honour: so that there shall not be any among the kings like unto thee all thy days. And if thou wilt walk in my ways, to keep my statutes and my commandments, as thy father David did walk, then I will lengthen thy days.*

This story is often cited for the fact that Solomon asked for wisdom to judge God's people and not anything for himself. This pleased the Lord, so Solomon received not only wisdom but also riches, honor, and long life. What most readers miss is how Solomon came to that opportunity. The answer is in the verses just prior to God's question:

1 Kings 3:3-4 *And Solomon loved the LORD, walking in the statutes of David his father: only he sacrificed and burnt incense in high places. And the king went to Gibeon to sacrifice there; for that was the great high place: a thousand burnt offerings did Solomon offer upon that altar.*

David had a heart after God,[130] and Solomon loved the Lord by walking in David's statutes. In the next verse, God gives Solomon the opportunity to ask for whatever he wanted. It is important to understand God did not grant Solomon the right to ask for anything while apprehensively hoping for the right answer. *He already knew the answer*, because Solomon had dedicated his whole heart to the Lord and walked in His statutes. This story is remarkable, but most believe it would not happen today. After all, it was in the Old Testament, and God does not do things like that today. That is not true to God's Word; He says He never changes:

Malachi 3:6 *For I am the LORD, I change not; therefore, ye sons of Jacob are not consumed.*

Hebrews 13:8 *Jesus Christ the same yesterday, and today, and forever.*

The reason Old Testament stories do not happen today is not that God has

---

[130] 1 Kings 11:4

changed; *it is because His people have changed.* The temporal distractions have increased as time has progressed, so many of God's people are not fully devoted to Him. I had decided at the beginning of this journey to *do whatever He requested and obey relentlessly* to determine if God would really perform His Word. I was way past that now; I knew He would not only perform it. *He wanted to perform it.* One morning, I was just finishing prayers, and the Lord declared: **"You have not because you ask not."**[131]

I acknowledged, "I know. I just don't know what to ask for." My prayers had always been for salvation, wisdom, insight, and knowledge for my leaders, as well as salvation for family members and others, the Lord would remind me of during prayer. For myself, I would only ask anything He saw in me, which was not of Him, to be pulled up and burned.[132] I finished praying and began to climb the stairs from the basement to the kitchen, and I heard: **"Ask me for something, and I will give it to you."**

I said aloud, "There is no way I just heard that," and I walked into the kitchen on my way to my office. As soon as I reached the office, He said it again: **"Ask me for something, and I will give it to you."** [133]

This time I knew what I heard was real; I knew this was serious because God always does what He says because He holds His Word above His name.[134] *I need to answer this,* I thought, so I sat down and took some time to think about what it was I really wanted. I wanted to be very deliberate; after all, this was a defining moment in my life, and I knew whatever I asked for, the King of the Universe *would be faithful to fulfill.* After about 20 minutes of contemplating, I asked myself, "What brings me joy?" Then I knew what it was; I said, *"All I want to do is talk about you."* That was truly what gave me the most joy - - when I was telling stories about who He was, what He had done, and how I had learned to know Him. It was at this point I realized *He already knew the answer.* He was not waiting anxiously, hoping I would choose what He wanted for my life. He knew what the answer would be because *He already had a hold of my entire heart;* my life's ambition was to please God, and He knew it, so the only answer I would give would be the desire He had placed in my heart.[135]

---

[131] James 4:2
[132] Matthew 15:13
[133] John 15:16
[134] Psalm 138:2
[135] Psalm 37:4

Meanwhile, He wanted to show me how to increase my faith by speaking His Word.

CHAPTER 5

Words: The Force Behind the Sword

Proverbs 18:21 *Death and life are in the power of the tongue: and they that love it shall eat the fruit thereof.*

A Question about Corrupt Communication

I was running a small group Bible study in my home, and for some unknown reason, church leadership was meddling with multiple small group Bible studies by directing people to leave one and attend another. This created a lot of confusion. "We know where it is best for people to learn," the leaders would say. I was perplexed, but I knew nothing could take place unless God allowed it. Shortly afterward, I got a call from a girl who had been attending the small group Bible study at my house. She was upset at how the leaders had treated her, and she vowed not to go back to church again. I told her of my feelings about how the leaders were operating the small group Bible studies, but I submitted to my authority and let the Lord determine the outcome. I was at peace, and I knew He saw everything that happened, so I refused to be offended. We talked a little more, and she thanked me and hung up. The next morning, I was praying, and I said to the Lord, "You know I speak this phrase every day about corrupt communication:

> *I let no corrupt communication proceed out of my mouth, but that, which is good to edifying, that it may bring grace to the hearer. I grieve not the Holy Spirit of God, whereby I am sealed unto the day of redemption.*[136]

However, I only know when I fail at it. I realize just after I say something I should not, and I ask for forgiveness and repent, but what about when I pass that test. I never see the good come when I do not allow corrupt communication to proceed from my mouth." According to James, that is not an easy thing to do:

---

[136] Ephesians 4:29-30

James 3:5 *Even so the tongue is a little member, and boasteth great things. Behold, how great a matter a little fire kindleth!*

Nonetheless, through all my failures in communication, there were some victories, so I just wanted to know what happened when I did it correctly when I stopped myself from saying something negative. No sooner had I finished praying than I received a text from the girl the day before. She said through our conversation; she was able to look past the unfair treatment and see the situation from a spiritual perspective; her relationship with the Lord transcends any mistreatment by any man or leader. She thanked me for the epiphany and went on her way. How amazing is God! He showed me the truth in that verse. The verse reads, "Let no corrupt communication..." That means if it is not corrupt – even if it *seems neutral*, He can use it to further His Kingdom. I had learned never to underestimate the power of words:

Proverbs 18:21 *Death and life are in the power of the tongue: and they that love it shall eat the fruit thereof.*

Matthew 12:36 But I say unto you, That every idle word that *men shall speak, they shall give account thereof in the day of judgment.*

I was also learning *to obey what I heard* is just as important; God had been using these experiences one after another to transform me to walk in the spirit and not after the flesh.[137] I had done my best in my relationship with the Lord to live according to my original proclamation to Him, "Tell me what to do, and I will do it," but now it was time to test my allegiance. I had been making decisions based on obedience and eternal consequences, but God designed the next test to determine my commitment to Him.

No Respecter of Persons

I had heard stories about the new leader in our organization at work; he was no pushover, he managed according to results, and since none of us knew him, there would certainly be no favoritism. He often used the Lord's name in vain, and the Holy Spirit had impressed upon me a Bible verse in Proverbs concerning speaking boldly against blasphemous conversation:

Proverbs 29:24 *Whoso is partner with a thief hateth his own soul: he heareth cursing, and bewrayeth it not.*

---

[137] Romans 8:5

After researching the Hebrew meaning of that verse, I realized it means: to hear the use of the Lord's name in vain and not oppose it; I was condoning it, and "taking away a portion of the evil." This causes the spiritual senses to become dull. The thief is Satan; passively to accept the use of the Lord's name in vain is partnering with evil. So, I knew when this leader visited our building for a meeting; I would have to talk with him about using the Lord's name in vain (because he often committed the infraction). Sure enough, ten minutes into the meeting, he began to curse. At the end of the meeting, he asked if there were any questions; I waited until most everyone had filed out of the room and got his attention before he left. I told him I had a question, and he stepped back into the room, so there was just the two of us. The Holy Spirit immediately instructed me to sit down, which put me in a position of submission. I then told him I recognized he was my superior, and I respected him. Not expecting to hear that, he quickly gave me his attention. I asked if he could refrain from using the Lord's name in vain; he surprisingly asked, "What did I say?" He had not even realized he was doing it. I mentioned how Satan constantly tries to demean Jesus' name because it is the most powerful name in the universe; I told him when he uses the Lord's name in vain, he undoes everything I pray for him every morning as my leader. He was pleasantly surprised, thanked me for bringing it to his attention, and said he would work on it. Then he shook my hand as we left the room. I did not realize until later, by following cues of the Holy Spirit, I had exhibited humility and the fear of the Lord all in one conversation. By doing that, God granted two spiritual things. I had brought upon myself "riches and honor, and life," and the enemy had lost access to me.

> **Proverbs 22:4** *By humility and the fear of the LORD are riches, and honour, and life.*

> **Proverbs 29:25** *The fear of man bringeth a snare: but whoso putteth his trust in the LORD shall be safe.*

The meaning of the word **safe *('sâgab* in Hebrew)** is *"especially inaccessible."* The Lord honors those who honor Him[138] , and His Word says I was in no manner to be afraid of a man:

> **Isaiah 51:12** *I, even I, am he that comforteth you: who art thou, that thou shouldest be afraid of a man that shall die, and of the son of man which shall be made as grass.*

---

[138] 1 Samuel 2:30

All I had to do is believe it *and do it.* Six months later, my leader visited our building for another meeting and *did not curse once.*

The Power of Speaking God's Word

There was a storm brewing at my workplace. I had been working from home for several years when there was a shift in personnel in our organization; we now had a new high-level leader. After some investigation, this new leader realized about 75 percent of the 800 people reporting in the organization were working at home. She decided everyone should report to the office, and the first item on the agenda for her very first meeting was *work locations.* The result was a new work-at-home policy would be forthcoming in the next few months. I had been working at home for about ten years, so I was concerned about the ramifications of the impending changes. *Working at home meant I had no commute time, which allowed me to continue devoting the first 10 percent of my day to the Lord,* changing that could jeopardize my overall spiritual growth and time with the Lord, and *I felt threatened.* While I was awaiting the decision, I was taking a shower one day, and the words suddenly came out of my mouth: "Walk in the light as He is in the light;[139] ask what you will, and it shall be done."[140] The Holy Spirit had recognized my agonizing over the situation at hand, so He pushed the words from my mouth to answer my own thoughts. I responded to Him with my request: I told the Lord a king was after my relationship with Him, and I needed the extra time in the morning to maintain it. I told Him this king was too big for me; I needed His help because nothing is too big for Him.[141] Two weeks later, management released the new work-at-home policy: There would be absolutely no working at home at any time, except for a select group of individuals, which happened to include our group of nine. However, the new leader was not finished yet. She slowly whittled away at the remaining group of engineers who worked at home, moving them into the office one at a time. I was still petitioning the Lord about this when my turn came. My boss called and asked if I was sitting down; I knew the news was not good. He told me my working at home days were over, and I would have to start reporting to the office. I readily accepted the change; after all, I knew God could see my plight, and somehow, He would take care of it. The immediate ramifications of the decision were not all-encompassing; I was able to continue working at home until my new work location was determined. A few weeks passed while my boss settled the details. One day, I got a call from my boss and was expecting to receive my new work location. Instead, he notified me the new high-level leader had

---

[139] 1 John 1:7
[140] John 15:7
[141] Jeremiah 32:27

accepted another position in the company. God showed me all I needed to do was ask, and He would act on my behalf. The new leader had accepted a new job out of my department, and I have been working at home ever since. By then, I had been fasting and praying in tongues regularly. Fasting produces spiritual authority by removing one of the essential needs of the flesh to survive (food).[142] This teaches the flesh the spirit will live regardless of the essentials needed by the flesh, therefore relinquishing dominion to the spirit. Speaking in tongues edifies the spirit,[143] promoting obedience while also communicating with God.[144] I had not actually spoken the words to ask the Lord for His intervention in this situation I had encountered, and God's Word says we have not because we ask not.[145] We must obey God's Word in order for the execution of His promises; since I had not asked, the Holy Spirit requisitioned the flesh and uttered a message directly out of my mouth. This is the power of fasting and praying in tongues: the physical power twins which generate the spiritual power twins: humility and the fear of the Lord.[146] Speaking *words* is powerful; speaking *God's Word* overcomes:

Revelation 12:11 *And they overcame him by the blood of the Lamb, and by the word of their testimony; and they loved not their lives unto the death.*

God spoke the universe into existence,[147] proving the physical is always subject to the spiritual. He also put it in His Word:

Zechariah 4:6 *Then he answered and spake unto me, saying, This is the word of the LORD unto Zerubbabel, saying, Not by might, nor by power, but by my spirit, saith the LORD of hosts.*

When Jesus was tempted in the wilderness, He used the written Word to rebuff the devil. And the devil said unto him, "If thou be the Son of God, command this stone that it be made bread." Jesus answered by saying, "***It is written***, That man shall not live by bread alone, but by every word of God." Satan then took Jesus to a high mountain and tempted Him, "I will give all this power to you if you will worship me." Jesus replied, "Get thee behind me, Satan: ***for it is written***, Thou shalt worship the Lord thy God, and him only shalt thou serve." The last time Satan tempted Jesus, he had finally

---

[142] *See* **Fasting** *in Chapter 2*
[143] 1 Corinthians 14:4
[144] 1 Corinthians 14:2
[145] James 4:2
[146] Proverbs 22:4
[147] Genesis 1:1- 2:1

caught on and used the **written** Word himself: He brought him to Jerusalem, and set him on a pinnacle of the temple, and said unto him, "If thou be the Son of God, cast thyself down from hence: **For it is written**, He shall give his angels charge over thee, to keep thee: And in *their* hands, they shall bear thee up, lest at any time thou dash thy foot against a stone." With His reply, **Jesus ended all temptation with the spoken word:** "**It is said**, Thou shalt not tempt the Lord thy God." Jesus knew the spoken Word was (and is) more powerful than the written word; He used this fact when tempted by Satan.[148]

Speaking God's Word with persistence will establish His truth in our lives, just as speaking evil will manifest evil:

> **Psalm 65:3** *Iniquities prevail against me …*

Strong's defines **iniquities** (*'avon* in Hebrew) as **a word, (as spoken of), (evil favoured).** The Ancient Hebrew Lexicon of the Bible defines **iniquities** as **an arrangement or placement of something creating order, an arrangement of words.** The word **prevail** (**gabar** in Hebrew) is defined by Strong's as **to be strong.** This verse says, "spoken evil is strong against me…" which is why deference to God's Word is critical. It protects us from spiritual laws we do not fully understand. His Word gives a command, that when obeyed, eliminates the consequences of speaking evil words, by eliminating the words themselves:

> **Ephesians 4:29** *Let no corrupt communication proceed out of your mouth, but that which is good to the use of edifying, that it may minister grace unto the hearers.*

Understanding the power of speaking God's Word, I began to daily read His Word aloud rather than silently, putting forth His Word into the atmosphere over my life. Therefore, the next problem I encountered, I decided to speak boldly and expect results. He gave me a command, and I obeyed it; then, He performed His Word, and although I should not have been surprised, I was fascinated at **how** He did it.

Coming Boldly to the Throne
I was experiencing problems with my private well, and it was the fall season. The control mechanism that called for water was sporadic; the pump did not seem to be responding properly. This was critical because our heating system was geothermal and depended upon well water to heat the house. It seemed

---

[148] Luke 4:3-13

the system was on the fritz; *maybe the well pump*, I thought. That was when I decided to implement boldness from the Word:

> **Hebrews 4:16** *Let us therefore come boldly unto the throne of grace, that we may obtain mercy, and find grace to help in time of need.*

I boldly said to the Lord, "I will not ask a man to fix something. You can fix." He then said something very peculiar. I would later understand He used this opportunity to grow my faith. He responded: "**Give $500 to the benevolence fund at the church.**"

I was not expecting that; I was in the process of remodeling my kitchen, so at the time, money was not easy to come by. However, I obeyed His command and gave the $500 to the benevolence fund. The Lord then revealed the answer to a question I had for many years; I had always read the story of the widow with the two mites and wondered how I could ever give that much from God's perspective, considering I was not financially impoverished.

> **Mark 12:42-44** *And there came a certain poor widow, and she threw in two mites, which make a farthing. And he called unto him his disciples, and saith unto them, Verily I say unto you, That this poor widow hath cast more in, than all they which have cast into the treasury: For all they did cast in of their abundance; but she of her want did cast in all that she had, even all her living.*

After this prayer, however, the Lord revealed to me how I could give just as the widow gave. He simply declared:

"**When you give out of your lack, you are giving as she gave.**"

After I gave the $500, I continued remodeling the kitchen and forgot about it. The well seemed to be doing better. Although it had moments of temporary failures, it recovered each time, and the heat worked throughout the winter. Then one day in midsummer, I was looking out the window during a thunderstorm, and suddenly, lightning struck a tree in my back yard. Accompanied by the deafening thunderous crash, a large blue flash jumped off the tree and hit the ground. Simultaneously, I heard a loud ratcheting coming from the basement. By the time I got down the stairs, the ratcheting had stopped, but when I looked at the well controller, no lights were flashing because it was completely dead. I asked God *why He struck my tree with lightning* because I know He directs it:

> **Job 28:26** *When he made a decree for the rain, and a way for the lightning of the*

thunder:

Job 37:3 *He directeth it under the whole heaven, and his lightning unto the ends of the earth.*

Job 38:35 *Canst thou send lightnings, that they may go, and say unto thee, Here we are?*

He did not answer my question because He knew I would soon discover why He directed lightning to the tree in my backyard. The lightning had "completely fried" the well controller panel, and it needed to be replaced at the cost of a thousand dollars. Insurance covered the $1000 cost of the well controller, so I got it replaced *at no cost.* As I was talking to the insurance adjuster, he asked me how big the tree was that the lightning struck. I told him it was about forty feet tall, but it was okay, it had a mark on the trunk, but there was no other damage. He proceeded to tell me they were going to give me the maximum they could for the tree. *It was five hundred dollars.* The Lord remembered the $500 I had given to the benevolence fund six months earlier; the insurance company reimbursed that exact amount. God returned it in full and *fixed the well for no cost.* In addition, the tree the lightning struck did not die; there was now a 16-foot long, four-inch-wide scar about 20 feet off the ground. Later in the year, I called a tree trimmer to clear some branches in my back yard. He asked me if I knew lightning struck the tree; I acknowledged I saw it happen. Looking at the mark, he was amazed the tree was still alive. The Lord showed me *He used His great power to strike my tree, not to hurt it, but to destroy my well controller and replace it at no cost.* How amazing is that! When I had come to His throne room boldly,[149] I was required to exercise faith; God will perform His Word for those who believe.[150] I knew exercising faith executed spiritual results, and faith comes by hearing and hearing by the word of God,[151] but I was about to learn a more basic truth about the Lord: His Word is Truth, and *its execution is required.* For this reason, He intervened to protect me from myself when taking communion.

His Word is Final: Communion
I was attending church on a Sunday, and frankly, my attitude was unacceptable. As the service continued, I caught myself criticizing how others were worshipping. "Lord, what is going on with me?" I exclaimed, "I need forgiveness for this." On top of that, it happened to be a communion

---

[149] Hebrews 4:16
[150] John 14:12-13
[151] Romans 10:17

Sunday. As the ushers distributed the bread, I was the only person sitting in an entire row, and the usher took the tray from the row in front of me and handed it to the person in the row behind. He overlooked me sitting at the end of the pew. When the ushers distributed the cup of grape juice, he overlooked me again. I declared to the Lord, "Wow, they actually missed me." The Lord said: **"You would not have refused it, so I blinded them to you."**

Moments later, the very usher who overlooked me, reached over gesturing for me to give him a cup I had never received. The Lord had truly blinded him to my presence as he had neglected to offer me the bread and cup. Thus, I realized two things; first, the Lord was indeed protecting me[152] from the written laws of His Word because God always fulfills His Word.[153]

> **Genesis 20:6** *And God said unto him in a dream, Yea, I know that thou didst this in the integrity of thy heart; for I also withheld thee from sinning against me: …*

The Lord had protected me from my own pride, as I would not have refused communion so as not to draw attention to myself. His Word is true, and He always fulfills it, regardless of whether He knows us; Taking communion unworthily has dire consequences:

> **1 Corinthians 11:24-30** *And when he had given thanks, he brake it, and said, Take, eat: this is my body, which is broken for you: this do in remembrance of me. After the same manner also he took the cup, when he had supped, saying, This cup is the new testament in my blood: this do ye, as oft as ye drink it, in remembrance of me. For as often as ye eat this bread, and drink this cup, ye do shew the Lord's death till he come. Wherefore whosoever shall eat this bread, and drink this cup of the Lord, unworthily, shall be guilty of the body and blood of the Lord. But let a man examine himself, and so let him eat of that bread, and drink of that cup. For he that eateth and drinketh unworthily, eateth and drinketh damnation to himself, not discerning the Lord's body. For this cause many are weak and sickly among you, and many sleep.*

The second realization was He genuinely loved me and knew I needed instruction on this important part of His Word, so He chose this instance to teach me of the Holy importance of communion. I never approached His Holy Communion the same way again. No sooner was this lesson finished than the next lesson began. It was in the realm of demon activity.[154]

---

[152] Genesis 20:6
[153] Psalm 138:2
[154] Mark 16:17

A Lesson in Thwarting Demon Activity

It was a spring day, and my granddaughter came to our house for a visit. Due to circumstances at her home, she had been living with other relatives since she was young; she was now about 11 years old and back living with her mother. However, this day, she and her mother were fighting. Consequently, her mother dropped her at my house for a visit. As her mother left for the evening, my granddaughter was terribly upset and locked herself in the bathroom. Attempting to alleviate the situation, I was passing notes to her under the bathroom door. All at once, the door opened and the paper came out like confetti, just to have the door slammed shut again. The Lord revealed to me this was a spiritual problem. I knew Jesus had asked demons their names[155] in the Bible, so I decided to ask, "What is your name?" to determine if it truly was a demon. Still in the process of sending notes under the door, I wrote, "What is your name?" and slid the note under the door. The reply promptly emerged on my side of the door; "MY NAME IS HATE," it read, and it was not my granddaughter's handwriting. The words were eerily crooked with scratch marks all over the paper. Therefore, I began writing a note to cast this demon out but remembered Jesus had cast out demons by speaking to them. I spoke through the closed door and told HATE: "In the name of Jesus, you no longer have any rights to her. Get out of her, and you will not come back. Be gone in the name of Jesus!" A few minutes passed, and the door opened, and my granddaughter walked out smiling and as loveable as ever; that was truly deliverance. Jesus said these things would happen:

Mark 16:17-18 *And these signs shall follow them that believe; In my name shall they cast out devils; they shall speak with new tongues; They shall take up serpents; and if they drink any deadly thing, it shall not hurt them; they shall lay hands on the sick, and they shall recover.*

Demons are subject to Jesus' authority in us; John declares there is no need to fear them:

1 John 4:4 *Ye are of God, little children, and have overcome them: because greater is he that is in you, than he that is in the world.*

Increasing Faith

One day, the Lord provided me with an opportunity to speak into a woman's

---

[155] Mark 5:9

62

life. I was searching for the renters of space in a small town in Maine, where my wife and I frequently visited on vacation. Instead, a new renter had taken the spot. We had a conversation about the previous renters, and I had told her I had been praying for them. She became intrigued, and I began to speak with her about Jesus; how He had been working in my life. As we began to speak, the people in the walkway suddenly dispersed; within moments, we were the only ones in the clearing crowded just moments before. She was deeply touched as I shared with her how the Lord had changed my life; her eyes filled with tears, and she sobbed as she listened. I felt as though I was standing beside myself, watching the Lord speak directly to her through me. *This was her day*, I thought, *the day the Lord chose to speak directly into her life.* After I had witnessed to her, she thanked me for speaking with her, and I actually replied with the words, "it is my job to glorify God's name, I am here to tell you about who He is." She said I was a nice person, and I replied, "That is Jesus Christ through me." I had told her it was my duty, which was the same as saying I was an *unprofitable servant*. Speaking those words increased my faith! The apostles asked Jesus to increase their faith in Luke 17, so Jesus told them a story about how to increase it. The last line in the story is where Jesus reveals the action that increases faith.

> **Luke 17:5-10** *And the apostles said unto the Lord, Increase our faith. And the Lord said, If ye had faith as a grain of mustard seed, ye might say unto this sycamine tree, Be thou plucked up by the root, and be thou planted in the sea; and it should obey you. But which of you, having a servant plowing or feeding cattle, will say unto him by and by, when he is come from the field, Go and sit down to meat? And will not rather say unto him, Make ready wherewith I may sup, and gird thyself, and serve me, till I have eaten and drunken; and afterward thou shalt eat and drink? Doth he thank that servant because he did the things that were commanded him? I trow not. So likewise ye, when ye shall have done all those things which are commanded you, say, We are unprofitable servants: we have done that which was our duty to do.*

The Lord told this story after the example of the mustard seed because this story takes faith just to believe it. Jesus exemplified what faith is and how He is the one who grows it[156] when we seek Him. Once we grasp that fact, we use that grasping to execute the second story to grow faith even further. In addition, notice that we only need small faith in the first story, like a mustard seed. When we use that small faith to seek Him diligently, then doing all He commands is possible. In the second story, Jesus reveals the next step to growing faith is to recognize it is our duty to spread God's kingdom, not to expect thanks but to say, "We are unprofitable servants; we have done that

---

[156] Hebrews 12:2

which is our duty to do." As for the woman, I never saw her again. It has been years since I met her, but I still pray for her daily in the hope she will come to know the Lord and be saved,[157] and see her in heaven so we can recount the day the Lord took her aside to speak directly into her life…

---

[157] 2 Peter 3:9

CHAPTER 6

What Do You Believe?

Matthew 6:24 *No man can serve two masters: for either he will hate the one, and love the other; or else he will hold to the one, and despise the other. Ye cannot serve God and mammon.*

Tithing

I had been tithing[158] for years because I knew this was not only good practice but from God's perspective, *it is required*.[159] God states we are not giving Him anything; He is receiving that which is *already His*. That is why in Malachi, He says we are robbing Him if no tithe is given – it is because He has already declared the first 10 percent of all increase is His. A life devoid of tithing will generate a curse:

> **Malachi 3:8-12** *Will a man rob God? Yet ye have robbed me. But ye say, Wherein, have we robbed thee? In tithes and offerings. Ye are cursed with a curse: for ye have robbed me, even this whole nation. Bring ye all the tithes into the storehouse, that there may be meat in mine house, and prove me now herewith, saith the LORD of hosts, if I will not open you the windows of heaven, and pour you out a blessing, that there shall not be room enough to receive it. And I will rebuke the devourer for your sakes, and he shall not destroy the fruits of your ground; neither shall your vine cast her fruit before the time in the field, saith the LORD of hosts. And all nations shall call you blessed: for ye shall be a delightsome land, saith the LORD of hosts.*

The Lord proved His Word by growing my faith through giving.[160] Campus Crusades invited my wife and me to a fundraising dinner because we had supported one of their people throughout the year. We decided to go, although we did not have the available resources, so we decided to give just

---

[158] Hebrews 7:2
[159] Malachi 3:8
[160] Hebrews 12:2

enough to cover our dinner – a hundred dollars or so. At the end of the night, the inevitable request for donations came, and I was prepared to give the hundred dollars when I distinctly heard the Lord say: **"What do you believe?"**

I replied, "I believe." He asked again, **"What do you believe?"**

I knew what He meant and felt this overwhelming peace[161] and calm deep inside that the Creator had just asked me if I genuinely believed what I had been saying for the past eight months:

"I immediately respond in faith to the guidance of the Holy Spirit within me. I am always in the right place at the right time because my steps are ordered of the Lord."[162,163] I had spoken that aloud daily for eight months, about 240 times. This was part of my daily devotions of reading aloud the book: *God's Creative Power*. The Lord had instructed me to hear[164] my own voice speak His Truth in order to grow my faith.[165] By speaking those words, I had come to *the right place at the right time* for an opportunity for God's blessing. My wife and I agreed to increase our offering to *$500*, and I checked the credit card box on the form and wrote in the amount; we had multiplied my original planned amount by five. This took place on a Friday night, and I never took a second thought of it all weekend. Not to be outdone, the Lord sent *$5000* from an unexpected source just three days later.[166] He had taught me about faith,[167] what it was to believe, *to act*, not just to hope. The Lord poured out a blessing for two reasons: I had been tithing, which allowed the heavens to be opened, and I acted, which executed faith, causing the blessing to occur.[168]

God vs. Mammon
The company I worked for had reached the inevitable end of a three-year contract with the union, upon which the union walked out of contract negotiations. As a software engineer in management, I knew this meant I would be working 72-hour workweeks to cover for union employees who were on

---

[161] Philippians 4:7
[162] Copied with permission from Charles Capps Ministries, Inc. God's Creative Power ® for Finances, p. 38
[163] Psalm 37:23
[164] Romans 10:17
[165] 1 Corinthians 3:7
[166] Luke 6:38
[167] Hebrews 11:1
[168] Malachi 3:10

strike. I was somewhat relieved in one sense, as 23 years earlier, I was a union employee in the same company, and we were out on strike for four months. Management assigned me to my usual job during this strike, albeit scheduled to work 72 hours a week. However, I was concerned about my relationship with the King of the Universe – no doubt, this strike would affect my relationship with God due to all the extra time working and commuting to the office. I told Him I did not want to give up my relationship with Him for money, but I had no choice – this would be mandatory work. Two days later, I got an email from my boss, *noting that no one working his or her regular job would be required to work overtime.* This was the first time in my 25 years with the company, there was a deviation from the standard overtime policy where all managers were required to work overtime during a work stoppage. It was then I realized the power of the Living God – He will do anything for us, according to His will.[169] The strike ended after only 15 days, and all was back to normal. A month later, the Lord said to me: "**You chose Me over money.**"[170]

I said, "That's right." A week or so later, our group had a conference call, and my boss told us we now had available (not forced) overtime for the next three months because we had a huge initiative to finish before the end of the year. I had to laugh as the Lord prepared me for the windfall by reminding me, I was committed to Him. So now, I could work overtime at my discretion and still maintain my relationship with Him. The overtime I was able to work was over six times what I gave up during the strike. That is the benefit of a friendship with the Creator. As the year wound down, I was speaking with a colleague who told me one of our group members worked the overtime but did not put in for the pay because he was concerned it would put him in another tax bracket. He had some rental property, etc. I thought about this and wondered why I did not have those things – after all, I was working the same job. Just then, the Lord spoke: "**You are rich.**"[171]

This was a direct reference to:

> **Proverbs 10:22** *The blessing of the LORD, it maketh rich, and he addeth no sorrow with it.*

Strong's defines **rich** (*âshar* in Hebrew) as **to grow.** In this exchange, the Lord had told me I chose Him over money, and, according to Him, I was

---

[169] 1 John 5:14,15
[170] Matthew 6:24
[171] Proverbs 10:22

rich not with the seen but the unseen.[172] I had been transformed to choose the eternal over the temporal, and I felt a particular closeness to Him now, but there was still more to understand concerning finances as I was about to learn.

Bring the Whole Tithe into the Storehouse

I had left my previous church because I was offended; I had not yet learned the lesson that God must direct, leaving one church for another. Because of my lack of understanding, I found myself at a new church, and it was not long before I was suspicious of exactly where my tithe was going. I complained to the Lord about this multiple times to no avail; the Lord did not answer me, because the answer was already in His Word:

> **Malachi 3:10** *Bring ye all the tithes into the storehouse, that there may be meat in mine house, and prove me now herewith, saith the LORD of hosts, if I will not open you the windows of heaven, and pour you out a blessing, that there shall not be room enough to receive it.*

However, I felt the church was misusing the funds, so I took justice into my own hands. One week, I took the tithe I would normally give to the church and gave the entire amount to a needy person who attended the church. *That fixes that*, I thought. The next day, I got a call from the needy woman thanking me for helping her, and I responded she was certainly welcome. *That was the right thing to do*, I thought, but as soon as I hung up the phone, the Lord said: **"You took credit for my money."**

> **Malachi 3:8** *Will a man rob God? Yet ye have robbed me. But ye say Wherein have we robbed thee? In tithes and offerings.*

Immediately I knew what I had to do. I painfully took *another 10%* of my paycheck and gave it to the church, in effect, giving the Lord His 10%, allowing the money I gave to the poor woman to be a gift in God's eyes. I quickly realized God sees the tithe as *already His*. He requires it, but also says He will "pour out a blessing, and *there shall not be room enough to receive it.*"[173]

The Vow

I had been tithing regularly and giving offerings[174] beyond the 10% tithe according to 2 Corinthians:

---

[172] 2 Corinthians 4:18
[173] Malachi 3:10
[174] Luke 6:38

2 Corinthians 9:7 *Every man according as he purposeth in his heart, so let him give; not grudgingly, or of necessity: for God loveth a cheerful giver.*

I had always attempted to give bountifully,[175] which is not difficult when disposable cash is available. It is just a matter of deciding to give to others instead of saving that money. All was going well until my wife retired. I decided to continue giving the following year as if she were still working, even though we lost virtually all our disposable income. I was so adamant, I confidently said to the Lord, "I am going to give offerings this year as I have been giving regardless of the drop in income."

That was a mistake because the Lord warns us not to pledge a vow:

Numbers 30:2 *If a man vow a vow unto the LORD, or swear an oath to bind his soul with a bond; he shall not break his word, he shall do according to all that proceedeth out of his mouth.*

Ecclesiastes 5:5 *Better is it that thou shouldest not vow, than that thou shouldest vow and not pay.*

Deuteronomy 23:23 *That which is gone out of thy lips thou shalt keep and perform; even a freewill offering, according as thou hast vowed unto the LORD thy God, which thou hast promised with thy mouth.*
There are many references to the seriousness of a vow, and Jesus confirms it:

Matthew 5:33-37 *Again, ye have heard that it hath been said by them of old time, Thou shalt not forswear thyself, but shalt perform unto the Lord thine oaths: But I say unto you, Swear not at all; neither by heaven; for it is God's throne: Nor by the earth; for it is his footstool: neither by Jerusalem; for it is the city of the great King. Neither shalt thou swear by thy head, because thou canst not make one hair white or black. But let your communication be, Yea, yea; Nay, nay: for whatsoever is more than these cometh of evil.*

I continued giving offerings as I had before until about mid-year. I assessed the finances and realized I could not sustain the outflow of cash I had pledged, so I stopped giving to a few places in order to maintain the finances. Then it happened. The refrigerator, the lawnmower, and the dishwasher all needed repair within a two-week period, to the tune of over $700. I immediately knew what had happened. The Bible says Satan goes before the Lord

---

[175] 2 Corinthians 9:6

to accuse the brethren:

> **Revelation 12:10** *And I heard a loud voice saying in heaven, Now is come salvation, and strength, and the kingdom of our God, and the power of his Christ: for the accuser of our brethren is cast down, which accused them before our God day and night.*

Satan knows the scriptures, and he accused me of not performing my vow; hence, he was able to operate in my life because of the sin:

> **Deuteronomy 23:21** *When thou shalt vow a vow unto the LORD thy God, thou shalt not slack to pay it: for the LORD thy God will surely require it of thee; and it would be sin in thee.*

The Lord told Cain if he did not do well, sin was lying at the door.

> **Genesis 4:7** *If thou doest well, shalt thou not be accepted? and if thou doest not well, sin lieth at the door. And unto thee shall be his desire, and thou shalt rule over him.*

Sin in this verse means *punishment;* since I broke my vow, I had sinned and suffered as a result. As soon as I realized what I had done, I quickly restored payment to all I had vowed and paid off all the repair bills with savings. That stopped any further breakdowns, and I continued to give offerings according to my vow. It was about a month later that I received an email at work informing me I had a monetary reward *from the previous year I had never cashed in.* That was extremely unusual, but indeed, the reward was valid. I was able to use it toward the repair bills. That is when I knew the ordeal was over. I had learned the lesson concerning vows the hard way, and, as painful as it was, I would not soon forget it.

CHAPTER 7

When Your Body is Writing Checks, Your Spirit Can Cash

Psalm 35:13 *But as for me, when they were sick, my clothing was sackcloth: I humbled my soul with fasting; and my prayer returned into mine own bosom.*

Strong's definition for humbled: self-affliction

Fasting

At this point, I thought I was doing everything spiritually I could, and one day when I was alone, those words came out of my mouth. I was contemplating all I had been doing to know God when I said aloud, "I am doing all I can," and the Spirit quickly instructed: **"You can fast."**

Through many years of attending various churches, my understanding of fasting was it "got the attention" of God and was implemented when praying itself was not enough. After hearing fasting was another action I could take, I decided to fast the next time I came across a situation that "warranted" it. I was not sure exactly what that situation would be but was determined to implement fasting into my life to obey this command. It was about two weeks later; I was praying for humility, and the Lord said: **"Fasting brings humility."**[176]

Still believing fasting was only for especially difficult circumstances, I told Him I would fast for a specific situation I was going through at the time. I had just taken action in obedience to the Lord's command, but it had become a long-drawn-out process, and all indications were it might not turn out well. I was now experiencing some apprehension about it and thought this situation called for fasting. It was just then the Lord said: **"I told you to do that;**

---

[176] Psalm 35:13

it's already done."

That statement blew me away. *He already had the solution* and, even though I could not see it, He reassured me that when I obey Him, *the situation is already solved – long before time reveals it.* He is the beginning and the end,[177] timeless, so time does not affect God. It was astonishing to hear the Master of the Universe tell me there is no need to be concerned about a matter because the future outcome *had already been determined.* That difficult situation did not settle down for quite some time, but it resolved beautifully. Time is not a constraint for God; He spoke of this situation as if it were in the past, while for me, the conclusion was several months in the future. When we obey His commands, He works on our behalf, and the situation is resolved with righteousness and equity.[178] I then recognized since I did not understand what He was telling me concerning fasting, He made it very clear: fasting regularly was to become a part of my life, not for any reason other than the obedience of fasting itself.[179] **"Fasting brings humility,"** He had said, and it is in His Word:

> **Psalm 35:13** *But as for me, when they were sick, my clothing was sackcloth: I humbled my soul with fasting…*

I began to practice fasting in order to become accustomed to functioning without food. There are many misconceptions about what exactly fasting is, but it really is quite simple. The Greek word for fasting in the Bible is **nesteuo,** and it means *to abstain from food (religiously): —fast.* This is an important truth because the enemy has twisted the word *fast* to mean "abstain from" and then add any word, e.g., "fast from television," etc. This has diluted the meaning, which limits the power of fasting Jesus intended. The only true fast is from food, as the Bible depicts (but God does allow provisions for those who may not be able to fast entirely from food – see next section). This is because humans need food to survive; fasting from our need for food promotes self-control over the flesh and brings humility. The verse below shows why God chose fasting from food to generate spiritual growth (in the definition of the word *quicken* in the Ancient Hebrew Lexicon of the Bible):

> **Psalm 119:50** *This is my comfort in my affliction: for thy word hath quickened me.*

---

[177] Revelation 22:13
[178] Proverbs 2:9
[179] Mark 2:20

Strong's defines *quicken* (*châyâh*) as *to live, to revive, quicken, recover, restore,* while the Ancient Hebrew Lexicon of the Bible defines *quicken* as *Live: This organ is seen as the life; as an empty stomach is like death but a revived stomach is life. Life: The revival of life from food or other necessity.* This is the reason fasting from food was chosen by the Lord; spiritually, it is like death and resurrection. It is important to understand the *original meaning* of God's commands. To obey is better than sacrifice;[180] fasting from food is obedience but abstaining from anything else is sacrifice. Jesus *commanded us* to fast:

> **Mark 2:18-20** *And the disciples of John and of the Pharisees used to fast: and they come and say unto him, Why do the disciples of John and of the Pharisees fast, but thy disciples fast not? And Jesus said unto them, Can the children of the bridechamber fast, while the bridegroom is with them? as long as they have the bridegroom with them, they cannot fast. But the days will come, when the bridegroom shall be taken away from them, and then shall they fast in those days.*

I decided to fast for multiple days, and as I was about to begin, I said to the Lord, "This is going to be brutal," to which He replied: **"My day is from sunset to sunset."**

He wrote it in His Word:

> **Genesis 1:5** *And God called the light Day, and the darkness he called Night. And the evening and the morning were the first day.*

Therefore, God's day begins just after sunset and ends at sunset the next day. That meant I could eat just before sunset and then again just after sunset of the next day, and from God's perspective, that was a complete one day fast. I had always fasted from the moment I awoke on one day until the morning I awoke on the next day. However, using God's perspective, I got credit for fasting while I was sleeping! I now fast from sunset to sunset according to God's schedule of a day. (So, a three day fast would be to eat just before sunset, then eat after sunset three days later). If you have never fasted before, it would be best to attempt a one day fast to allow your body to learn how to function without food. Then increasing the number of days will not be overwhelming. Also, inquire of the Lord as to how long to fast for any issue. Be sure to hydrate often, as fasting without enough water will produce muscle cramps. Also, when returning from a fast, be sure to come back slowly with vegetables or soups. Meat should not be eaten on the first meal after a fast

---

[180] 1 Samuel 15:22

because your body needs to reboot back into the digestive mode with more easily digested foods.

There was one more inherent rule when fasting, and it is throughout chapter 58 in the book of Isaiah: ***obedience trumps fasting.*** Fasting without executing obedience in other areas of our spiritual walk garners no spiritual results. Obedience is the foundation of all God's principles; *without obedience, any action in the spiritual realm is futile.* This is true because ***obedience is the most basic staple of salvation.***

> **Hebrews 5:9** *And being made perfect, he became the author of eternal salvation unto all them that obey him;*

God's Provision for Exceptions

The Lord lays out general commands for those who follow Him, but He sometimes provides exceptions in the details of those commands, so He does not exclude groups of people from the potential benefits. Numbers 9:4-13 provides an example of an exception. The Jews were to keep the Passover feast on the 14th day of the *first* month, but contact with a dead body defiled some, not allowing them to keep the Passover. Moses inquired of the Lord, so He granted an exception: anyone unclean or on a journey afar off could keep the Passover on the 14th day of the *second* month. However, God provided this exception for only those who were unclean or on a journey at the time of Passover. All others were cut off from the people if they did not bring the offering at the appointed time.

This means *God does allow for exceptions in cases where obeying Him would be a hardship.* Therefore, in the case of fasting, exceptions are available for those with medical conditions, etc. who are unable to abstain from food. In these cases, God will accept abstaining from something else. However, the Lord must choose the substitute for us to realize the spiritual benefit. Those who cannot fast from food must inquire of the Lord to determine the adequate substitute from which to abstain. The Lord provides the spiritual benefits for those who obey, so the substitute must be of *His choosing.* Also, notice the Passover command: if a man is *not unclean,* he must observe the first Passover and cannot choose the second. That means we cannot choose a substitute if fasting from food is truly practical. If we choose a substitute but fasting from food is indeed viable, then God most likely will not award the spiritual benefits (as in the Passover example above). The Lord knows the heart,[181] so if there is a question, the Lord must be included in the decision of whether a substitute is valid in order to determine if He will allow it.

---

[181] Jeremiah 17:10

The Lord had imparted to me; personally I was to fast consistently. Incorporating fasting will be specific to our relationship with the Lord; He may instruct to fast occasionally, when a situation arises, or to fast consistently. The only way to know for sure is to inquire of Him.[182] I would later discover God commanded me to fast because it brings humility, which is an essential part of building a deep relationship with Him. At this time, however, I was not aware of the reason for fasting, but out of obedience, I began fasting weekly.

Physical Benefits of Fasting: Health

God does command us to perform actions for our own health, both physically and spiritually. There are several proven health benefits from fasting. Mark Mattson is a professor of neuroscience in the Johns Hopkins School of Medicine and serves as chief of the Laboratory of Neurosciences at the National Institute on Aging. His research on fasting in a *Johns Hopkins Health Review* article:

> "According to research conducted by neuroscientist Mark Mattson and others, cutting your energy intake by fasting several days a week might help your brain ward off neurodegenerative diseases like Alzheimer's and Parkinson's while at the same time improving memory and mood. Mattson's studies have built on decades-old research establishing a connection between caloric intake and brain function. In laboratory experiments, Mattson and his colleagues have found that intermittent fasting—limiting caloric intake at least two days a week—can help improve neural connections in the hippocampus while protecting neurons against the accumulation of amyloid plaques, a protein prevalent in people with Alzheimer's disease. "Fasting is a challenge to your brain, and we think that your brain reacts by activating adaptive stress responses that help it cope with disease," says Mattson." [On fasting two non-consecutive days per week:] "I hope it's not a fad," says Mattson, who is currently working on a study involving obese subjects at risk for cognitive impairment and the effects of intermittent fasting. "There's a lot of science behind it, and the science is only increasing." [183]

The National Institute on Aging reveals fasting is indeed healthy.

---

[182] 1 Samuel 23:4
[183] http://www.johnshopkinshealthreview.com/issues/spring-summer-2016/articles/are-there-any-proven-benefits-to-fasting; Joe Sugarman

"Emerging evidence suggests that intermittent dietary energy restriction might improve overall health and reduce risk factors for diabetes and cardiovascular disease in humans," Mattson says. "Our new findings in laboratory animals provide evidence that similar intermittent eating patterns can enhance the beneficial effects of aerobic exercise on endurance performance. Research supported by NIA has also focused on the effects of intermittent fasting. During fasting, the body uses up glucose and glycogen, then turns to energy reserves stored in fat. This stored energy is released in the form of chemicals called ketones. These chemicals help cells—especially brain cells—keep working at full capacity. Some researchers think that because ketones are a more efficient energy source than glucose, they may protect against an aging-related decline in the central nervous system that might cause dementia and other disorders."[184]

In the article "Fasting Makes Our Cells Resilient to Stress," Douglas Bennion, Martin Wegman, and Michael Guo, from the University of Florida, found the following:

"We found that in response to fasting every other day, the cells made more copies of a gene called SIRT3, which is part of a pathway that works to prevent free radical production and improve cellular repair processes. We also found a significant decrease in levels of circulating insulin, a sign that the participants' bodies were more responsive to this hormone. This is important because when we become less sensitive to insulin, we are at risk for diabetes.

One somewhat surprising finding is that **when participants took daily oral supplements of Vitamin C and E, the benefits from fasting disappeared**. It seems that because the cells were relatively sheltered from experiencing any oxidative stress that may have been caused by fasting every other day, they didn't respond by increasing their natural defenses and improving their sensitivity to insulin and other stress signals.

This suggests that **low levels of environmental stress from things like fasting are actually good for our bodies** and that antioxidant supplements, while potentially good at certain times, might actually prevent our normal healthy cellular responses in other situations."[185]

---

[184] https://www.nia.nih.gov/health/calorie-restriction-and-fasting-diets-what-do-we-know

[185] https://www.bluezones.com/2019/01/fasting-makes-our-cells-resilient-to-stress/

Bennion, Wegman, and Guo also noted that free radicals damage cells, but fasting may help.

"One way that our cells can become damaged is when they encounter oxidative stress. And preventing or repairing cell damage from oxidative stress is helpful against ageing. This stress happens when there is higher-than-normal production of free radicals, such as reactive oxygen species. These are unstable molecules that carry highly reactive electrons.

When one of these free radicals encounters another molecule, it may either give up an electron or take another electron. This can result in a rapid chain reaction from molecule to molecule, forming more free radicals, which can break apart connections between atoms within important components of the cell, like the cellular membrane, essential proteins, or even DNA. Anti-oxidants work by transferring the needed electrons to stabilize the free radicals before they can do any harm."[186]

"Although fasting seems to help our cells combat damage from this process, it isn't clear exactly how that happens. Free radicals can be generated by poorly functioning mitochondria (the powerhouses of the cell). The switch between eating normally and fasting causes cells to temporarily experience lower-than-usual levels of glucose (blood sugar), and they are forced to begin using other sources of less readily available energy, like fatty acids. This can cause the cells to turn on survival processes to remove unhealthy mitochondria and replace them with *healthy* ones over time, thus reducing the production of free radicals in the long-term."

The Lord, in His infinite wisdom, charged us to fast for spiritual reasons, knowing it would benefit the human body in physical means. The spiritual benefits are even greater because they cause us to grow more intimate with Him.

Those benefits are the spiritual growth received for the obedience itself as well as the humility granted by fasting.[187] Fasting is *how to acquire* humility, and the benefits of humility are extraordinary; and I was about to understand the power of humility itself.

---

[186] https://www.bluezones.com/2019/01/fasting-makes-our-cells-resilient-to-stress/
[187] 1 Kings 21:27-29

Spiritual Benefits of Fasting: Hearing from the Lord through Submission

Fasting brings clarity to hear from the Lord because we are submitting to the Lord with the most powerful physical action we can take. When tempted in the wilderness, Jesus put his flesh into submission to His spirit by fasting. Thus, when questioned by Satan, all His answers were directly from the Word of God; there was no logical reasoning but direct access to spiritual answers. When Jesus continued resisting the devil, Satan departed according to the Word of God:

> **James 4:7** *Submit yourselves therefore to God. Resist the devil, and he will flee from you.*

When we fast, we submit the flesh to the spirit, allowing us to hear from the Lord because the reasoning of the flesh has been put under submission. This is proven in the Bible in Psalm 119:50.

> **Psalm 119:50** *This is my comfort in my affliction: for thy word hath quickened me.*

The word affliction relates to *humbled* and proves fasting is afflicting the soul.

> **Psalm 35:13** *But as for me, when they were sick, my clothing was sackcloth: I humbled my soul with fasting; and my prayer returned into mine own bosom.*

Strong's defines **humbled (ânâh)** as **abase self, afflict** while the Ancient Hebrew Lexicon of the Bible defines **humble** as: **afflict, humble.** So, we know the phrase *in my affliction* in Psalm 119:50 refers to fasting.

In Psalm 119:50, Strong's defines **word ('imrah)** as speech, and the Ancient Hebrew Lexicon of the Bible goes deeper and defines the **word** as: **continue: A continuation of segments that fill the whole.** That is the description of **revelation knowledge**; knowledge given directly by the Lord; it is the meaning of scripture not readily understood.

The Septuagint (Greek Translation of Hebrew scriptures) allows cross-reference from Old Testament Hebrew to the New Testament Greek. In this case, the **word ('imrah)** translates to the word **oracle** in only three verses in the New Testament, meaning "an utterance of God." Webster's 1828 Dictionary defines **oracle** as "*the place where answers were given,*" and "*the communications, revelations, or messages delivered by God.*"

Spiritual Benefits of Fasting: The Currency of the Spiritual Marketplace

There is a spiritual marketplace, and although scarce information is available, it does exist. Jesus counsels us to buy gold and white raiment from Him:

> **Revelation 3:18** *I counsel thee to buy of me gold tried in the fire, that thou mayest be rich; and white raiment, that thou mayest be clothed, and that the shame of thy nakedness do not appear; and anoint thine eyes with eyesalve, that thou mayest see.*

The spiritual marketplace is where trading is executed in the spiritual realm; physical actions have spiritual effects that precipitate the buying and selling of spiritual fruits as well as access to valuable spiritual relationships. For example, wisdom is a spirit, and we are encouraged to develop a relationship with her as well as understanding.

> **Proverbs 7:4** *Say unto wisdom, Thou art my sister; and call understanding thy kinswoman:*

The relationship with wisdom is purchased, as is the relationship with understanding and truth:

> **Proverbs 23:23** *Buy the truth, and sell it not; also wisdom, and instruction, and understanding.*

How to purchase in the spiritual marketplace:

> **Isaiah 55:1** *Ho, every one that thirsteth, come ye to the waters, and he that hath no money; come ye, buy, and eat; yea, come, buy wine and milk without money and without price.*

Strong's defines **thirsteth** (**tsâmê'** in Hebrew) as **thirsty**, literally or figuratively; but the Ancient Hebrew Lexicon of the Bible (AHLB) gets even more granular:

> ac: **Thirst** co: **Dry** ab:?: The pictograph y is a picture of a man on his side representing the hunt; them is a picture of water. Combined, these to mean "hunt for water." *Fasting from water or food.*

This verse reveals *fasting is the method to buy wine and milk* without money or price. This process is further explained by Psalm 119:50.

> **Psalm 119:50** *This is my comfort in my affliction: for thy word hath quickened me.*

The word **quickened (châyâh in Hebrew)** is defined in Strong's as **to live, whether literally or figuratively.** The AHLB further breaks it down:

> "When the stomach is empty, one is famished and weak, and when it is filled, one is revived. This organ is seen as life; as an empty stomach is as death, but a revived stomach is life."

Fasting is a form of resurrection; that is why fasting must be from food to encompass spiritual benefits. This is further explained by Proverbs 9:2; Wisdom is preparing the table:

> **Proverbs 9:2** *She hath killed her beasts; she hath mingled her wine; she hath also furnished her table.*

In this verse, the word **wine (yayin in Hebrew)** is translated as **fermented.** That is important because the Webster's 1828 definition of fermentation is as follows:

> **FERMENTATION**... *It may be defined, in its most general sense, any spontaneous change which takes place in animal or vegetable substances, after life has ceased.*

Wine is received through the process of fermentation, which is a spontaneous change that takes place after death, and Ephesians 5:18 likens the Holy Spirit to wine:

> **Ephesians 5:18** *And be not drunk with wine, wherein is excess; but be filled with the Spirit;*

We know the Spirit (wine) is received through spontaneous change following death, fasting is referred to as a form of death, and Isaiah 55:1 says those who thirst (fast) can buy wine and milk without price.

Fasting is the currency of the spiritual marketplace, but obedience opens the door.

Therefore, we know fasting generates a form of spiritual currency, which gives us access to the attributes of the Holy Spirit. The Holy Spirit contains the fruits of the spirit: love, joy, peace, longsuffering, gentleness, kindness, faith, meekness, and temperance,[188] and those fruits are found in **goodness,**

---

[188] Galatians 5:22-23

righteousness, and truth.

Ephesians 5:9 *(For the fruit of the Spirit is in all goodness and righteousness and truth;)*

Goodness is defined as virtue, and **virtue defined is nothing more than voluntary obedience to the truth**. It always comes back to obedience because obedience trumps fasting, but the two are inextricably linked. Through the obedience of fasting, we receive access to the Holy Spirit and all His attributes, which, in turn, grant increased power to obey.

Spiritual Benefits of Fasting: Humility

Humility: Empirical Evidence

I was at the doctor's office for a routine physical, but unknowingly, I was about to realize the result of years of fasting; and the Lord would use my own mouth to perform it. As she entered the room, the nurse practitioner made "small talk:" she asked what I did for a living. "I am a software engineer," I replied, then she mentioned her son was thinking about going into that field; he was currently weighing his options. "Where did you go to school?" she asked. I had a bachelor's degree in computer science and two master's degrees from a very reputable school. In fact, I had just finished 20 years of night school just four years earlier that my employer had funded. *This was the moment to show the education I had amassed, a moment to boast without guilt*, I thought. After all, she had asked, so it would be most assuredly acceptable to *answer the question*. It was at this point the **Holy Spirit intervened and answered the question for me**. "Where did you go to school?" she asked, and out of my mouth came the answer unbeknownst to me: "**Narragansett.**" *That was my high school*, I thought. *I had no idea where that answer came from; it certainly was not the answer I had planned to give.* Then it hit me. Jesus said by the overflow of the heart, the mouth speaks,[189] and what had proceeded from my mouth had come **directly from my heart**. Just then, the Lord imparted: **"I have seen what you have been doing; now, I am showing you what I have been doing."**

It had taken four years, but the Lord rewarded me with evidence of humility within my heart.

Many pray for humility, but true humility is a fruit of the spirit purchased through fasting.

---

[189] Matthew 12:34

81

All the time I had been fasting over the past 18 months, *He had been working on my heart.* I had not *seen any results from fasting* but continued in obedience because the Lord had told me *fasting brings humility.* Four years earlier, I had arrogantly said to Him, "There is no way a bag lady can be ahead of me in the kingdom of God," and He had replied, **"You better believe it."** The Lord had replaced the arrogance with humility; and, at the same time, revealed the spiritual success of carefully following His commands. I had performed the physical act of fasting through obedience, and He performed the spiritual removal of pride and replaced it with true humility. I believed what the Lord said: **"Fasting brings humility**;" and because I believed it, I did it; and because I did it, He performed what He said:

> **Luke 1:45** *And blessed is she that believed: for there shall be a performance of those things which were told her from the Lord.*

I had erroneously believed somehow education and knowledge made a difference in the kingdom of God, when in reality, knowing God is zero percent "head knowledge" and 100 percent heart.[190] I had thought education mattered, and it took four years to learn God instead of values of obedience. *Everything else comes from Him*; thinking I was better than others because of education or *any other reason* was in opposition to God's Word:

> **Philippians 2:3** *Let nothing be done through strife or vainglory; but in lowliness of mind let each esteem other better than themselves.*

Recognizing pride in self is futile because deception is a consequence of pride.[191] It is impossible to be humble by our own doing. The enemy has twisted the meaning of humility to be defined by man's standards, so it is even more difficult to understand true humility:

> **Colossians 2:18-19** *Let no man beguile you of your reward in a voluntary humility and worshipping of angels, intruding into those things which he hath not seen, vainly puffed up by his fleshly mind, And not holding the Head, from which all the body by joints and bands having nourishment ministered, and knit together, increaseth with the increase of God.*

In this verse, the word ***voluntary*** means *to determine with an active voice.* That means *voluntary humility is false humility.* Therefore, true humility is *involuntary.*

---

[190] Jeremiah 30:21-22
[191] Obadiah 1:3

The word *involuntary* means that it is independent of will or choice. That is because true humility is a spiritual result of the physical act of fasting (abstaining from food). True humility is never displayed through voluntary means; it is a spiritual fruit, not a physical action. True humble actions are a result of humility, while humble actions that generate internal pride are the epitome of false humility. ***True humility is a result, not an action. It cannot be chosen; it is a fruit of the spirit[192] and must come from joining our spirit with the Lord.[193]*** It is something that happens spiritually, not something that is done physically. The most significant benefit of humility is found in Psalm 10:17:

Psalm 10:17 *LORD, thou hast heard the desire of the humble: thou wilt prepare their heart, thou wilt cause thine ear to hear.*

The Lord **prepares the heart** and **listens intently** *to the humble*. Without a doubt, there is no greater reward from acquiring humility; the Lord Himself prepares the heart. Strong's defines the ***heart*** (*lêb* in Hebrew) as ***understanding;*** wisdom builds the house, and *understanding establishes it*.[194] The Ancient Hebrew Lexicon of the Bible defines ***understanding*** (*tabûn* in Hebrew) as ***to set something firmly in place, either physically or with words.*** Understanding sets the house firmly in place, and understanding is in the heart. When the Lord prepares the heart, *He is setting a firm foundation for the spiritual house:*

1 Peter 2:5 *Ye also, as lively stones, are built up a spiritual house, an holy priesthood, to offer up spiritual sacrifices, acceptable to God by Jesus Christ.*

This is the same house He refers to in Luke 6:48:

Luke 6:48 *He is like a man which built an house, and digged deep, and laid the foundation on a rock: and when the flood arose, the stream beat vehemently upon that house, and could not shake it: for it was founded upon a rock.*

The Lord used this experience to affirm humility is one of the characteristics that build a firm foundation on the rock; He would soon reveal there are several more characteristics which fully establish the foundation, that when implemented, actually bring about abundant life.[195]

---

[192] Galatians 5:22-23
[193] 1 Corinthians 6:17
[194] Proverbs 24:3
[195] John 10:10

Four years earlier, the Lord revealed I had acquired the fear of the Lord. Now on this day, He had informed me I had also found the path to true humility, which could have meant only one thing: I was now on the path to the second half (riches and honor and life) of Proverbs 22:4:

> **Proverbs 22:4** *By humility and the fear of the LORD are riches, and honour, and life.*

However, it would not be that simple. The Lord had a plan for my life, and it would require intense training to bring to fruition.

CHAPTER 8

I AM: Your Exceeding Great Reward

Genesis 15:1 After these things the word of the LORD came unto Abram in a vision, saying, Fear not, Abram: I *am* thy shield, *and* thy exceeding great reward.

Seven Words

I had faithfully continued in daily devotions, chasing humility through fasting, and planting seeds (speaking God's Word), when I awoke one morning to the words of the Lord, and I immediately knew what He meant: **"That phrase has seven words."**

The Lord was referring to the statement He had imparted several years before: **"You have the feet of a priest."** It may seem cryptic to hear He speaks just a few words at a time, but He imparts all the details directly to the mind. He may say four words and dump four paragraphs of information explaining it. So, this morning, He was talking about the phrase He had mentioned years earlier; I stopped and counted the words and realized, "yes, that's right." Not that I expected God to be *wrong*, but I still did not understand *why* He mentioned there were exactly seven words in that phrase. Moments later, I opened my Bible to begin devotions, and my reading happened to be the story of Abraham and Isaac. The Lord had instructed Abraham to sacrifice his son, the essence of his promise, in order to prove Abraham did not hold Isaac above his relationship with God. When Abraham was about to go through with it, the Lord stopped him:

> **Genesis 22:10-12** *And Abraham stretched forth his hand, and took the knife to slay his son. And the angel of the LORD called unto him out of heaven, and said, Abraham, Abraham: and he said, Here am I. And he said, Lay not thine hand upon the lad, neither do thou any thing unto him: for now I know that thou fearest God, seeing thou hast not withheld thy son, thine only son from me.*

Genesis 22:16-18 *And said, By myself have I sworn, saith the LORD, for because thou hast done this thing, and hast not withheld thy son, thine only son: That in blessing I will bless thee, and in multiplying I will multiply thy seed as the stars of the heaven, and as the sand which is upon the sea shore; and thy seed shall possess the gate of his enemies; And in thy seed shall all the nations of the earth be blessed; because thou hast obeyed my voice.*

Strong's defines **sworn (shaba** in Hebrew) as **to be complete, to seven oneself, i.e., swear (as if by repeating a declaration seven times.) Seven (sheba`**in Hebrew*)* is defined as **the sacred full one,** and *full* means **completion and perfection**. When I read the definition of *sworn*, I instantly knew the reason He had said there were seven words in the phrase, "**you have the feet of a priest**" was because *He had sworn that to me*. In addition, the definition of the word **seven** means to be complete or perfect. He had spoken and **therefore created** my future, and God was now determined to fulfill it. I would eventually discover His definition of *perfect* was not the same as mine,[196] and since His command is for us *to be perfect*,[197] *it must be attainable*. I said to Him, "You swore that to me!" The spirit rushed through my body, confirming it (a massive chill all at once).

A Diamond
One day as I was praying, the Lord again reminded me of years earlier, my wife had asked the Lord if she should marry me. The Lord said: "**It is up to you. He is a diamond in the rough.**"

I was feeling melancholy as I meditated on the words *diamond in the rough…* and immediately, the Lord said: "**I called you a diamond.**"

Ordinary carbon placed under pressure and heat over a period of time forms diamonds. The Lord says He tests our hearts. The testing of the heart through trials and temptations produces a "spiritual diamond," an obedient, hardened soldier. The Lord tries the hearts;[198] Strong defines the word **tries (bâchan)** in Hebrew as **to test (especially metals) to investigate: —examine, prove.** In Paul's letter, he instructs Timothy to endure hardness as a good soldier of Jesus Christ.[199] Strong's defines the word **hardness (kakopatheo)** as **endure afflictions (hardness), suffer trouble.** Paul also says we please God by separating ourselves from this life:

---

[196] Isaiah 55:9
[197] Matthew 5:48
[198] Proverbs 17:3
[199] 2 Timothy 2:3

2 Timothy 2:4 *No man that warreth entangleth himself with the affairs of this life; that he may please him who hath chosen him to be a soldier.*

Thus, when the Lord called me a diamond, He was encouraging me. I had made progress towards the goal He had set for me:

Psalm 16:11 *Thou wilt shew me the path of life: in thy presence is fulness of joy; at thy right hand there are pleasures for evermore.*

Strong's defines *evermore* (*netsach* in Hebrew) as **properly, a goal,** *i.e.,* **the bright object at a distance travelled towards, truthfulness, confidence, perpetual, strength, victory.** This was encouraging, to be sure. The Lord was not finished yet; He would provide several encouraging circumstances over the next two years. God was transforming me; now He was going to confirm it through experiences...

An Extraordinary Confirmation

The Lord had prepared an extraordinary event He would use to overwhelm me with His encouragement. My wife, stepson, and I had planned a 12-day trip to the Greek islands, and the island of Patmos was on the itinerary, so we were sure to book the excursion to the Cave of the Apocalypse. This is where John received the Revelation, and I was intent on visiting it because I thought perhaps the Lord would speak to me there. I decided to take my tallit (prayer shawl) and wear it inside the cave to venerate the Lord in this holy place. As the time came for the tour to the cave, I put on my tallit and walked down the many steps to the place where John dwelled when he received the book of Revelation. When we entered, we saw several benches, and I promptly took a seat. I pulled my tallit over my head and began speaking in tongues quietly to worship the Lord in this sacred grotto. After a few minutes, my wife notified me a tour group was coming, and I had to leave to make room for the new influx of people. As we left the grotto, my wife informed me a woman had stooped over to see my face as I was praying. Odd, to be sure, but we continued back to the small ship that carried about 250 passengers from one island to the next. The next day a peculiar occurrence took place. My wife was taking my picture on the ship when the same woman from the grotto asked if she could also take my picture. My wife said, "Sure, can I ask why?" The woman said: **"He has the hands, arms, and feet of a priest."**

That was shocking because five years earlier, He had spoken to me: *"You have the feet of a priest."* Back then, I was not sure if the Word was truly from the Lord, because He used a friend in my local church to speak His Word. As my wife shared the encounter, she noted the woman who requested my picture was present at the grotto the day before, and she had leaned over to look around the tallit to see my face. I was not aware because I had my eyes closed at the time.

The next day, I was taking pictures on the Greek island of Santorini and felt drawn away from the group. I found my way to a church; there was a crowd of people in the courtyard. In order to take a picture of the church only, I had to tip the camera up and away from the ground level. Seconds later, as I took the camera down, the same woman from the grotto and her husband were standing in front of me. *We were the only three people in the courtyard.* That was a miracle because there was no way the crowd could have cleared out of the courtyard in the ten seconds that I was taking the picture. They approached me, and the woman said: **"You have the hands, arms, and feet of a priest."**

Then she asked me to place my hand over my heart as she took my picture. The experience was surreal; I was overwhelmed with awe. It was indisputable: The King of the universe had spoken a message to me years before, and now He had confirmed it. I was not sure what it meant at the time, but I knew this was an intensely personal encounter with the One True Living God; He had articulated the same obscure message *by two completely different people over 5000 miles and five years apart.* I would soon realize my assessment of the situation was not completely clear. After she took my picture, I began telling the woman and her husband of my experiences concerning God as if to verify with them what she was saying had some merit. Her husband touched my shoulder and said, *"It radiates right off of you,"* and they promptly turned and walked back toward the village. I sat down to consider what had happened. *This was serious business,* I thought, *a true milestone in my relationship with God.* As I was contemplating the magnitude of what just happened, I realized it was getting late, and I needed to get back to the parking lot to catch the bus back to the ship. I hurriedly climbed the path to the top of the cliff where my wife and stepson were waiting on the bus. As I was about halfway there, *I saw the woman and her husband walking back toward the church where we spoke – away from the waiting buses.* I would never see them again. There were just moments before the bus left for the 30-minute drive to rendezvous with the ship. I quickly made my way to the parking lot and boarded the bus just in time. On the bus ride to the ship, I told my wife of the incredible encounter I had just experienced. As we talked, we uncovered a few odd details about the woman we had both encountered separately. For instance, when each of us saw her, she was always wearing the same clothing. We saw her twice on the ship, but neither she nor her husband was present in group photos or any of the photos we took throughout the trip on a ship of just 250 passengers. One instance was that our group from the ship went to the grotto; the woman was not in our group but was in the grotto during our visit. That made no sense – only one group went to the grotto from our ship. We discussed in detail the times and places we had seen them and determined we had most likely encountered *two angels*. The first time the Lord spoke this message, I did not believe it. He waited five years and sent me 5000 miles from home and spoke it again with more detail. As I pondered this, He imparted: **"Now, you will believe it."**

I was overwhelmed; and realized He had orchestrated the divine meeting. I was not sure of the full meaning of the message, but God would eventually reveal it. God calls things that are not as though they are,[200] He does not always speak in clear terms because He wants to reveal parts of His Word over time. His approach amazed me at each revelation[201] on the journey toward the goal[202] He had set for me. This updated phrase had more information than in the first message (hands and arms), so I looked up the meanings of hands, arms, and feet in Hebrew in two verses:

> **Exodus 35:16** *The altar of burnt offering, with his brasen grate, his staves, and all his vessels, the laver and his foot,*

> **Genesis 49:24** *But his bow abode in strength, and the arms of his hands were made strong by the hands of the mighty God of Jacob.*

Strong's definition for the **foot** is an **office,** while the definitions for **hands** and **arms** are **power** and **force,** respectively. Thus, the phrase can be stated as such: **"You have the power, force, and office of a priest."**

The Lord made me want to "live up" to what He had said. I wanted to become how He saw me, and this is the true power of His Word. *He creates the future by speaking it.*[203] I began to realize this is why knowing Him is of the highest priority; He reveals His secrets to those who fear Him:

> **Psalm 25:14** *The secret of the LORD is with them that fear him; and he will shew them his covenant.*

---

[200] Romans 4:17
[201] Galatians 1:12
[202] Psalm 16:11
[203] Romans 4:17

I was beginning to understand *the secret of the Lord* is the path to knowing Him, and knowing Him *is* abundant life. That is why He told Abram He (God) is Abram's exceeding great reward:

> **Genesis 15:1** *After these things the word of the LORD came unto Abram in a vision, saying, Fear not, Abram: I am thy shield, and thy exceeding great reward.*

I was starting to *get it.* By obeying Him, I came to know Him, and by knowing Him, He revealed the pieces of the path to knowing Him more intimately; God was transforming me to fulfil His original plan from the beginning of time. Then I was able to see the desire He had placed in my heart *and receive that desire through Him.*

Holiness

One morning I was praying in devotions, and the Lord revealed *devotions are holiness.* He said: "**Holiness, without which no man shall see the Lord; this is holiness.**"

This was directly from Hebrews:

> **Hebrews 12:14** *Follow peace with all men, and holiness, without which no man shall see the Lord.*

Holiness is whole, entire, or perfect in a moral sense; *set apart.* The Bible commands us to be holy:

> **1 Peter 1:15** *But as he which hath called you is holy, so be ye holy in all manner of conversation.*

Strong defines **conversation** (**anastrepho** in Greek) as **behavior.** We cannot achieve holiness in and of ourselves; nonetheless, holiness is required. Holiness is a *result* – it is the behavior resulting from internal moral values. The moral values expected are beyond our capability as humans due to our sinful nature. However, when we become partakers of the divine nature, holiness is attainable:

> **2 Peter 1:4** *Whereby are given unto us exceeding great and precious promises: that by these ye might be partakers of the divine nature, having escaped the corruption that is in the world through lust.*

We become *partakers of the divine nature* by joining our spirit with the Lord, who is holy:

1 Corinthians 6:17 *But he that is joined unto the Lord is one spirit.*

In order to join with His spirit, I invested time with Him in devotions; and devotions *set me apart.* The Lord *had to know me* in order for me to enter heaven;[204] *how* I know Him is through *my devotions* – reading His Word and talking with Him in prayer. My devotions joined my spirit with His, so *He knows me*, and from His perception, *I am holy.* The following month, the Lord revealed He had given me a reward. This further affirmed the *rewards He gives relating to eternity.* He rewards us with spiritual revelations and spiritual gifts which cause us to know Him more deeply:

Genesis 15:1 *After these things the word of the LORD came unto Abram in a vision, saying, Fear not, Abram: I am thy shield, and thy exceeding great reward.*

The Reward.

I had posted a testimony about living for eternity on a Christian discussion forum and received a reply, "What are your eternal goals?" I had to think about that for a few days, and I realized I had one eternal goal. I had mentioned to the Lord that when I see Him, I do not want Him to say, "Well done," but rather *"Extraordinarily well done."* Knowing God that way will require some serious ***doing*** of the Word here on earth, *but it is possible to amaze the Creator.* After all, Jesus marveled at a man in the Bible:

Matthew 8:5-*10* *And when Jesus was entered into Capernaum, there came unto him a centurion, beseeching him, And saying, Lord, my servant lieth at home sick of the palsy, grievously tormented. And Jesus saith unto him, I will come and heal him. The centurion answered and said, Lord, I am not worthy that thou shouldest come under my roof: but speak the word only, and my servant shall be healed. For I am a man under authority, having soldiers under me: and I say to this man, Go, and he goeth; and to another, Come, and he cometh; and to my servant, Do this, and he doeth it. When Jesus heard it, he marvelled, and said to them that followed, Verily I say unto you, I have not found so great faith, no, not in Israel.*

I posted on the discussion forum that I wanted the Lord to say, *"Extraordinarily well done,"* to which I received only one reply. It was from a woman I had never heard from before and have never heard from since:

---

[204] Matthew 7:21-23

"YOU have captured the essence of HIS heart through desperate pursuit,[205] and He has rewarded[206] you with the revelation[207] of the unveiled truth to set others free[208] and to enter His Kingdom on earth as it is in heaven.[209] The kingdom is within."[210]

I was astonished! How could it be that the King of the Universe would provide *specific details* of what He was doing to my heart? However, He did, and it was surreal. It was then I understood the definition of diligently seeking God is in *desperate pursuit*. Then the Lord revealed the second half of Hebrews 11:6 had been executed in my life:

> **Hebrews 11:6** *But without faith it is impossible to please him: for he that cometh to God must believe that he is, and that he is a rewarder of them that diligently seek him.*

The word **desperate** in Merriam-Webster's 1828 dictionary means "*Without care of safety; rash; fearless of danger; as a desperate man.*" This is remarkably similar to the definition of the fear of the Lord, which is to do absolutely anything necessary not to disappoint Him through unconditional, immediate, and complete obedience. I had been learning of the rewards and consequences of *obedience to completion* and what it meant to delight God; it requires hearing His voice and doing His commands – no matter the consequences.[211] The fear of man is when one shapes their behavior to please men; the fear of the Lord is when one bases their behavior on delighting God. Delighting God will undoubtedly have earthly consequences because it often conflicts with pleasing men. This is by God's design because we learn to fear the Lord through suffering.[212] I understood this in theory, but over the next two years, I would come to understand it through actual life events. The other part of this word from the Lord was, "***you have been rewarded with the revelation of the unveiled truth.***" I did not exactly understand what that meant at the time, but I would come to recognize the unveiled truth is *God's perspective*. It is being able to separate temporal earthly aspirations from the eternal path of life[213] and making godly decisions based on that knowledge.

---

[205] Hebrews 11:6
[206] Psalm 19:9-11
[207] Galatians 1:12
[208] John 8:32
[209] Romans 14:17
[210] Luke 17:21
[211] Psalm 15:4
[212] Hebrews 5:8
[213] Psalm 16:11

A Vision: The Treasure

One morning, I had a vision while I was praying. I was on a stone path with vines on both sides, standing before an old, heavy, medieval wooden door, the kind with the heavy black hinges. I was knocking at the door,[214] and suddenly it opened. Out flowed jewels and diamonds – all pure and transparent, so much treasure[215] it was knee-deep and knocked me over. This was a foreshadowing of Isaiah 45:3:

> **Isaiah 45:3** *And I will give thee the treasures of darkness, and hidden riches of secret places, that thou mayest know that I, the LORD, which call thee by thy name, am the God of Israel.*

The Lord had already told me I was *rich* and would soon call me by name. This was an important milestone because He was revealing to me that I was accruing rewards in heaven:

> **Matthew 6:20** *But lay up for yourselves treasures in heaven, where neither moth nor rust doth corrupt, and where thieves do not break through nor steal:*

Meanwhile, the Lord was determined to show me the path
of life through overcoming adversity.

The Path to Righteousness

> **Psalm 16:11** *Thou wilt shew me the path of life: in thy presence is fulness of joy; at thy right hand there are pleasures for evermore.*

My oldest stepdaughter was to be married, and we had not seen eye to eye since I became part of the family; our spiritual differences only strained the relationship, so she resisted allowing me to attend the ceremony. However, her mother would not attend unless we went together, so just a week before the wedding, my stepdaughter capitulated and allowed me to attend. I was not aware of the scrutiny I was under at the reception, but through God's grace, my demeanor was unruffled. I volunteered a few times to help the bride with items others had forgotten or needed retrieval from various cars in the parking lot. At one point, I found myself walking through this quaint New England harbor alone with the bride while we searched for the car containing the shoes she needed for the reception. She and I talked, and all was

---

[214] Matthew 7:7
[215] Isaiah 45:3

well, the closest we had been in quite some time. She appreciated all I had done, and I was openhearted as we strolled back to the reception. As the reception progressed, I mentally noted there were two people across the table that had offended me in the past, so I disregarded them and spent the time talking to the man seated to my right. This went on for the entire evening, and as I was leaving, the Lord convicted me that my conduct was not quite right; I should have included the people across the table rather than ignoring them. Once home, my wife noted how cordial I had been, given the pressure I was under, but I quickly conveyed I could have done better because I disregarded people seated at our table. She brushed that aside and told me how several people were amazed at my pleasant manner throughout the event. The next day, I attended church, and there was an altar call after the service. I do not exactly remember what the altar call was for, but I remember thinking, "I don't need to go up for that." Yet I felt this tug, a slight uneasiness in the heart; this was the Holy Spirit prompting me to the altar, so I obeyed. While I was at the altar, I was talking with the Lord about the people I had ignored the day before. He lightheartedly said: **"Repent!"**

I smiled and said, "OK!" Just then, a woman gently took hold of my arm and said, *"The Lord wants you to know He is pleased with you; keep doing what you are doing. He is well pleased."* The Lord was pleased because I had discounted the praise of men concerning my actions at the reception, and instead exhibited concern because, *while not seen by most*, my actions were not acceptable by God's standards. He uses the praise of men to test our obedience:

> **Proverbs 27:21** *As the fining pot for silver, and the furnace for gold; so is a man to his praise.*

> **Romans 2:29** *But he is a Jew, which is one inwardly; and circumcision is that of the heart, in the spirit, and not in the letter; whose praise is not of men, but of God.*

Although I had displayed appropriate behavior according to the wedding guests,[216] I recognized my heart was not right. As soon as I confessed it, He revealed *He was well pleased; I was astonished at His words, and frankly, it took me a few days to collect myself.* About a week later, I was reminiscing over what had happened, and I realized that for the Lord to speak those words, I must have found something. It was just then He said: **"You found the path to righteousness."**[217]

---

[216] 1 Samuel 16:7
[217] Psalm 5:12

His Word confirms it:

1 John 1:9 *If we confess our sins, he is faithful and just to forgive us our sins, and to cleanse us from all unrighteousness.*

He knew my behavior bothered me, so He pulled me toward the altar. I confessed my sin, and He performed His Word[218] and forgave me. The amazing thing about knowing God is that He directs and guides; all the intricate details about *what to do and when* are not necessary, He provides all of that. I just prepared my heart to hear His still small voice[219] and obeyed it; then, *He rewarded me for obeying Him.* His Word also says, without faith, it is impossible to please Him; He confirmed from *His perspective*, I had faith because I had executed the first part of Hebrews 11:6:

Hebrews 11:6 *But without faith it is impossible to please him: for he that cometh to God must believe that he is, and that he is a rewarder of them that diligently seek him.*

James 2:21-23 records that God counted Abraham's faith unto him for righteousness.[220] That is how the Lord revealed His Word when He said, "**You found the path to righteousness.**" God counted Abraham's faith unto him as righteousness, and faith is required to please God.

The Bible records another reward connected to pleasing God, and when the Lord speaks, He performs His Word. Therefore, when He said He was pleased, within the next two weeks, three of my enemies made peace with me:

Proverbs 16:7 *When a man's ways please the LORD, he maketh even his enemies to be at peace with him.*

I did not search out my enemies; the Lord *made* three separate people approach and make peace with me. With that, the Lord had fulfilled in my life the first half of Hebrews 12:14:

Hebrews 12:14 *Follow peace with all men, and holiness, without which no man shall see the Lord:*

---

[218] Jeremiah 1:12
[219] 1 Kings 19:12
[220] James 2:21-23

God gave me the grace to not only endure this situation but succeed in it. I could be strong in grace because grace is *the divine influence of the heart and its reflection in the life* (Strong's definition of the Greek word for **grace. charis**); how much influence grace had in my life was determined by the commitment of my submission to the Lord. I trusted God for the outcome of **every** situation, no matter the result, even *if I thought it was unfair* (because God uses unfair situations). That trust *provided my attitude was right,* led to great blessing. Trusting God always prioritized His best interest in my life, *no matter what the situation looked or felt like;* it allowed situations to unfold with no attempt to manipulate circumstances in my favor or flee from them. Trusting God meant *not* taking offense to those involved in the situation, and perceiving that *God was using them to perfect me no matter how they made me look or feel.* When I successfully *understood* this, I was able to do it successfully; and it is then that God perfects.[221] The more situations I submitted to God in my life, the more humility I was given and *the more grace (power) I received.*[222,223] Humility promotes grace in the heart, and when we allow grace to influence our heart, our life reflects that divine influence through the evidence of the fruits of the Spirit (love, joy, peace, patience, gentleness, kindness, faith, humility, and self-control).[224] That reflection, in turn, promotes humility (one of the nine spiritual fruits), which garners more grace:

> **2 Peter 3:18** *But grow in grace, and in the knowledge of our Lord and Saviour Jesus Christ. To him be glory both now and forever. Amen.*

> **John 1:16** *And of his fulness have all we received, and grace for grace.*

We achieve successful obedience to all Jesus' commands in the Bible through knowing Him.[225] The Bible instructs us to follow peace with all men;[226] however, peace is a fruit of the Spirit, which God grants when He is pleased.

Physical Rain – A Foreshadowing

My wife and I decided to take a trip to always balmy, weather perfect, San Diego, California. To our surprise, when we arrived, it rained half an inch in the first 24 hours we were there. As I was looking out the window at the

---

[221] Psalm 138:8
[222] James 4:6
[223] 1 Peter 5:5
[224] Galatians 5:22-23
[225] Matthew 6:33
[226] Hebrews 12:14

ocean through the pouring rain, I perceived in my spirit[227] that the rain was coming down **because** we were visiting. I said to my wife, "It is raining because we are here." The San Diego Union-Tribune reported this as the wettest day in May in drought-ridden San Diego in nine years. The Living God of Israel, who created *everything* and commands the weather[228] , sometimes uses physical instances to foreshadow spiritual events,[229] and I knew this was one of those times. I realized this journey would never be about me,[230] but rather about the blessings God would shower on others by blessing me. This was a physical representation of the spiritual vision of the little white house in the cornfield when I saw all the corn stalks. I said to the Lord, "But it is not raining." He replied, **"It is raining *inside* the house."** Several weeks later, He would grant the gift to accomplish the desire He had placed in my heart:[231] to speak about Him.

Called by Name

It was just two and a half weeks after we returned from San Diego when an anointed international evangelist came to preach at our small church in New England. He had been preaching for over 30 years all over the world. I spent most of the morning catching people that were "slain in the spirit," which is to say they fell over backward[232] by the power of God. The evangelist was about four feet away from my wife, and when he prayed for her, the power of the Holy Spirit knocked her right over. The morning service ended, but there was another service that evening; I felt the draw of the Holy Spirit to attend the service that night. I was again on duty to catch people as they fell backward; at one point, there was no one left in line. The evangelist looked directly at me and said, "You don't need me to pray for you; you have already got it." The evangelist had never met me before that day and had no idea who I was. How could he know the depth of my relationship with the Lord? There are servants who have a deep relationship with the Lord and can see beyond the natural into the spiritual. They can see the spiritual flag the Lord places on those who fear Him:

Psalm 60:4 *Thou hast given a banner to them that fear thee, that it may be displayed because of the truth. Selah.*

---

[227] 2 Samuel 5:12
[228] Job 28:23-26
[229] Jeremiah 51:63-64
[230] Philippians 2:3
[231] Psalm 37:4
[232] John 18:6

The Hebrew word for banner *nec* means flag. Therefore, the Lord had placed a flag on my spirit when He had determined I feared Him. This evangelist had a deep relationship with the Lord and was able to see it. The evening continued, and I found myself just to the right of the evangelist as he was praying for another man. He proclaimed, "You have the gift of communication: speaking and writing." The man was flabbergasted and somewhat refuted the claim as if he did not know or understand what was being said. *I wonder if that was for me,* I thought, *maybe it was "wrong guy, close by."* There was no way I could verify that thought, so I moved on with the crowd as the evangelist moved over to the left side of the church. I was now standing behind a man he was about to pray for when the evangelist said to him, "Do you have any relatives or friends named Scott?" The man said, "No, but he is standing right behind me." The evangelist looked at me in complete shock and asked, "Your name is Scott?!" "Yes," I replied. He exclaimed, "**Wow!**" He backed up several steps, clearly astonished, and shouted, "**Wow! The Lord put that name right in my *spirit!***" The Lord God of Israel had called me by name:[233]

> **Isaiah 45:3** *And I will give thee the treasures of darkness, and hidden riches of secret places, that thou mayest know that I, the LORD, which call thee by thy name, am the God of Israel.*

The evangelist was clearly astonished as if that had never happened to him in 30 years of ministry. When he was asking the man if he knew anyone named Scott, I was standing just behind him. The evangelist was *off by one person* just as he was when he proclaimed the gift of speaking and writing. This was the Lord showing me it indeed was the *"wrong guy, close by"* on the other side of the sanctuary. The evangelist had not recognized the gift in the man, but rather, *the Lord had granted me that gift through the evangelist.* When the Lord mentioned my name, He was letting me know He granted the gift; He did not want me to ascribe the granting of the gift from a man but from God Himself. The evangelist then looked at me and said, *"Your tongue is being loosed. You will prophesy to men to whom you have never prophesied before."* The Lord had fulfilled the promise He had made years before when He said, "**Ask Me for something, and I will give it to you.**" I had replied, "All I want to do is talk about you"; that request was now fulfilled with the gift of communication: speaking and writing. *The spiritual rain had begun.*

---

[233] Isaiah 45:3

CHAPTER 9

The Revelation of the Unveiled Truth

Isaiah 45:3 *And I will give thee the treasures of darkness, and hidden riches of secret places, that thou mayest know that I, the LORD, which call thee by thy name, am the God of Israel.*

From my perspective, I had been diligently seeking God through relentless obedience, and I was about to discover the Living God agreed. While I was praying one summer morning, I had a vision; it was a revelation of pillars supporting a house. Each of the pillars corresponded to actions I implemented through obedience in my journey over the past five years. The Lord revealed the spiritual value of the physical actions and how they built a foundation upon a rock. The rock was Him, and the actions were pillars built to support the house.[234]

---

[234] Luke 6:48

The Seven Pillars

Figure A

Therefore whosoever heareth these sayings of mine, and doeth them, I will liken him unto a wiseman, which built his house upon a rock. And the rain descended, and the floods came, and the winds blew, and beat upon that house; and it fell not: for it was founded upon a rock

Matthew 7:24-25

Devotions | *Tongues* | *Tithes & Offerings* | *Speaking God's Word* | *Fasting* | *Obedience* | *Perseverance*

He is the Rock, his work is perfect: for all his ways are judgment: a God of truth and without iniquity, just and right is he. Deuteronomy 32:4

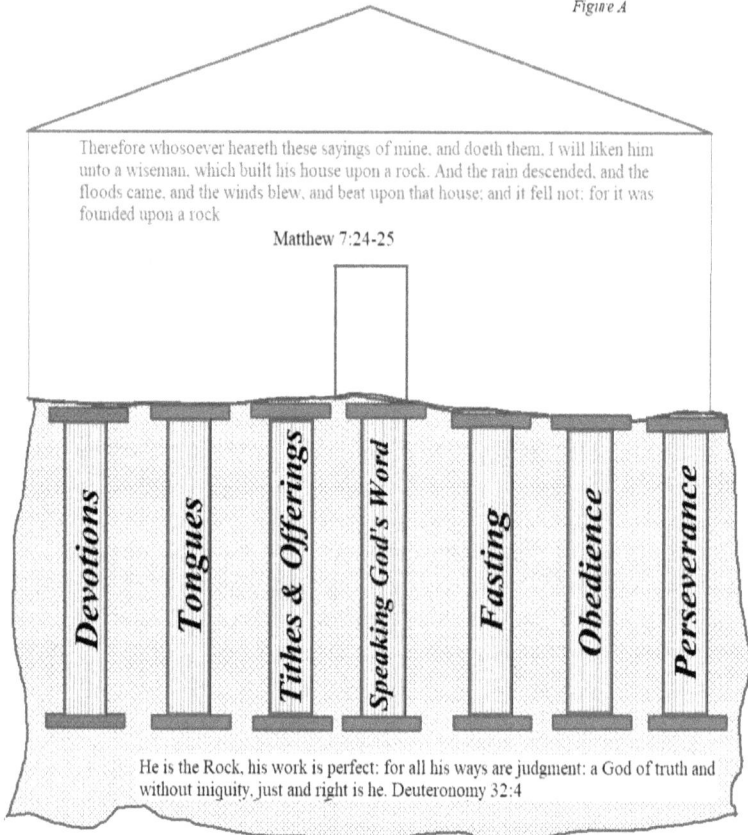

Revelation knowledge is powerful because it is often personal and always a depth of understanding in God's Word that is not readily available. Paul, who was a "Hebrew of Hebrews"[235] and highly educated in the law, understood revelation knowledge is not the knowledge of men, but the knowledge of God:

> **Galatians 1:11-12** *But I certify you, brethren, that the gospel which was preached of me is not after man. For I neither received it of man, neither was I taught it, but by the revelation of Jesus Christ.*

> **Ephesians 3:1-4** *For this cause I Paul, the prisoner of Jesus Christ for you Gentiles, If ye have heard of the dispensation of the grace of God which is given me*

---

[235] Philippians 3:4-6

to you-ward: How that by revelation he made known unto me the mystery; (as I wrote afore in few words, Whereby, when ye read, ye may understand my knowledge in the mystery of Christ)

Paul most certainly performed the seven pillars:
Devotions – Paul constantly communed with the Lord[236,237]
Tongues – Paul spoke in tongues "more than you all."[238]
Tithes and Offerings – Paul "suffered loss of all things."[239]
Speaking God's Word – Paul preached[240,241]
Fasting – Paul fasted[242,243]
Obedience – Paul was obedient unto the faith and heavenly vision[244,245]
Perseverance – Paul persevered through tribulation and suffering[246,247]
Paul said the God of peace would be with those who learned to do as he did:

> **Philippians 4:9** *Those things, which ye have both learned, and received, and heard, and seen in me, do: and the God of peace shall be with you.*

Doing these physical acts generated the spiritual growth that brought Paul into an intimate relationship with the Lord. Even the evil spirits knew Paul:

> **Acts 19:13-15** *Then certain of the vagabond Jews, exorcists, took upon them to call over them which had evil spirits the name of the Lord Jesus, saying, We adjure you by Jesus whom Paul preacheth. And there were seven sons of one Sceva, a Jew, and chief of the priests, which did so. And the evil spirit answered and said, Jesus I know, and Paul I know; but who are ye?*

The evil spirits did not recognize the exorcists who were using Jesus' name

---

[236] Acts 16:25
[237] Romans 1:9
[238] 1 Corinthians 14:18
[239] Philippians 3:8
[240] Acts 15:35
[241] Acts 20:7
[242] Acts 9:8-9 [Saul = Paul]
[243] Acts 13:2-3
[244] Romans 1:5
[245] Acts 26:19-20
[246] 1 Timothy 1:16
[247] 2 Corinthians 11:24-28

to cast them out, but they did acknowledge they knew both Jesus and Paul. Of course, they recognized Jesus, but they also recognized Paul because he had joined his spirit[248] with the Lord through enacting The Seven Pillars.

I implemented all these pillars in various stages of my journey, and up to this point, I believed the perseverance pillar was simply a culmination of continuously performing the other six pillars. I would soon learn; however, I had not yet fulfilled the perseverance pillar, and it would be the most challenging to complete. It was the pillar of the present; I needed to implement it in order to complete the building of the house; I would soon embark on the fulfillment of that pillar, which would involve suffering I had not yet experienced. Meanwhile, I received another revelation; this one was of the relationship between trust and fear. This vision was of a mathematical truth that He would expound upon to reveal the depth of His abundant life.[249]

Abundant Life

Figure B

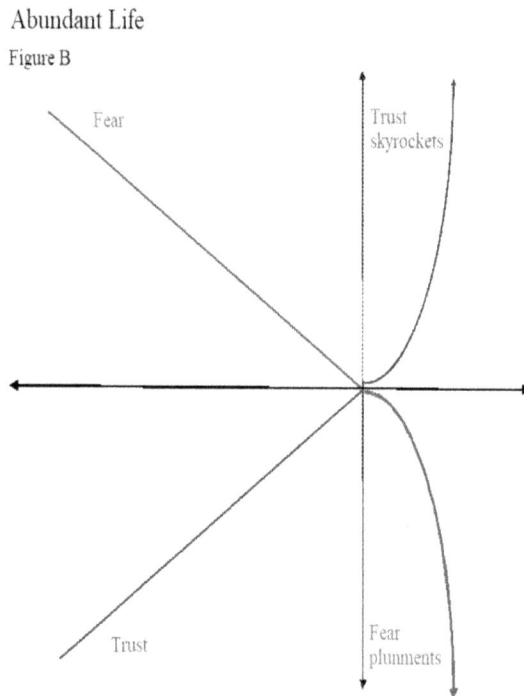

The vision shown above was the picture I received from the Lord. As

---

[248] 1 Corinthians 6:17
[249] John 10:10

trust increases, fear decreases. Once trust and fear intersect, trust exponentially increases while fear exponentially decreases. There are mathematical functions that create these curves, and the details that define this picture are not coincidental. As I added more information, God revealed more of the revelation until the diagram was complete:

Figure C.

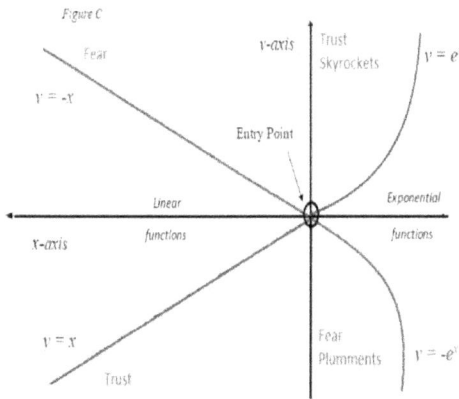

Abundant Life

John 10:10

The thief cometh not, but for to steal, and to kill, and to destroy: I am come that they might have life, and that they might have it more abundantly

What it is:

Abundant Life is receiving God's perspective to live for eternity.

How it is lived:

Spiritual growth becomes priority. Everyone and everything else are secondary. The goal is to have a perfect heart in God's eyes and become the very person He called you to be by living His perfect will for your life.

How to receive it:

Abundant Life cannot be manufactured. It is a reward given to those with a committed and dedicated relationship with God through doing his Word. **Doing God's Word is accomplished by continually practicing The Seven Pillars.**

e = a transcendental number having a value ≈ 2.71828183
that is the base of natural logarithms

Figure C

Fear

$y = -x$

x-axis

Trust
Skyrockets

$y = e^x$

Entry Point

Linear functions

Exponential functions

x-axis

$y = x$

Trust

Fear
Plummets

$y = -e^x$

Mt 16:27 For the Son of man shall come in the glory of his Father with his angels: and then he shall reward every man according to his works.
Greek: works (praxis): practice. i.e. (concretely) an act; by extension, a function:—deed. office. work.

Function (Merriam Webster definition)
1: professional or official position : OCCUPATION
2: the action for which a person or thing is specially fitted or used or for which a thing exists : PURPOSE
3: any of a group of related actions contributing to a larger action

Exponential (Webster's 1828 dictionary)

EXPONENTIAL. a. Exponential curves are such as partake both of the nature of algebraic and **transcendental** ones. They partake of the former, because they consist of a finite number of terms, though these terms themselves are indeterminate; and they are in some measure **transcendental**, because they cannot be algebraically constructed.

Experiencing Abundant Life is an *exponential function* of The Seven Pillars

transcendental function, (Encyclopedia Britannica)

In mathematics, a function not expressible as a finite combination of the algebraic operations of addition, subtraction, multiplication, division, raising to a power, and extracting a root. Examples include the functions log x, sin x, cos x, ex and any functions containing them. Such functions are expressible in algebraic terms only as infinite series. In general, the term transcendental means nonalgebraic. See also transcendental number.

Webster's Dictionary

tran·scen·den·tal
tran sen den(t)l/ *adjective*

1. of or relating to a spiritual or nonphysical realm.

"the transcendental importance of each person's soul"

2 MATHEMATICS
(of a number, e.g., e or π) real but not a root of an algebraic equation with rational roots.

The mathematical functions that create each curve on the x and y-axes are linear on the left and exponential on the right. The arrow from left to right represents time. Keeping God's commands (obedience) causes trust to increase and fear to decrease until a critical point where trust overcomes fear; this is where abundant life begins. Matthew 16:27 (on the left side of the illustration) reveals Jesus will reward every man according to his works; this is not salvation, because salvation is a gift. [250] The definition of works is a *function*, or *the action that a person is specially fitted for, or that for which a thing exists.* The first commandment is to love the Lord with all our heart, mind, and soul,[251] so the function God made us for is to *love Him.* Also, on the left side of the diagram, the word *exponential* is defined as *transcendental.* The curves defining fear and trust on the right side of the diagram are exponential and, therefore, transcendental curves. Transcendental functions are *infinite,* and the word transcendental itself is defined as *"of or relating to the spiritual or nonphysical realm."* This vision essentially shows the results of performing the seven pillars, a representation of spiritual sowing and reaping:

2 Corinthians 9:6 *But this I say, He which soweth sparingly shall reap also sparingly; and he which soweth bountifully shall reap also bountifully.*

Meanwhile, the Lord was about to reveal an amazing revelation of the origin of the icthus symbol.

A Vision: The Icthus Revelation

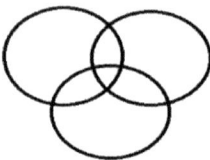

I asked the Lord to show me something about Him, and I received a vision of three circles. The vision slowly filled in with detail until I realized the revelation was concerning the origin of the **icthus**. The icthus is the "Jesus fish" many Christians displays as a symbol of their faith, and I was amazed at the understanding of the importance of the icthus. Have you ever seen "Jesus Fish?" It is the Greek letters "ΙΧΘΥΣ" inside a fish symbol.

---

[250] Romans 6:23
[251] Matthew 22:37

What it means:
Icthus (ΙΧΘΥΣ): Greek for "fish")
ΙΧΘΥΣ spells "Fish" in Greek. ΙΧΘΥΣ is an acrostic poem. Acrostic poems use the first letter of each line to spell out something. **Iota** is the first letter of Iesous or Ιησους, which is the Greek spelling of Jesus. **Chi** is the first letter of Christos or Χριστός, which is Greek for Anointed. **Theta** is the first letter of Theou or θεοῦ, which is the possessive form of the Greek word for God. **Upsilon** is the first letter of Huios or γἱός, Greek for Son. **Sigma** is the first letter of Soter or Σωτήρ, the Greek word for Savior.

Jesus Christ, God's Son, Savior
This is a special symbol; it reveals Jesus is the Son of God, and He is the Savior. The use of the symbol originates in the first century A.D., and Christ-followers still use it today. The fact that it is an acrostic poem is amazing; after all, this reveals Jesus as the Savior and the Son of God, but the question is: Why a fish? Many believe this is because the apostles were "fishers of men," etc. The Bible uses the Greek word ΙΧΘΥΣ multiple times for the word "fish" in the New Testament. In ancient times, followers of Jesus would write half of the symbol
and wait for another believer to finish the symbol:

This would tell the first person they were now in the presence of another believer; this is how followers of Christ could determine if it was safe to talk about Jesus without persecution.

The Revelation of the Origin of the Icthus
The revelation is not of the icthus itself; that is well known. The revelation is of the *origin* of the icthus. Why do the letters that reveal Jesus Christ as the Son of God and the Savior mean "fish?" In addition, where did the shape of the symbol originate? The revelation is the story of sanctification (holiness). It shows a man can only be sanctified (made holy) through Jesus, which is why it is so important to **know Him.** Many believe they know Him; however, whether we know Him **will be**

determined by Him, not us. How do we know that we know Him? *By keeping His commands:*

> **1 John 2:3** *And hereby we do know that we know him, if we keep his commandments.*

> **Many believe holiness is unattainable, but true followers know that holiness is required,[252] it comes through sanctification, and sanctification is accomplished through obedience.**

It all comes down to **obedience!** The revelation was pieced together over the course of four days. This is the importance of the icthus, where it came from, and why it is a fish. One piece of the revelation not shown on the following figure is this: Instinctively when connecting the circles, I wrote the words "Holy Ghost" numerous times to emphasize His Presence as well as the shape of the icthus within the intersecting circles. Afterward, I was curious about the number of times Jesus used the words "Holy Ghost" in the Bible; He spoke those words *thirteen* times. I quickly went back to the revelation figure to count the number of times I had written "Holy Ghost" in the icthus: *it was thirteen.*

---

[252] 1 Peter 1:15-16

Icthus (ΙΧΘΥΣ): Greek for "fish"

ΙΧΘΥΣ actually spells "Fish" in Greek. ΙΧΘΥΣ is an acrostic poem. Acrostic poems use the first letter of each line to spell out something. Iota is the first letter of Iesous or Ιησους, which is the Greek spelling of Jesus. Chi is the first letter of Christos or Χριστός, which is Greek for Anointed. Theta is the first letter of Theou or θεοῦ, which is the possessive form of the Greek word for God. Upsilon is the first letter of Huios or γἱός, Greek for Son. Sigma is the first letter of Soter or Σωτηρ, the Greek word for Savior.

Jesus Christ, God's Son, Savior

The Father, Jesus and the Holy Ghost are one.[11] The Holy Ghost forms the icthus that incorporates God with Jesus. This icthus directs God toward man

Holiness

I AM

Righteouness

Holy Ghost

ΙΧΟΥΣ

But we are all as an unclean thing, and all our righteousnesses are as filthy rags; and we all do fade as a leaf; and our iniquities, like the wind, have taken us away.[1]

But to him that worketh not, but believeth on him that justifieth the ungodly, his faith is counted for righteousness.[2]

Follow peace with all men, and holiness, without which no man shall see the Lord.[3]

But seek ye first the kingdom of God, and his righteousness; and all these things shall be added unto you.[4]

* The cross of Jesus touches God the Father vertically while simultaneously touching man horizontally.

† The sword of the Spirit exists in the cross. Hebrew meaning of kissed: "equip with weapons"

Man must come to God through Jesus. The Holy Ghost and repentance create the icthus that is the gateway between Jesus and man. This icthus directs man toward God.

Mercy and truth are met together; righteousness and peace have kissed each other.[12]

I am the way, the truth, and the life: no man cometh unto the Father, but by me.[5]

I am the door: by me if any man enter in, he shall be saved, and shall go in and out, and find pasture.[6]

For they verily for a few days chastened us after their own pleasure; but he for our profit, that we might be partakers of his holiness.[8]

And for their sakes I sanctify myself, that they also might be sanctified through the truth.[9]

Looking unto Jesus the author and finisher of our faith; who for the joy that was set before him endured the cross, despising the shame, and is set down at the right hand of the throne of God.[9]

To open their eyes, and to turn them from darkness to light, and from the power of Satan unto God, that they may receive forgiveness of sins, and inheritance among them which are sanctified by faith that is in me.[10]

[1] Isaiah 64:6
[2] Romans 4:5
[3] Hebrews 12:14
[4] Matthew 6:33
[5] John 14:6
[6] John 17:19
[7] John 10:9
[8] Hebrews 12:10
[9] Hebrews 12:2
[10] Acts 26:18
[11] 1 John 5:7
[12] Psalm 85:10

"The Revelation of the Icthus"

01/28/2016

The revelation of the icthus shows three circles: one for Man, one for Jesus, and one for God (I AM). This diagram depicts the relationship of the icthus: Jesus Christ, God's Son, Savior. The illustration shows how Jesus' circle in red interconnects and creates an icthus between Jesus and God; God's circle contains holiness and righteousness; two attributes God requires man to be present with God. Jesus is *God's Son,* and the intersection is orange – which is created from the blood of Jesus (red) and the light of God (yellow). *Jesus is the Savior* is illustrated where the Jesus circle interconnects and creates an icthus between Jesus and Man. Psalm 85:10 reveals the cross where the two icthus meet. Mercy is found in Man's circle and righteousness in Jesus' circle; God's circle contains peace, and the truth is shared by Jesus and God. This cross contains the sword of the Spirit because Psalm 85 *equips with weapons*:

107

Psalm 85:10 *Mercy and truth are met together; righteousness and peace have kissed each other.*

Strong's definition of ***kissed (nashaq*** in Hebrew) means ***to equip with weapons.*** The Ancient Hebrew Lexicon of the Bible defines ***kissed*** as ***touching in battle with weapons.***

The Holy Ghost Interlocks Man with Jesus and Jesus with God; Jesus, with repentance, also provides for the remission of sins. I received this vision because I asked[253] the Lord to show me something about Him. I was puzzled when the three intersecting circles appeared, and I quickly wrote them on a piece of scrap paper that still hangs on the wall in my office. God revealed this vision over the course of four days; as I wrote each part, He revealed more until it was finished; I am still amazed every time I see it. That was a revelation revealed to me by the King of Kings to show me the depth of His Word simply because I asked!

---

[253] James 4:2

CHAPTER 10

Whom Shall I Fear?

Psalm 27:1 *A Psalm of David. The LORD is my light and my salvation; whom shall I fear? the LORD is the strength of my life; of whom shall I be afraid?*

Holy Spirit Appointed

The church board member elections were imminent, and I had been asking the Lord what action to take in the event the church asked me to serve on the board. I had served as a board member for another church in the past, and I was not overly eager to serve in that capacity again; although, I felt I could certainly help with all the Lord had taught me. I had begun inquiring of the Lord six months prior to the election for direction on whether to accept a nomination if requested. I knew whether I served was not my choice, but God's. After a few weeks, He said: **"If there is no election, take the job; otherwise defer."**

That sounds great, I thought, *no matter what happens, this will be the Lord's decision, not mine.* I knew from experience that inquiring of the Lord in these circumstances was always better than making my own decision. That is because situations do not always unfold as expected, and following the Lord's will always garner a positive outcome *to those who obey Him*,[254] whether physical blessing, which can be readily identified or spiritual growth not so easily detected by man's perception. The verse that references this truth is Romans 8:28.

Romans 8:28 *And we know that all things work together for good to them that love God, to them who are the called according to his purpose.*

---

[254] Romans 8:28

After a series of events transpired, I would later learn that, while nominated to be a member on the board, the nominating committee rejected my status. Nonetheless, a week before the election, the leadership of the church called and asked if I would consider filling a vacancy on the board. I asked if there would be an election and was told there would be none. Therefore, in obedience to the Lord, I accepted the position. Later, I would discover five people had rejected the position before leadership offered it to me. Given the circumstances, I was sure the Lord had appointed me to help spiritually guide the church. I could not have been more wrong in my assessment; this would begin the most challenging phase of my journey. The Lord had placed me in this position in order to test my allegiance to Him, *but ten months would pass before that testing would begin.*

The Paradox
Initially, I had some adverse experiences as a board member, but I chalked them up to the normal assimilation of the new position. However, the Lord was about to turn up the heat.

> **Proverbs 17:3** *The fining pot is for silver, and the furnace for gold: but the LORD trieth the hearts.*

I received a fasting devotional from my leader who wanted the Board members to follow it over the forty days of Lent. The problem was that the "fast," as it was called, referred to abstaining from things such as "isolation," "willful sin," "spiritual self-protection" (whatever that is), and the list went on. The book continually used the word "fast" when referring to abstaining from anything and everything. I knew this was not true fasting because these are negative *behavioral attributes*, which Jesus referred to as evil fruit. The fruit of the Spirit comes from walking in the Spirit,[255] and walking in the spirit originates from an intimate relationship with God.[256] This book was claiming one could *"work on the bad fruit"* and call it fasting, when, in reality, the fruit is the *result* of the spiritual inner man's relationship with God:

> **Matthew 7:17-19** *Even so every good tree bringeth forth good fruit; but a corrupt tree bringeth forth evil fruit. A good tree cannot bring forth evil fruit, neither can a corrupt tree bring forth good fruit. Every tree that bringeth not forth good fruit is hewn down, and cast into the fire.*

---

[255] Galatians 5:16-25
[256] 1 Corinthians 6:17

We cannot work upon the fruit itself; a tree does not "work" at producing fruit – the fruit is a result of a healthy or unhealthy tree. I had been fasting for the previous two years and fully understood the definition of fasting, and why the spiritual benefits of fasting are only acquired through the physical act of abstaining from food (or approved exceptions-see chapter seven God's Provisions for exceptions). While abstaining from other things (e.g., television, sports, etc.) may be admirable and may even aid in drawing closer to God, the act of abstaining from food produces supernatural progress of the inner man. The word *fast* in the Old Testament Hebrew means: *to cover the mouth*[257] while *fast* in the New Testament Greek means *to abstain from food.*[258] Psalm 35:13 says humility comes from fasting. Unfortunately, today's society has swapped out the word "fast" for the word "abstain," so anytime anyone abstains from *anything*, it is called a fast. That is a dilution of the word "fast" as God originally intended and gives the impression that abstaining from anything will garner the spiritual benefits of true fasting. The Lord speaks about the "fast that He has chosen"[259] in Isaiah 58. He uses the word *fast* seven times in that chapter, and *every time* it refers to *covering the mouth* (not eating). Understanding this, I knew I could not participate in this devotional with the other board members because it was not Biblical. The Lord had brought to my attention; I must obey my leader, so I could not simply ignore the directive; I had to tell him I could not follow through and the reason why. This was tantamount to placing my promise on the altar, obeying God, and effectively watching His promise die (I would someday speak about Him). I knew the power of obedience and strove to obey authority in every situation, but my conviction was first to God, then my leaders. If there were any discrepancies, I had to obey God, even to my own detriment.[260] I sent an email explaining I could not participate with the new devotional, and my leader subsequently summoned me to his office. He assured me the church community had accepted this book. I attempted to convince him my conviction was valid, but he was not persuaded and bluntly told me I had spiritual pride, and I was not a team player. This is a common misconception when evaluating pride versus humility. True humility comes from above; it is a fruit of the spirit[261] and has only one quality: confidence in God. Pride is confidence in self and is often displayed by boldness or even false humility, which is an outward display of humility while inward pride subsists. False humility emerges when seemingly humble people have confidence in themselves.

---

[257] 2 Samuel 12:22
[258] Matthew 9:15
[259] Isaiah 58:6
[260] Psalm 15:4
[261] Galatians 5:22-23

On the other hand, a person showing boldness can be truly humble while displaying *seemingly* prideful qualities. How then, can one discern whether someone is prideful or humble? This can be tricky because pride has many traits, some of which are hidden. Paul tells us to be bold[262] , which may *look like pride* to the undiscerning eye; however, *the difference between pride and humility is where the trust is placed.* Regardless of a display of boldness or timidity, one who places trust in God is humble, while one who places trust in themselves is prideful.[263] Confidence in God is often misunderstood as pride, especially when disagreement exists.

The enemy (Satan) had not been able to crack into my life; he knew I had found true spiritual growth comes from relentless obedience. Therefore, he craftily sent a false devotion (to break into my devotional time *and* crack my foundation) through my leader; I knew honoring and obeying him was equivalent to honoring and obeying God. This was a well-set trap because if I alienated this leader, it was unlikely that I would ever see God's promise come to fruition in my life (or so I thought). There were two driving forces: obedience and the promise. However, I knew I must obey God in *all* situations; obedience to Him trumps all other authority. Obedience to God in difficult situations was the ultimate display of faith and humility, i.e., confidence in God. Therefore, regardless of the consequences, I enacted what was deep within me - the fear of the Lord. Across from me, my leader was not convinced of my conviction to obey the Lord, but it was then that the Holy Spirit saved me; I spoke of some indisputable incidents where God had intervened in my life and how God had called me by name. I began to share. I had found the treasure in the field and sold all I had to buy that field.[264] I was still in the process of communicating the story to my leader when I began sobbing to the point where I could no longer speak. That was when the veil was lifted from my leader's eyes, revealing I was a servant of God willing to do whatever it took to obey Him - even if it meant not obeying the leader himself (he backed off of his original assessment I had spiritual pride). The leader was profoundly moved; I was permitted to forgo the devotions with no ramifications. I had placed God's promise to me (speaking about Him) on the altar, and the Holy Spirit had rescued me from the brink of disaster. I realized God had tested me to determine whether I would follow Him or

---

[262] Ephesians 3:12
[263] James 4:6-7
[264] Matthew 13:44

forsake His command in order to follow the promise. Just two weeks later, the Lord gave me a dream[265] of encouragement.

Encouragement in the Jungle

Shortly after I had laid my promise on the altar,[266] the Lord encouraged me through a dream. The dream was noteworthy because it was predicated upon a dream from years earlier before I had begun the journey to know the Lord. Eight years previous, I had a dream where I was in a grocery store, and a tiger was stalking me; I warily made my way to the store's exit, just in time to dash to the back seat of a waiting car. I quickly slammed the door just in time to escape the tiger's ferocious jaws. I had long since forgotten about that dream until I received another dream from the Lord, which included a tiger; this dream was to encourage me to stir up the gift.[267] I was in the jungle outside a bungalow at night, burning brush with a flamethrower, and suddenly, I heard a bone-chilling roar from the forest. I swiftly scanned the tree line just in time to encounter a large tiger in full attack mode: teeth fully visible and charging toward me at full speed. The tiger pounced and was airborne, intending to strike me with full force. I quickly redirected the flamethrower, and, as I let it loose on the tiger, he disappeared. Immediately, the flamethrower became a fire poker, and I quickly canvassed the area, prepared to engage in hand to hand combat, but no other tigers emerged.

2 Timothy 4:17 *Notwithstanding the Lord stood with me, and strengthened me; that by me the preaching might be fully known, and that all the Gentiles might hear: and I was delivered out of the mouth of the lion.*

Interpretation

1. *Jungle*: This world[268]
2. *Bungalow*: God's umbrella of protection[269]
3. *Burning brush*: Taking back ground the enemy had stolen[270]
4. *Night*: The last days[271]
5. *Tiger*: Evil spirit[272]

---

[265] Psalm 16:7
[266] James 2:21
[267] 2 Timothy 1:6
[268] Ephesians 6:12
[269] Psalm 34:7
[270] 1 Samuel 30:8
[271] 2 Timothy 3:1
[272] 1 Peter 5:8

6. **Flame thrower.** Prayer in tongues[273]
7. **Fire.** Holy Spirit[274]
8. **Fire poker.** Sword of the Spirit[275]

The dream was powerful because it contrasted the dream from eight years earlier. Looking back, I believe the interpretation of the first dream is that I was attempting to buy and sell in the spiritual marketplace.[276] The tiger was a demon that chased me off because I had no protection from the Lord; I had no authority to be in the market.[277] This is proof I did not know God, even though outwardly it *looked like I was saved.* I could not claim 1 John 4:4:

> **1 John 4:4** *Ye are of God, little children, and have overcome them: because greater is he that is in you, than he that is in the world.*

Since I did not have the Lord, the demon easily ran me off. The second dream, however, proved I had prevailed by relying on God, *not my own works.* I had joined my spirit with the Lord,[278] and *greater was He that was in me than he that was in the world.*[279]

> **2 Chronicles 13:18** *Thus the children of Israel were brought under at that time, and the children of Judah prevailed, because they relied upon the LORD God of their fathers.*

Strong's definition of **prevailed ('âmats** in Hebrew) means to **be courageous (of good courage),** and Webster's 1828 dictionary defines **courage** as n. [L, *the heart.] Bravery; intrepidity; that quality of mind, which enables men to encounter danger and difficulties with firmness, or without fear or depression of spirits; valor; boldness; resolution.* It is a constituent part of fortitude, but **fortitude** implies patience to bear continued suffering. ***The courage that grows from constitution often forsakes a man when he has occasion for it; courage, which arises from a sense of duty, acts in a uniform manner.*** This means when a man is appointed to a position, courage often fails him; *when a man acts from a sense of duty, courage is enacted from within and carried out with conviction.* This is because of fortitude itself. Fortitude arises from joining our

---

[273] 1 Corinthians 14:4
[274] Luke 3:16
[275] Hebrews 4:12
[276] Revelation 3:18
[277] John 10:1
[278] 1 Corinthians 6:17
[279] 1 John 4:4

spirit with the Lord, which provides strength through faith, and through belief, there is access to the power of grace. That builds confidence and gives us fortitude, which is the strength to bear suffering and encounter danger with composure.

Spiritual Contempt

About two months later, my leader again summoned me to his office as he voiced his displeasure with my position on another issue regarding the church board. That surprised me, but not as much as the next statement. He admonished, "You know there is a well-stated quote, *you can be so spiritual that you are no earthly good.*" I had heard of that statement, but, when I checked God's Word, I found it was untrue:

> **Colossians 3:2** *Set your affection on things above, not on things on the earth.*

I was beginning to understand my spiritual convictions were not valued, but I did not yet have a complete understanding of *why* God had placed me on this church board. At one point, my leader referred to me as a "truth-teller" in a derogatory way. The Lord had enlightened me that through rejection, my leader was actually blessing me.[280] There would be one more incident before the Lord would reveal to me exactly what my role was – because it certainly was not looking like it was as a *spiritual advisor*

The Lord told Zechariah it is by His *Spirit*:

> **Zechariah 4:6** *Then he answered and spake unto me, saying, This is the word of the LORD unto Zerubbabel, saying, Not by might, nor by power, but by my spirit, saith the LORD of hosts.*

The truth is the physical realm is principally subject to the spiritual. God used words to create the physical universe[281] , and miracles throughout the Bible were supernatural results of God, who is a *Spirit.*[282] It is of the utmost importance to be heavenly minded because the mind fixed on the heaven is the one which fulfills the will of God.[283] Spiritual mindedness prompts obedience, where physical actions generate spiritual fruit. The actual physical actions do not generate growth in the spirit; it is the *obedience* of those actions.

---

[280] Luke 6:22
[281] Genesis 1:1
[282] John 4:24
[283] 1 Peter 4:1-2

Many choose what they consider noble actions of the New Testament[284] to fulfill their understanding of God's will in their lives, not comprehending God's chosen plan.[285]

Many pray to know the will of God for their lives, but obedience is what reveals it.

He gives meat to those who fear Him:

Psalm 111:5 *He hath given meat unto them that fear him: he will ever be mindful of his covenant.*

That meat contains the will of God:

John 4:34 *Jesus saith unto them, My meat is to do the will of him that sent me, and to finish his work.*

The Holy Spirit has given each of us unction[286] for a specific purpose He has chosen for us to fulfill. When we discover God's true purpose through seeking Him[287] rather than choosing an action to honor Him, He reveals to us His True Plan for our lives, which, through obedience, brings abundant life because God grants His God-given desires in our lives when we delight in Him.[288] This True Plan is what God originally intended, but it is a mystery[289], and we must discover it by developing an intimate relationship with Him. Upon drawing near to Him,[290] He reveals the magnificent plan He has for each of us, and the unction is given. Merriam Webster defines **unction** as that *which excites piety and devotion*. To understand this gift fully, we must understand the meaning of **piety** (Webster's 1828 dictionary). **"piety in principle** is a compound of veneration or reverence of the Supreme Being and love of his character or veneration accompanied with love; and **piety in practice**, is *the exercise of these affections in obedience to his will and devotion to his service."*

---

284 Matthew 25:35-40
285 Jeremiah 29:11-13
286 1 John 2:20
287 Luke 11:9-10
288 Psalm 37:4
289 Ephesians 1:9
290 James 4:8

This is how to *live* what God has created for each of us individually to achieve. It is by *obedience* when we give our will over to God's will for our lives,[291] that is when we receive the unction (*anointing*) to perform the life He has planned for us, not as a task, but as a treasure and joy with which God is glorified.

Meanwhile, I had heard about the Year of Jubilee in the Bible, that it was a time of setting free, and I was about to experience that concept in multiple ways.

---

[291] Matthew 10:39

CHAPTER 11

The Law of Liberty: The Year of Jubilee

Leviticus 25:10 *And ye shall hallow the fiftieth year, and proclaim liberty throughout all the land unto all the inhabitants thereof: it shall be a jubile unto you; and ye shall return every man unto his possession, and ye shall return every man unto his family.*

Part 1: An Opportunity to Teach

God designates a specific time every 50 years as the Year of Jubilee, the year of liberty.[292] It is a special year calculated by the Hebrew calendar and the exact date of the year it begins can vary slightly depending upon the calculation used. Nonetheless, the calculation for the Year of Jubilee generally begins and ends in September. This is significant because the church scheduled me to teach a class about knowing God on the very first day of the year of Jubilee – a year of liberty, *a year of setting free.* God had told me I was **"rewarded with the revelation of the unveiled truth to set others free..."** so this was God's *perfect timing.* The timing was also note-worthy because the last year of Jubilee was 50 years earlier, the year I was born; I would turn 50 during this year of Jubilee – *which occurs once every 50 years.* I had prepared the class and rehearsed multiple times to include all the necessary information over the 8-week time slot. It took a vast amount of time to prepare, and as the date got closer, I prayed I would not be nervous, but able to confidently present God's Word and demonstrate how *doing God's Word* is what actually brings us to a more intimate relationship with Him. *Then it happened.* One week before the class was to begin, my leader notified me that I was required to include participation in the class. I went home that Sunday, completely crushed. In no way would I be able to include participation and cover everything I had practiced. All the timing was now off; there was no way to make it work. That night, I was talking to the Lord, and I told Him I did not want to do it; I was extremely discouraged. The next morning my reading included Isaiah 10:15:

---

[292] Leviticus 25:8-12

Isaiah 10:15 *Shall the axe boast itself against him that heweth therewith? or shall the saw magnify itself against him that shaketh it? as if the rod should shake itself against them that lift it up, or as if the staff should lift up itself, as if it were no wood.*

Through His Word, the Lord had assured me the most important part of teaching this class was that I obeyed the directives set before me; no matter what I had planned, it was of the utmost importance to obey the authority allowing me to teach. I was the axe in this verse, and who was I to boast myself against the one who was my authority? I fully submitted myself as soon as I finished reading that verse. The Holy Spirit said: **"Do not worry; I will be teaching the class through you."**

Therefore, each Sunday, as I entered the classroom, I gently put on the "spiritual handcuffs" waiting for me on the podium. These "handcuffs," as I saw them, were the restraints that made it exceedingly difficult to convey the information I had prepared. However, because I was careful to abide by the requirements, the class was extremely successful; over the course of eight weeks, the average attendance was 30 to 40 people – a sizeable lot for this church. I realized while I was teaching about obedience, I was doing *it*, and that made all the difference. I would understand the meaning of this verse over a year later:

Ephesians 6:20 *For which I am an ambassador in bonds: that therein I may speak boldly, as I ought to speak.*

The 1828 Webster's Dictionary defines the word **bond** in Greek as "*manacles*"; and defines the word **manacles** as *"to restrain the use of natural powers."* The spiritual manacles restrained my natural powers to teach and allowed the Holy Spirit to teach through me. Obedience was *the primary reason* the class was successful. The success of the class was threatening to other leaders in the church, and it was evident when, just after the class ended, I was approached by a leader in the church who actually *berated* me: "You think you are going to speak in this church again?!" I had experienced more subtle rejection from the leaders for some time leading up to this altercation, so it was not completely surprising. Leadership saw me as more of a threat than a benefit even though the foremost goal of any church is to grow its members spiritually.[293] In my time there, I had witnessed several parishioners impeded from using their gifts; some left the church, and others remained offended. A church with offended members is a church truly devoid of its overall

---

[293] Philippians 3:14

goal.[294] Many church leaders lean toward controlling the church rather than letting the spirit flow because of discord in their past.

One of the churches I attended experienced an attempted takeover by the board ten years prior to my arrival, and the ramifications were still evident. Another church was very fearful of a takeover, and I later discovered they themselves had captured the hearts of a portion of another congregation to start their own church. One morning as I was praying for the leader of that church, the Lord showed me the story of David and Absalom. David had ordered the killing of Uriah the Hittite in order to secure his widow for himself.[295] The Lord told David that because of this, the sword would never leave David's house. The vision the Lord gave me (which I relayed to that leader) was since he had taken a part of another church's congregation to start his own church, the fear of the same event happening to him would never leave him as long as he continued running a church. The church I was now attending also experienced a split some 20 years prior and an attempted takeover just a few years prior to my arrival. I believe the fear of a split or attempted takeover happening again was one of the reasons the leadership disparaged my reputation, the other being a spiritual issue within the church itself, which would soon become evident. Meanwhile, the year of Jubilee was about to become evident in my finances.

Part 2: Financial Freedom

I had mentioned to the Lord "off the cuff," I would like to eliminate my debt. I knew the company I worked for was due to negotiating another contract with the union later that year. I was sure there would be a work stoppage. Years earlier, when I encountered this same situation, I told the Lord I was concerned a work stoppage would affect my relationship with Him, so He changed the work rules, and I remained unaffected. This time, however, my relationship with Him was much more solid, and I had come to believe the Lord would answer my request because I believed His Word:

> **John 15:7** *If ye abide in me, and my words abide in you, ye shall ask what ye will, and it shall be done unto you.*

The deadline came and went with no work stoppage, but the union did not agree to a contract; they decided to keep working and negotiating after the contract deadline. There were very few signs of rumbling within the ranks, and it seemed as though work-life had returned to normal. Then suddenly,

---

[294] 1 Corinthians 10:32
[295] 2 Samuel 12:9-12

out of nowhere, the union walked out of negotiations and called a strike in the following year; it was a surprise to virtually everyone except me. I surmised what had happened; the Lord had waited for the contract to expire and then allowed time for people to prepare for a strike He would set in place during the year of Jubilee. The year of Jubilee is a special time when debt is erased, and there is a "setting free" of God's people. During the work stoppage, my boss originally assigned me to work in my existing job eight hours a day with no overtime pay. However, just before the original contract deadline, he reassigned me to a different group in the city to work 72 hours a week. It was then I knew God was setting up the necessary plans to grant my request. I reported to the new location on the first day of the strike to help cover for workers who had walked off their jobs. I had a unique title that paid me differently than most managers; that title stipulated I must be paid *double time* for any time worked over 51 hours. I had no doubt this was God's doing; He often prepares the groundwork of His miracles far in advance of when they occur. My title had changed two years earlier, and since no managers received regular overtime pay (all were on salary), I never expected there to be a provision in the overtime rules, which compensated my title differently from others. We were in the heart of the city, so there would undoubtedly be a picket line we would have to cross to get into work. I understood the logistics of picket lines as I spent four months in the union picketing during a strike many years before. During this strike, there was widespread concern there would be harsh picketers we would be forced to face twice a day, as we came into work for 12-hour shifts. However, there was nowhere near the number of picketers we had expected – only about 20 or 30. Furthermore, they were not overly aggressive, although verbally abusive. Once inside the building, managers gave us work assignments to cover the responsibilities of those union workers who were outside picketing. It was not long after we had begun; I would hear the Lord's name in vain on a regular basis. The Holy Spirit again impressed upon me the same Bible verse He did earlier concerning speaking boldly against blasphemous conversation:

Proverbs 29:24 *Whoso is partner with a thief hateth his own soul: he heareth cursing, and bewrayeth it not.*

I knew I would have to "speak up" against this evil, and so it began. One man used the Lord's name in vain, and I shot back "That won't help you," to which he replied, "What did I say?" That is how the enemy has designed our sinful nature; blasphemous expressions are prevalent, and we simply repeat what we have heard as children without giving it a second thought.

God's Word states death and life are in the power of the tongue,[296] so from God's perspective, words are **immensely powerful**. Understanding that, I explained to him the importance of blasphemous words; how they are detrimental to his health. He quickly obliged and watched his words, mostly because he was using blasphemous phrases without knowing it. That is the enemy's plan: to demean the name of the One True God as a routine part of normal daily language. Another woman was sitting close by and heard our conversation. I strode back to my cubicle and continued working, and it was not long before I heard them both catching and stopping each other from using blasphemous phrases. However far, they were from truly knowing God; their normal language practice was hindering their progress toward that end. Once they understood the ramifications of blaspheming God, they immediately changed their behavior. Understanding God's Word is extremely important, as He notes a lack of knowledge destroys us:

> **Hosea 4:6** *My people are destroyed for lack of knowledge: because thou hast rejected knowledge, I will also reject thee, that thou shalt be no priest to me: seeing thou hast forgotten the law of thy God, I will also forget thy children.*

Every day, the picketers would yell their insult of choice: "Scabs!" As we entered the building in the morning and as we exited in the evening. About two weeks after enduring these insults, the Lord brought me to the story of Cain in Genesis:

> **Genesis 4:7** *If thou doest well, shalt thou not be accepted? and if thou doest not well, sin lieth at the door. And unto thee shall be his desire, and thou shalt rule over him.*

I decided to look up each word in the Hebrew language to get a deeper understanding of the verse. The word **accepted**, in Hebrew, means **an elevated or leprous scab.** A scab was considered acceptable, high, and exalted because it rises above the skin. Therefore, while the picketers believed they were saying something derogatory, God heard *they were actually blessing us as we entered and exited the building.* I revealed this to other managers working with me, and soon after, they would say as we approached the picket line: "**We are about to be blessed!**" There was no priest blessing us as we went into the building or when we came out; instead, there were angry picketers yelling the word *scab,* but the Lord wanted me to know He was blessing my coming in and going out:

---

[296] Proverbs 18:21

Deuteronomy 28:6 *Blessed shalt thou be when thou comest in, and blessed shalt thou be when thou goest out.*

This underscores the importance of understanding; without it, I would never have known the picketers were blessing rather than verbally abusing us. God says understanding is of the utmost importance:

Proverbs 4:7 Wisdom *is the principal thing; therefore, get wisdom: and with all thy getting get understanding.*

One morning during the second week of the strike, I felt the unmistakable tingling of the beginning of a cold sore and immediately knew this was from lack of sleep due to my arduous schedule. I was still committed to giving the first 10 percent of the day to the Lord – even during the strike. Although this was challenging, I was dedicated to continuing with my routine devotions. This meant during this 72-hour workweek; I was probably sleeping about five hours per night. In the past, I would often get cold sores when I lacked sleep, and at this point, I knew there was no way I could catch up; the results could be disastrous, as this was the first indication my immune system was struggling to keep up with my taxing schedule.

On top of that, I had decided to continue regularly fasting, so my immune system was at a distinct disadvantage. I sat at my desk, considering the ramifications of this seemingly harmless cold sore; with no substantial sleep in sight, I knew I was in trouble. I said to the Lord, "I can't have this. They are going to say, 'he is not sleeping enough or eating enough – that is why he is getting sick.'" I marched to the men's room to determine my next course of action. When I looked in the mirror, it had disappeared; no sign of a cold sore, no tingling, nothing. I would never encounter another cold sore during the entire strike. God had understood my concern. I could not represent Him with power if I were sick while honoring Him. However, His Word said I had to ask,[297] so when I brought my petition to Him, He was more than willing[298] to oblige. I would again ask Him for healing a few days later when the woman sitting next to me became intensely ill, so ill that she was out of work for two days. Shortly after she left, I began sneezing, and our manager asked me if I should be coming to work, assuming I had contracted the same virus. That night I got back to the hotel and was getting worse by the minute; again, I said to the Lord, "I can't have this." The next morning,

---

[297] James 4:2-3
[298] Luke 5:12-13

I awoke and was completely healed[299] – there was no evidence I had even been remotely ill.

One afternoon we were eating lunch in the break room and discussing what time each of us awoke in the morning to begin the grueling 12-hour shift after negotiating an extremely difficult commute for upwards of an hour. A few people noted they got up at the latest possible time, 5:50 a.m., and others at 5:00 a.m. to start the drive at 6:00 a.m. When asked, I told them I routinely awoke at 3:00 a.m. in order to complete my devotions before heading to work. One astounded woman looked at me and exclaimed, "You don't even look tired!" Prioritizing time with God, the Creator had executed His Word in my life:

> **Proverbs 3:24** *When thou liest down, thou shalt not be afraid: yea, thou shalt lie down, and thy sleep shall be sweet.*

The word **sweet** in this verse means "to *barter, to exchange one item for another.*" This, in fact, is what God had done. He exchanged the time I invested in devotions with Him for the benefits of sleep, making my physical body undergo the regeneration obtained by deep rest. We were required to stay in the building during the strike, so breakfast and lunch were provided. One day the vendor brought Chinese food, and someone brought us all fortune cookies. We each received a fortune cookie, and I had no reservations about it. I understand many may find it unconventional that, knowing God, I would accept a fortune cookie. However, I have seen God use many secular people, places, and things to speak into my life, so I rely solely on the Holy Spirit to determine what to avoid and what is acceptable. In this case, there was no check in my spirit when I received the cookie, and when I opened it, I understood why. We went around the table, each of us reading our "fortune," which amounted to a bunch of silly sayings until I read mine: *"Truth is an unpopular subject. It is unquestionably correct."* There were about 150 people in that building and five of us on the sixth floor. The chance of me receiving that message was roughly one-half of one percent. The Lord had used this moment to encourage me in the face of persecution from church leaders; I was told not to speak the truth in board meetings because others were offended.[300]

As the strike wore on, everyone was guessing when it would end, and rumors were rampant. On the fifth week, some of the group were sent to work from

---

[299] Isaiah 53:5
[300] Matthew 24:10

home to save money on hotels, and the rest of us were wondering how long it would be before we would be sent home also. In the sixth week, I had a vacation scheduled. I could take the vacation even in the midst of the strike because it was prepaid (otherwise, vacations were not allowed). I was thinking about cancelling so I could take advantage of the incredible paychecks. I asked the Lord what I should do; and one morning as I was walking toward the picket line, He said:

"Look at that man (referring to a man who was scheduled to return home the following day). He wanted to see the city. However, he worked every day, thinking he had plenty of time; he did not take the opportunity, and now he is gone. If you choose not to write (I was charged with continuing to write this book during the break) **during the vacation in Florida, you will miss what I have to tell you."**

That was all I needed to hear, so I took the scheduled vacation. As I rested by a pool in the sun, I pondered a question I had been poring over for years: If God truly was no respecter of persons,[301] how could each man receive different measures of faith and grace?[302,303] The Lord revealed the proven Biblical truth that the time a man invests with God directly correlates to the measure of grace and faith given to him. ***That truth is written:***

> **2 Corinthians 9:6-7** *But this I say, He which soweth sparingly shall reap also sparingly; and he which soweth bountifully shall reap also bountifully. Every man according as he purposeth in his heart, so let him give; not grudgingly, or of necessity: for God loveth a cheerful giver.*

This verse refers to the giving of *resources*, but most everyone associates it with money. However, the verse has multiple meanings, and money is the *secondary meaning*. The primary meaning is *how I sow my time and will* determine the measure of faith[304] and grace[305] I receive from Him. The spiritual aspects of this verse are the primary meaning, because the next verse reveals, "God is able to make all *grace* abound toward you."[306] Grace is *the divine influence on the heart and its reflection in the life*. This is a direct reference to reaping spiritually for

---

[301] Romans 2:11
[302] Romans 12:3
[303] Ephesians 4:7
[304] Romans 12:3
[305] Ephesians 4:7
[306] 2 Corinthians 9:8

devoting *time and will* in devotions; that are obeying the first commandment.[307] The requirement of *the will, coupled with obedience,* is noted:

Isaiah 1:19 *If ye be willing and obedient, ye shall eat the good of the land:*

Additionally, in 2 Corinthians 2:6, the word **soweth** (**speirō** in Greek) means *to scatter,* and the root word **spaō** means to *draw out.* Looking at Proverbs 20:5, we see a man of understanding draws out deep counsel:

Proverbs 20:5 *Counsel in the heart of man is like deep water; but a man of understanding will draw it out.*

And understanding comes from relentless obedience:

Psalm 111:10 *The fear of the LORD is the beginning of wisdom: a good understanding have all they that do his commandments: his praise endureth for ever.*

The Lord said He would limit portions for those who have forgotten Him:

Jeremiah 13:25 *This is thy lot, the portion of thy measures from me, saith the LORD; because thou hast forgotten me, and trusted in falsehood.*

2 Corinthians 9:6-8 reveals the order of spiritual matters:

1. Sowing time and will bring ***intimacy with God***[308]
2. When He decides we truly know Him, ***He provides the measures of grace and faith*** needed to continue growth - ***His unction***[309] to achieve beyond our natural ability both physically and spiritually - for us to succeed in performing good works *chosen by Him,* which glorify Him.
3. This measure of grace is used (with the measure of faith - we must believe the measure of grace exists and is able to do that which He said it would) to abound in every good work, and has everything needed to succeed in the work He calls us to fulfill. When we ***do the good work we were called to do using the grace He gives***

---

[307] Mark 12:30
[308] Galatians 6:8
[309] 1 John 2:20

us to do it, the measure of grace is increased[310][311] in order for us to progress in His plan, which is *to perfect us.*

This is an important concept to understand because the enemy has convoluted the truth to confuse some by attempting to fulfill this truth without understanding. They do not draw near to know God, but rather believe doing works through their own righteousness[312] *will bring about a relationship with Jesus.* In that case, Jesus has already spoken what he will say to them:

> **Matthew 7:21-23** *Not everyone that saith unto me, Lord, Lord, shall enter into the kingdom of heaven; but he that doeth the will of my Father which is in heaven. Many will say to me in that day, Lord, Lord, have we not prophesied in thy name? and in thy name have cast out devils? and in thy name done many wonderful works? And then will I profess unto them, I never knew you: depart from me, ye that work iniquity.*

The strike was still ongoing, and we all had our predictions of when it would end. None of us chose the correct date, but before I went on vacation, I revealed to everyone the next paycheck would pay off the remainder of my debt. The strike ended while I was in Florida, and the next paycheck I received paid my debt down to *zero.* I had asked the Creator of the Universe to clear my debt, and He obliged during His Year of Jubilee. Could it be God had granted my request? There is no doubt in my mind that He did,[313] and to prove it, He pushed the strike date out from the original deadline to allow striking workers to prepare, and He ended it on *the exact day* my debt reached zero.

Part 3: Cannot Touch the Will
There was roughly a month left to the Year of Jubilee, and the Lord had removed His grace from my wife's employment situation. She had been working for 17 years at the same job as an executive assistant. However, it had gotten unbearable due to several reasons. She had inquired of the Lord as to what to do and told Him she needed to hear from Him directly. The following Sunday, we planned to update her resume after church. There was a guest speaker at the church, and his message was about how he was a pastor in the same church for 17 years. He explained how the Lord had told him it was time to leave, and he had asked his daughter for help with his resume.

---

[310] 2 Peter 3:18
[311] John 1:16
[312] Isaiah 64:6
[313] Matthew 21:22

My wife was stunned; the 17-year timeframe was all she needed to hear; she had gotten direction from the Lord; it was time to leave. When she got to work the next day, she planned to have a discussion with her boss to give a three-month notice to be sure he would have ample time to replace her. I received a call from her a few hours after she got to work; she said her boss had talked her into staying three more *years* until *he retired.* Immediately I felt a panic come into my heart, and I quickly explained to my wife we had heard from the Lord in multiple ways, including that He had answered her request to hear from Him directly. I spent the next few minutes trying to convince her she needed to revisit the conversation with her boss and stick to her plan of retiring. When I hung up the phone, the Lord said: **"That is what it is like, I cannot make the decision for them; I can only try to convince them of what to do."**

Having no control over a situation is the effect of free will. When my wife got off the phone, she said to the Lord, "My boss is going to have to broach the subject; I don't want to ask for another meeting with him." She said a few minutes later, her boss walked in the door and asked, "So are we ok?" She said, "No, we are not," and the conversation took off from there. When she got home, she told me she had given her notice and her boss, while not happy about it, accepted her resignation without reservation. The Lord had released my wife from her work obligations along with other family obligations in order to prepare her for a new direction in life. He had cleared her path to fulfill what I had been praying for her for quite some time: that she would have the time and energy for uninterrupted devotions to daily draw nearer to Him. One day as she was getting ready for work during her three-month notice, she was getting her resume together, and the Lord said to her: **"Where you are going, you don't need a resume."**

The very day she retired; the Holy Spirit told her: **"You are going to have a beautiful life."**

The Holy Spirit gently guides us[314] through the journey God has set in place for us before the foundation of the world.[315] All we need to do is hear Him; then take the necessary action to follow His lead…

---

[314] John 16:13
[315] Ephesians 1:4

128

CHAPTER 12

He Teaches My Hands to War and My Fingers to Fight

Psalm 144:1 *A Psalm of David. Blessed be the LORD my strength, which teacheth my hands to war, and my fingers to fight:*

The Beginning of Suffering

I was still on the church board, and there were concerns that church attendance was decreasing, and it was affecting the church's bottom line while also hindering the building program. By now, I had undergone more than a few conversations with my leader about a myriad of issues, so I knew he was averse to discussing anything to do with my assessment that there was a Jezebel spirit in the church. Knowing what I know now, I would not recommend this course of action, but back then, I thought it was the only avenue to a solution. I had seen the spirit of Jezebel manifest itself multiple times in the church (as did others), so we decided to begin fasting and praying to force it out. My wife and I, along with another couple, fasted once a week and prayed about it regularly. We seemed to be making progress when one day I said to the Lord, "I am doing all I can; I cannot do anything more than fast and pray." Immediately, the Holy Spirit showed me a vision of Jehu when he was on the way to destroy Jezebel. "Who is on my side?"[316] He asked. At that point, I knew I needed more people to fast and pray with me on this matter. The following week, I approached a woman and asked her to join us; she agreed. I felt I should include my leader in this endeavor, but I knew he did not believe there was a Jezebel spirit in the church. That notion was proven the very next Sunday when my leader's wife overheard, we were praying against the Jezebel spirit; she was furious and immediately informed my leader. It was not long before I was in the office to explain who-what-when-where and why. He asked me why I did not ask his permission to do this. "Quite frankly," I said, "I don't think you believe there is a problem." He went on to generalize about spiritual warfare and specifically mentioned he *did not want Jezebel's name mentioned in the church.* That statement was

---

[316] 2 Kings 9:32

remarkable, but not surprising. Although he noted he thought I did it from the best of intentions (which was true), the result of that meeting was the cancellation of the class I was supposed to teach within the next few weeks. He simply told me they would run the same classes on Sunday morning they were running on Thursday nights; Sunday morning was supposed to be my slot. I felt rejected and disheartened, and the following day, the Holy Spirit said: "**You don't need a man.** "[317]

Wow, I thought, *God will fulfill the promise, but it will not be through this church.* The Lord knew I would need encouragement at this time, as I literally saw the path to the fulfillment of His promise destroyed before my very eyes. Before meeting with my leader, I told the Lord if this class did not transpire, I would write this book to completion. Once the class was cancelled, I began doing exactly that; I was now on the Lord's path, not my own. The next morning, I was praying and discouraged over the cancellation of my teaching opportunity, and I said to the Lord, "I really don't even want to pray or fast against this Jezebel spirit." Immediately Jesus said:

"I had the same problem. In my hometown, they did not believe, so there was nothing I could do;[318] you have a leader that doesn't believe; there is nothing you can do."

Jesus gave to man the power to limit His ability based upon faith.[319] This also proved another point: the Lord looks at the heart, not the outside circumstances.[320] The Lord searches the heart and judges the *motive*;[321] the reason for my actions was to extricate the spirit *for* my leader, not to override him. Although I am sure there would be many who would say my actions were wrong, God did not reprimand me. He revealed to me *the reason for the results.*[322] I would soon see. He caused even my *mistakes* to prosper.[323] His Word says He *checks the motives*:

> **Proverbs 16:2** *All the ways of a man are clean in his own eyes, but the LORD weigheth the spirits.*

---

[317] Romans 8:31
[318] Mark 6:4-6
[319] Matthew 9:29
[320] 1 Samuel 16:7
[321] Jeremiah 17:10
[322] Proverbs 16:2
[323] Psalm 1:3

Into the Pit

Years earlier, an acquaintance from a job-related website sent me an email, and at the time, he referenced the life of Joseph in Genesis 39. He said through all the difficult circumstances, the Lord kept Joseph and had favor on him. Then he said, *"the spirit of Joseph is on your life,"* and the Lord's hand was on me, and He was giving me a favor. Back then, I could not really see the life of Joseph relating to mine, but it was now four and a half years later, and the difficult circumstances had just begun. I told my leader all I wanted to do was teach. So once he took away my class, I began to view the church as a jail, a place where I was required to attend (I had learned not to leave until God allowed me), but could not exercise my gift of teaching to help others. I would not leave without the Lord's blessing, but no doubt, it was unpleasant to attend; and it was going to get worse before it got better. Through these difficulties, however, I was about to learn the true reason the Lord brought me to this place.[324]

An Occasion to Fall

After my leader cancelled my class, I did not need availability to teach in September, so my wife and I decided to take a vacation. We booked a hotel to a warm island, unaware there would be a festival there that week. When we arrived, the hotel lobby was so loud we could not hear the desk clerk. It was the "Electric Festival," they said, a very loud, pounding, annoying repeated beat of music called "Techno." Our hotel was "base camp" for this event for four long days. The third day we were approaching the lobby and accompanying the usual deafening music, there was a pool party going on. We were curious as to what was happening, although we knew it could not be good. My wife suggested we check it out, and upon arriving, we could see it looked like Sodom and Gomorrah had come to our hotel pool. We stayed for about 10 minutes, which, in retrospect, was 10 minutes too long. That night, the room next to ours was boisterously playing the same distressing music all night. I attempted to drown it out with the television. Normal volume was at about level seven; I had it up to level 32 to no avail. Eventually, I had to turn it down because I was driving *myself crazy*. I could not sleep for hours, but *my wife was fast asleep next to me*. Exasperated, I exclaimed, "How can she sleep through this?!" The Holy Spirit quickly answered: **"You were responsible for this"**

I knew right away that I had opened a door for the enemy to torment me by attending the debauchery at the pool. I also understood that regardless of who suggested the idea, God held me responsible as the head of the marriage.[325] The following night we walked right past and went to our room. Of course, there was no noise at all from the room next door that evening; however, the crucial test would come in the morning of the next day.

Before I began this journey with the King of the Universe, I had attended church for many years; I read my Bible on a schedule to complete it "through in a year." I was deceived into believing that because of my church attendance and Bible reading, I knew God. The thing about not knowing God is you do not know that you do not know Him until you truly know Him. The life I was living looked upright to man; in fact, I had been a board member in multiple churches. However, because I was deceived, pornography easily ensnared me, a "secret sin" unseen by men, yet the Lord sees all the ways of man.[326] I had come to the end of myself, and at that moment, I looked up to the sky and asked the God I had been supposedly following all my life, "Who are you?" At that moment, everything changed; the One who died to save us all had been waiting my whole life to hear me speak those words. He has been answering that question ever since, *and so began the making of a Godly Warrior.* The addiction to pornography was quickly lost in the pursuit to know and understand the Creator of the Universe; however, Satan, the tempter, knew my past and would soon test me to determine my allegiance to the King. Satan must obtain permission from God in order to tempt us,[327] but God will not allow temptation beyond what we are able to bear; He always provides an escape.[328] The reason the Lord allows temptation is to provide the opportunity to overcome and mature in the spirit; in fact, through temptation is how we are perfected.[329] God's intention is for us to go from glory to glory;[330] the word glory here means honor.

At the hotel, Satan had requested to test me[331] in the area of pornography, and the Lord allowed it to provide me with an opportunity to overcome. Crafty as he is, when Satan got the permission, he did not just attempt to steer me toward pornography. He held nothing back and produced a woman

---

[325] Ephesians 5:23
[326] Proverbs 5:21
[327] Job 1:7-12
[328] 1 Corinthians 10:13
[329] James 1:2-4
[330] 2 Corinthians 3:18
[331] Job 1:6

live and in color. Our hotel owned a private island and provided a boat taxi to the island every 20 minutes. My wife and I decided to rise early and catch the first boat of the day in order to secure chairs on the beach. We arrived early enough to get one of the tiki huts for shade, which was great because the sun became intense very quickly, and shade was a necessity to stay on the beach for any length of time. My wife decided to take a walk along the beach and asked if I wanted to come along. I declined, as I had a slight sunburn from the day before and did not want to make it worse. It was early, and for the most part, the beach was empty; there were upwards of 50 empty chairs to my right, and all the chairs were facing the beach (including mine) with the sun rising on my left. I began working on writing notes in my journal, and after about 20 minutes, I looked across the beach to determine the whereabouts of my wife. It was then I caught a glimpse of the woman in the chair directly next to mine. She had turned the chair towards me, so she was lying in the sun facing me, positioned in a risqué and lewd manner. She had removed her bikini top and placed a straw hat over her face as if to say, *you can lust over me; I will not embarrass you with eye contact.* After I overcame the initial shock, I began gathering our stuff. My wife arrived just then and asked why I was packing up to leave. I quietly uttered, "Take a look," as I motioned to my right; she glanced over and immediately understood it was time to leave. We walked the 50 yards to the boat taxi, which arrived just as we approached the dock, and settled on another beach from the main island. Satan knew I did not even need to touch her to fail this test; he just needed me to lust over her so he could accuse me of adultery to the Lord. Satan knows the scriptures and attempts to use them against us:

Matthew 5:27-28 *Ye have heard that it was said by them of old time, Thou shalt not commit adultery: But I say unto you, That whosoever looketh on a woman to lust after her hath committed adultery with her already in his heart.*

I quickly removed myself from the temptation and sidestepped the snare Satan had beguilingly prepared.[332,333,334,335] The Lord's plan for us is always to overcome and grow spiritually throughout life. Satan often plays into God's overall plan in his overwhelming desire to thwart progress, but the Almighty God is the Master Planner and knows through overcoming temptation, we obtain strength and wisdom to handle the next temptation encountered on the journey to receive His promise. The reason God allows temptation is

---

[332] James 4:7
[333] 2 Timothy 2:22
[334] 1 Corinthians 6:18
[335] Galatians 5:16

because He knows how to deliver the godly;[336] He is aware of the capability to overcome the temptation and the spiritual growth that will result versus the possibility of failing. In this case, Satan saw me as a prime target because, when my leader cancelled my class, I believed I witnessed the destruction of the path to God's promise in my life. He attempted to use my past sin in a time of weakness because I knew the cancellation of the class was likely the end of any future teaching in that church, and it looked like the end of the promise as well. This was my first encounter similar to the story of Joseph, who endured the same test[337] just prior to being thrown in jail.[338]

Set Apart

Returning from vacation, I began to withdraw and disassociate myself with those closest to my leaders. Primarily, I avoided specific leaders intimate with the workings of the church. I was not sure if this was an offense or it was correct behavior, so I inquired of the Lord: was my behavior acceptable, or should I be more cordial? It *seemed* like I had an offense, but I needed to know what to do. The Lord sent the Spirit right through me, confirming all was well.[339] He told me to continue doing what I was doing;[340] He was perfecting my leader through me. Then I read this scripture, and God confirmed it:

> **Proverbs 21:23** *Whoso keepeth his mouth and his tongue keepeth his soul from troubles.*

I was still a little uncomfortable with the silence, so I inquired of the Lord again just to be sure all was well. That night, I was on my way to a prayer meeting at the church, and as I turned the corner, the church sign bellowed with bold letters: **"A wise man once said: Nothing."**[341] This newfound silence was pure obedience for me until I read 2 Timothy:

> **2 Timothy 1:1** *Paul, an apostle of Jesus Christ by the will of God, according to the promise of life which is in Christ Jesus.*

This verse does not seem to apply until the Greek meaning of the word ***apostle*** is defined: *set apart, it usually denotes separation, departure, cessation, abstain from*

---

[336] 2 Peter 2:9
[337] Genesis 39:12
[338] Genesis 39:20
[339] Psalm 39:2
[340] Psalm 39:9
[341] Proverbs 17:27

associating with; withdraw self. God does not say anything not already in His Word; once I found this conduct was in His Word, following through was effortless. However, life at home was heating up, and I was about to gain a true understanding of loving my neighbor.

An Offense, the Dream, and Prison

Luke 17:1 *Then said he unto the disciples, It is impossible but that offences will come: but woe unto him, through whom they come!*

After ten years, several minor annoyances with my next-door neighbor had developed into a full-blown offense, so I inquired of the Lord as to what to do about it. Just a few days later, I had a dream; I was a passenger in a pickup truck; I did not recognize who was driving, but as we were traveling, I saw my neighbor suddenly appear from underneath the tarp in the back of the truck. I was livid. We stopped at a bridge, and I threw my neighbor over the bridge into the water. He got out of the water and stood next to me, but I threw him back over the bridge, and he returned. This happened about ten times, and then I woke up. I know the Lord visits us in the night seasons,[342] so I knew He was speaking to me about this situation. I asked the Lord to help me know how to clear this offense, not to just "fake it until you make it," but to understand how to release an offense. *Just two days later,* I received a text from my neighbor asking what it was he did wrong, and how he remembers our relationship used to be. He apologized if he offended me in any way and asked to bury the hatchet. Many would say this was quite a coincidence, but I knew *God was at work* because I was asking for His help to obey His commands. In this case, I was asking for help on exactly how to do the second commandment – love my neighbor as myself.[343] I replied to the text and, of course, apologized and told him I had been praying about this relationship, and no doubt, this was the Lord's doing. I expected this would be a gradual restoration of the relationship. The next day I was outside raking leaves, and I saw him walking toward me in his driveway. It was just then these words came out of my mouth: **"That man is the key to your future."**

The words had audibly come out of *my own mouth.* This is how the Holy Spirit can override the flesh and deliver a message through fasting and praying in tongues. One of the attributes of fasting is we give the spirit control over the flesh; while praying in tongues is communication with God, but the message

---

[342] Psalm 16:7
[343] Matthew 22:39

given is not in our native language and therefore not understood.[344] If we give the spiritual authority to override the flesh through fasting,[345] then a message from praying in tongues can be delivered directly in our native language *using the mouth* at the appropriate time. This is a primary attribute of the Godly Warrior: engaging in fasting and praying in tongues to overcome the flesh with the will of the spirit.

> *Praying in tongues receives a message to the spirit, yet the mind does not understand. Fasting gives the spirit control over the flesh. The spirit has received a message and has dominion; it overcomes the flesh at an opportune moment and speaks the message in the native tongue.*

Hearing those words, audibly was powerful, so I was sure to engage my neighbor in conversation. I waved and said a few words over the bushes, separating our property and began raking again. When I looked up, I was surprised to see him standing right in front of me. He shook my hand and hugged me. I realized this would not be a gradual return to our old relationship. I was not ready for "full restoration," but that is the very definition of forgiveness:

Mark 11:25 *And when ye stand praying, forgive, if ye have ought against any: that your Father also which is in heaven may forgive you your trespasses.*

Forgive in this verse means to remit, which is defined as to restore. **Restore** means to return to a person, as a specific thing, which he has lost, or which has been taken from *him and unjustly detained*. This man was not going to go away; the Lord had deliberately placed him in my life to sharpen me.[346] I was beginning to understand the meaning of the second commandment:

Matthew 22:39 *And the second is like unto it, Thou shalt love thy neighbour as thyself.*

I had to ask myself, do I ever feel love for myself? The answer was no; *I just took actions to care for myself.* The word **love** in that verse (**agapeo** in Greek) means *embracing especially the judgment and the deliberate assent of the will as a matter of principle, duty, and propriety: a decision of the head).* That was a major revelation; the Lord was saying I did not have to *feel* love for my neighbor; rather I had

---

[344] 1 Corinthians 14:2
[345] Psalm 35:13
[346] Proverbs 27:17

to make a decision (of the head) *to take actions to love my neighbor.* I made that decision through the deliberate assent of my will and sense of duty to the Lord. This meant I was to love my neighbor as a matter of duty, and it was acceptable to not *feel* that I loved him; *taking the actions to love him* was acceptable to God. The following Sunday, I arrived at the church early to pray before the service.

As I went to the prayer room, a friend of mine was the only one present; my friend and I prayed for a few minutes when I asked him how things were going. He said there was not enough time to tell everything, but he was going through some tough times. I told him I had a dream and shared the story about my neighbor; and how God strategically placed him there to sharpen me. My friend was astounded as he told me he had a dream about a person in his life with which he was extremely annoyed. He woke up furious. The fact that this person was present in his dream is what made him "flip out," as he described it. I told him it means God would not remove that man from his life. God put him there to refine my friend, just as He placed my neighbor in my life to refine me. As soon as we finished our conversation, we walked to the church sanctuary for the start of service, and he repeated that he was "blown away" by our conversation. After praise and worship, just as the service was starting, the Holy Spirit imparted to me: **"You just interpreted a dream from within the prison."**

This experience was extraordinarily similar to the story recorded in Genesis of Joseph when he interpreted two dreams from within the jail.[347] Remarkably, even in all the things that had happened to Joseph (thrown into the pit, sold in slavery, and falsely accused of adultery), he was still able to use the gift God gave him to help others even though his own life seemed to be on a downward spiral.

> *If you can inspire others with the wonder of His glory when you can't see it in action in your own life, then you are getting close to the fulfillment of the promise because that's exactly what Joseph did.*

I now had a very small inkling of what that felt like, and it was this: Once I had personally experienced the awesomeness of God's power, there was no thought of turning away from it. *No matter what was happening*, I focused my eyes on the eternal.[348] This was my second encounter similar to the story of

---

[347] Genesis 40:12
[348] 2 Corinthians 4:18

Joseph, who interpreted a dream from within the jail to help another even though he himself was under duress. The following week, my friend shared how he had given a gift to the man with whom he had an offense, effectively restoring his relationship with him.[349]

A few weeks later, one of the leaders of the church spoke from behind the pulpit that she had a vision of *someone sitting in a jail cell with the door open.* I immediately knew the Lord was telling me He saw my plight, and although it was unpleasant, it would not last; soon, God would set me free.[350] I was willingly attending a church that, for me, was a spiritual jail cell. My leader would not allow me to use the gift God gave me to teach others about Him, yet I stayed in the situation *out of obedience to the Lord.* In the flesh, there is no doubt I did not want to go back to that church; however, I continued because the Lord had not released me to go elsewhere. This was perseverance in action as well as the fear of the Lord, which brings wisdom, knowledge, and understanding. [351, 352] I would soon realize understanding is enormously powerful. Spiritual understanding of a situation accomplishes courage to persevere, no matter the consequences, no matter the suffering. That is why the Lord's Word says *with all your getting get understanding.*[353]

> *Understanding and doing God's Word is of the greatest importance; hearing it only has the greatest consequences.*

The Lord had provided more encouragement throughout the next few months. A guest speaker came to the church and said, "*God did not put this inside you to tease you. He is going to fulfill it.*" That struck a chord in me, and the Lord used it to propel me forward through the difficulties I had been experiencing. Then the Lord provided an exclamation point to that statement late December in a devotional. The devotional read "**I have spoken it; I will also bring it to pass**" and went on to provide stories from the Bible where the Lord honored His Word. *The daily devotional was on my birthday:*

> **Isaiah 46:11** *Calling a ravenous bird from the east, the man that executeth my counsel from a far country: yea, I have spoken it, I will also bring it to pass; I have purposed it, I will also do it.*

---

[349] 1 Corinthians 13:8
[350] Isaiah 10:27
[351] Psalm 111:10
[352] Proverbs 9:10
[353] Proverbs 4:7

Turning the Key

Although the Lord had told me my neighbor was the key to my future, I was not completely sure about what to do concerning him. The relationship was still somewhat strained, but better than it had been in the recent past. *Then it happened.* My neighbor took an action that would force a change one way or the other, and my response would determine the direction.

I heard some noise and looked across my driveway to determine the source. There it was: a large crane and workers with chain saws cutting branches off one of my trees close to the border of my neighbor's property. Furious, I wasted no time in halting the decimation of my tree. As I arrived, I could see no sign of my neighbor, so I yelled at the workers to cease their activity. The workers complied just as my neighbor appeared from his garage. What ensued was a "heated discussion" at best. I knew *legally* he could cut those branches leaning over his property, but I was flabbergasted he would proceed without prior notification. In fact, he did utter the word "legal" at one point, which absolutely infuriated me. With no remedy in sight, I went back to my house and watched as the workers systematically dismantled my tree. I could see no solution to the relationship with my neighbor after that incident, although I knew he wanted us to be okay with one another. *Easy for him to say*, I thought, *he did not suffer the loss.* I knew this would either break the relationship permanently or be a catalyst for change; according to the second commandment, I had to make sure to preserve the relationship, no matter what had happened.

> *Loving your neighbor is a command accomplished through actions, not feelings. It is a conscious choice of the will, a matter of principle and duty - a decision of the head. There need be no feeling of love; it is an act of obedience with no expectation of reciprocity.*

This is not going to be easy, I thought, but the Lord imparted an answer providing I was willing to go through with it. I was aware it was not the incident itself that had me contemplating walking away from this relationship, but rather, the numerous annoyances over a lengthy period. The solution the Lord had given me incorporated another command He had given:

Matthew 28:19-20 *Go ye therefore, and teach all nations, baptizing them in the name of the Father, and of the Son, and of the Holy Ghost: Teaching them to observe all things whatsoever I have commanded you: and, lo, I am with you alway, even unto the end of the world. Amen.*

My neighbor texted me, hoping this would not come between us. I immediately replied and told him we needed to talk, as this incident was not the issue, but a symptom of a larger problem. We got together, and I told him of the other numerous annoyances, and we agreed to work together to solve them. I knew in order to preserve the relationship, we would need to spend time together, and I used that time to teach him more about observing God's principles, which drew him closer to the Lord. We met once a month for lunch, which caused our relationship to become closer. I prayed for him daily, and eventually, I was able to love him as I loved myself.

Just a week later, the Lord revealed the importance of the *key*. He had likened my spiritual journey to one of planting seeds, rain, and growing crops, and when I found the meaning of the word key, I understood why it was so important to my future:

> **Isaiah 22:22** *And the key of the house of David will I lay upon his shoulder; so he shall open, and none shall shut; and he shall shut, and none shall open.*

This verse reveals Jesus has a key that will spiritually open and shut doors no man can change. Therefore, when the Spirit told me "that man is the key to your future," He was saying He would open or shut the doors to the promise based upon my obedience to His word concerning my neighbor. I looked up the Hebrew meaning of the word key in that verse; Strong's definition of *key* (*maphtêach* in Hebrew) means an **opener**. The root word for *key* is *pâthach,* and it means **to plough**. Thus, the phrase really means, **"that man is the plough needed to fulfill your dream."** I was planting seeds, and the Lord would provide the rain, but I still needed to till the soil:

> **Hosea 10:12** *Sow to yourselves in righteousness, reap in mercy; break up your fallow ground: for it is time to seek the LORD, till he come and rain righteousness upon you.*

In this verse, the words *fallow ground* (*niyr* in Hebrew) mean *ploughing*. The Lord had protected me by imparting His command at the precise time I needed it. I was obliged to love my neighbor, and by imparting that we are to teach others to observe His ordinances, the Lord showed me *how* to love my neighbor, *regardless of his behavior towards me.*

CHAPTER 13

Rejected by Man, Approved by God

2 Timothy 2:15 *Study to shew thyself approved unto God, a workman that needeth not to be ashamed, rightly dividing the word of truth.*

A Bishop

Our church had a service where parishioners were to give testimonies rather than having our Pastor preach a traditional sermon. As I was sitting in the congregation listening to these testimonies, I could not help myself; I let out a quiet laugh to the Lord and said, "Are you kidding me? This is unbelievable. You gave me this gift of communication, and the leaders *know* the extraordinary things you have done in my life, yet here I sit, watching others do what you ordained me to do." The Lord did not reply. To me, this was being dragged out of my jail cell and publicly flogged, very discouraging, to say the least, but I knew this was part of growing spiritually through perseverance. With more pain comes more spiritual growth if we handle it from God's perspective, but it still hurt while it was happening. That is why the Bible says, "With all of your getting, get understanding"[354] because, with understanding, it is much easier to persevere. I asked the Lord if He could repair my relationship with the church leaders; it never seemed quite right. After all, even when the relationship was at its best, it was still a strain, and I could not figure out why. There was just nothing more painful than watching others do what God promised I would do. I knew I could inspire others, but my leader simply would not allow me to do it in this church. The next morning in my devotions, I read:

1 Peter 2:12 *Having your conversation honest among the Gentiles: that, whereas they speak against you as evildoers, they may by your good works, which they shall behold, glorify God in the day of visitation.*

As usual, I looked up the words to determine their meaning in Greek, and I came across the meaning of **visitation** as *superintendence, specifically the Christian*

---

[354] Proverbs 4:7

141

episcopate: - the office of a bishop. To understand the meaning further, I referenced the word **Bishop** in Webster's 1828 Dictionary:

BISHOP, *noun*

1. An overseer; a spiritual superintendent, ruler, or director; applied to Christ. Ye were as sheep going astray but are now returned to the shepherd and *bishop* of your souls. 1. Pet.2.

2. In the primitive church, a spiritual overseer; an elder or presbyter; one who had the pastoral care of a church.

The same persons are in this chapter called elders or presbyters, and overseers or bishops. ***Scott, Comm.*** Acts 20:1.

There it was, *my name* amid the definition of a Bishop: *a spiritual overseer, elders or presbyters, and overseers or bishops.* ***Scott, Comm. Acts 20:1.*** The Lord had directed me to this passage to show me this is how He sees me, and not to be concerned about man's thoughts. This reference of "*Scott*" refers to Rev. Thomas Scott (1747-1821), an Anglican Bible Commentator. Not only does this entry have my first name, but also the word commentary is abbreviated as "Comm." The Lord had given me the gift of communication. The Bible verse referenced in Webster's definition was Acts 20:1, and it read:

> **Acts 20:1** *And after the uproar was ceased, Paul called unto him the disciples, and embraced them, and departed for to go into Macedonia.*

Strong's defines the word **departed (exerchomai** *in Greek)* as *to depart (out of), escape, get out.* This meant it would not be long before I would be set free to begin living God's Promise: to speak about Him. I asked my brother, who is a mathematician, to calculate the probability of this occurrence. The King James Bible has 783,137 words, and the Webster's 1828 Dictionary contains 70,000 words. I had read the Bible through in two years and five months (882 days). The probability I would read one particular word in the Kings James Bible (1 in 783,137) that is also the exact word found in the Webster's 1828 dictionary with the name "Scott" in the definition (1 in 70,000) on that one particular day of reading through the Bible (1 in 882) is 1 in 12,097,141,712,031 *(one in 12 trillion).* No coincidence, to be sure - that is the extraordinary precision of a very personal relationship with the King. I have a plaque on the wall in my office that perfectly depicts an intimate relationship with the King of kings:

That Incredible Christian
From the Radical Cross by A.W. Tozer: "That Incredible Christian"

> *At the heart of the Christian system lies the cross of Christ with its divine paradox. The power of Christianity appears in its antipathy toward, never in agreement with,*

142

the ways of fallen men. The truth of the cross is revealed in its contradictions.

The Christian soon learns that if he would be victorious as a son of heaven among men on earth, he must not follow the common pattern of mankind, but rather the contrary. That he may be safe, he puts his life in jeopardy; he loses his life to save it and is in danger of losing it if he attempts to preserve it. He goes down to get up. If he refuses to go down, he is already down, but when he starts down, he is on his way up.

He is strongest when he is weakest and weakest when he is strong. Though poor, he has the power to make others rich, but when he becomes rich, his ability to enrich others vanishes. He has most after he has given most away and has the least when he possesses most.

He may be and often is highest when he feels lowest and most sinless when he is most conscious of sin. He is wisest when he knows that he knows not and knows least when he has acquired the greatest amount of knowledge. He sometimes does most by doing nothing and goes furthest when standing still.

He loves supremely One whom he has never seen, and though himself poor and lowly he talks familiarly with One who is King of all kings and Lord of all lords, and is aware of no incongruity in so doing.[355]

It was at this time the Lord revealed why He had brought me to this church. Upon my first arrival, the leaders asked me if I was an evangelist. According to the definition above, I was ordained to do the very work for which my leaders were responsible: to be a spiritual overseer, an elder or presbyter, to have the pastoral care of a church. Knowing that revelation, coupled with the fact that these leaders had seen their church split and survive an attempted takeover, I understood their wariness; my relationship with them was strained at best. I would come to understand it was not the Lord's intention for me to become part of this church's culture, but rather to *endure suffering because of it.[356]* Since I began this journey, I had acquired the Lord's perspective through years of obedience, studying, and testing from experiences the Lord had brought me through; it was with great excitement I began attending this church. The first year seemed promising as I spent numerous hours attending Bible studies, teachings, etc. to assimilate and become acquainted with the people of the church. The second year also looked promising as my leader allowed me to facilitate a few Bible studies, running DVD's of preachers and discussing them afterward. However, when I was elected a board member, the trouble began; I was reprimanded many times for speaking the truth, which was frustrating because I was able to understand situations from God's perspective but was belittled for thinking too spiritually.

---

[355] Tozer, A. W, The Radical Cross
[356] Philippians 1:29

At one point, I disagreed with the leaders concerning their dealings with a business, and I voiced my concerns to them. Another board member agreed but chose to remain quiet. My leader characterized me as a "truth-teller" in a derogatory way, and he subsequently considered me a troublemaker. From then on, I generally kept my opinions to myself and voted along with the majority to maintain unity.[357] I was ashamed to go to church after my leader canceled my class because I had told others I would be teaching that September; but the Lord encouraged me with His Word:

> **1 Peter 4:16** *Yet if any man suffer as a Christian, let him not be ashamed; but let him glorify God on this behalf.*

> **2 Timothy 1:12** *For the which cause I also suffer these things: nevertheless, I am not ashamed: for I know whom I have believed, and am persuaded that he is able to keep that which I have committed unto him against that day.*

I knew the problem I was experiencing with my leader was because we did not see situations in the same manner. He did not discern the spiritual ramifications I perceived, but now I knew this was by the Lord's design. I understood the spiritual solution to the existing problems, but my leader labeled me a troublemaker for attempting to reveal those solutions to the decision-makers. Jesus reminded me when He was on earth, He was healing people – *which had never been done before in the history of time* – and *was rebuked, and they sought to kill Him because He healed on the Sabbath.*[358] Jesus did these things by instructions from the Father[359] that He might learn obedience through suffering.[360] Jesus' suffering was not just about physical pain from the Roman military; it was much more. It was also rejection,[361] rebuke,[362] hatred,[363] emotional and verbal abuse,[364] and mockery.[365] Not to mention taking on the sins of the world.[366] Jesus endured all the suffering that we will ever experience in our lives -- in three years

---

[357] Ephesians 4:3
[358] John 5:16
[359] John 8:28
[360] Hebrews 5:8
[361] Luke 9:22
[362] Mark 8:32
[363] John 7:7
[364] 1 Peter 2:23
[365] Mark 10:34
[366] 1 John 2:2

of ministry. He had the spiritual solution to their problems, but they did not believe Him[367] , and if we suffer likewise, we are to *rejoice*:

1 Peter 4:13 *But rejoice, inasmuch as ye are partakers of Christ's sufferings; that, when his glory shall be revealed, ye may be glad also with exceeding joy.*

Coming Up Short

Our church had been experiencing some financial difficulties, and we were meeting to discuss the cause and effect of the situation at hand. There were a few easily recognizable issues as to why the finances were coming up short. Church leadership gave multiple reasons as to what had happened, and undeniable circumstances explained each issue. We watched attendance slip; some people moved away while others had stopped giving altogether. This was taking its toll on the bottom line, and the church overseers were coming to attend our meeting to help determine how and why this happened, and conceivably resolve how to reverse the financial slide that had been occurring over the past few months. Although it was explainable by circumstances, the root of the problem was not easily discerned. It would be through understanding true forgiveness by overcoming an offense that the Lord would reveal to me the key to resolving this predicament.

Overcoming Another Offense

I had encountered an offense with my unsaved stepdaughter, and words cannot describe the disrespect and dishonor she displayed to my wife and me in our home. I was disappointed and perturbed, to say the least, and it took many days before it was no longer at the forefront of my mind. I took it personally, although she had admitted she had problems with authority in the past. One day after I had calmed down, I was praying about this offense and told the Lord I wanted to know how to overcome an offense like this; I really wanted to know. I did not want to just let time pass and hope the anger subsided. I wanted to know true forgiveness; how to *forgive without conditions attached.* I had been wrestling with the situation for a few months, although the Lord had allowed my relationship with Him to remain close during that time. Usually, when something like this was not resolved soon after it happened, He would step back slightly, and I would feel a separation between us. This time, however, all seemed well, but the unforgiveness toward my stepdaughter was still there. I asked Him about it from time to time and told Him I wanted this situation cleared up, but I had a few problems. First, I thought she needed to understand what she did was hurtful and disrespectful, and she needed to apologize. Second, she needed to know we would not

---

[367] John 6:36

tolerate this behavior in the future, and there would be dire consequences for any reoccurrence. I was so upset one day as I was talking with the Lord; I reminded Him of His Word that things could not go well with her because she dishonored her parents.[368] I thought I would remind Him, as I was sure He had forgotten because I did not see any ramifications in her life due to her actions.

A few months after the initial offense, a guest speaker arrived at our church, and his message was on forgiveness. I had forgotten I asked the Lord months before to know how to forgive the way He had intended. While I was aware, I had this unforgiveness problem, I expected I already knew the content of the speaker's message. The message was as I had anticipated, but then he named the very issues I was having. He said, "We need to forgive as the Lord forgave us.[369] Jesus didn't say 'well I didn't think you would do *that*' or, 'What if they do *that same thing* again?'" In my thoughts, I was dealing with those very two issues. Did it mean I just had to act as if it never happened? What about the risk of her doing it again? Surely, she had to understand this behavior was unacceptable and would not be allowed at *any* time in the future. Yet, here I heard the speaker describing God's forgiveness. He forgave *no matter what we did*, and He said we are to forgive *seventy times seven* even for the same offense.[370] Even then, that forgiveness would never approach the forgiveness He gave us, as we have all sinned.[371] The sermon went on to describe that Jesus took the risk on us; He knew it was possible we would commit the same sin He previously forgave, but He forgave us anyway. I have heard many speak (and have said it myself in the past) of forgiveness: "I will forgive that person, but I will never trust them." Hearing this sermon, I now understood we do not need to trust the person, but rather *the Creator*. When we forgive, we forgive the person with no conditions, as if the infraction never happened. We reinstate the person to exactly where they were in the relationship before the offense, and we trust God to handle future events. Thus, forgiveness and trust are intricately linked.

Many forgive but withhold trust; this is because trust is ascribed to the offender. True success in forgiveness is accomplished by forgiving the offender and trusting God. This way, we forgive like Jesus, forgiving the next infraction before it is even committed.

---

[368] Ephesians 6:2-3
[369] Matthew 6:12
[370] Matthew 18:22
[371] Romans 3:23

We must also recognize God determines what is best for us; if He determines that to grow spiritually, we need to forgive the exact same offense again, then He will allow it. To understand He is omnipresent,[372] omnipotent,[373] and omniscient[374] is of utmost importance because knowing that we are able to trust Him with all circumstances, He is a loving Father and will not allow circumstances that will hurt us, but only those who grow us spiritually. After the sermon, I went to the altar to talk to the Lord about the incident; I was still concerned about the likelihood of it happening again. A friend came to pray with me, but it turned out to be a venting session for me. I was still angry that I had to allow this unruly child to come into my house and disrespect her mother and me. As I left the church, I decided I was going to forgive and reinstate her to her position in my life with no conditions, even though I did not know how. This is the type of love in the Bible known as *agape* love, which is a *decision of the head* (a matter of principle; a deliberate assent of the will) and not the heart, whereas *phileo* love is the *love of the heart* which can be felt toward another. *Phileo* love is usually the type of love reciprocated to someone, while agape love is God's love, which enables us to love the unlovable. The next day, my stepdaughter arrived at our house, and unlike the past few months, I left my office and found my way to the kitchen where I heard her talking with her mother. I quickly engaged in the conversation, and we were soon talking as if the past had never happened. Within minutes, I had completely let go of the offense and trusted that even if she were to have a sudden outburst, I would simply take it in stride. While she was speaking, the Lord showed me her future and the difficulties and hardships that would ensue because of her lack of respect for authority. As I could see the trouble ahead for her, I felt compassion; God had taken agape love (the decision of the head) and moved it to the heart (*phileo* love) because I had obeyed His Word. I had taken action to obey Him, so He did the work I could never do myself because I had never understood *it was spiritual*. That is how true forgiveness is completed; when I took the step toward reconciliation in faith *and trusted the outcome to God*, He was faithful to restore the relationship in full. The offense was released, and no longer had a hold on me. As soon as I had forgiven my stepdaughter, the Lord immediately revealed to be the reason for the financial troubles at the church; *it was unforgiveness*. It was one week until the financial meeting at the church, and He wanted me to convey *at that meeting* the reason for the church's financial problems was due to unforgiveness.

---

[372] Hebrews 4:13
[373] Revelation 19:6
[374] 1 John 3:20

With All of Your Getting Get Understanding[375]

The morning before the overseers came to our church to discuss our financial shortcomings; the Lord had reminded me I must disclose that unforgiveness was the reason for the church's financial difficulties. The next evening when the meeting began, I was nervous but determined to obey His command. As the meeting progressed, I felt my heart begin to pound faster. When one of the overseers alluded to a more open atmosphere for board members to share their thoughts, my entire chest and esophagus began to throb uncontrollably.[376,377] It was so overwhelming, I wondered if others in the room noticed; I actually told the Holy Spirit, "I need to wait until the leader stops speaking." The Holy Spirit had caused all my internal systems to go haywire to be sure I succumbed to His bidding. As soon as the opportunity arose, I disclosed the Lord had revealed to me the problem with the church finances. My leader gave me permission to share the revelation, so I explained the experience I had with my stepdaughter. As I began to convey the details of my lesson in forgiveness, the Holy Spirit overwhelmed me with His presence, which caused me to weep as I spoke. Ironically, the speaker who preached the for-giveness message *was one of the overseers at the meeting.* I explained what I had learned; we must forgive *no matter the circumstance with no strings attached.* Eve-ryone agreed with the story until I revealed, "So forgiveness and trust are closely related. *We trust not the person, but God when we forgive.* If God decided my character must be built by allowing the exact same infraction I had already forgiven to happen again, then so be it." This means that, in effect, I was already determined to forgive the infraction *even before it happened again.* That generated blank stares in the room, and I knew they did not understand the concept – even the speaker who spoke on forgiveness was dumbfounded. My leader allowed me to continue; I explained the unforgiveness issues that needed to be resolved in order to alleviate the church's financial deficiencies. Each of the three leaders who needed to forgive gave excuses and reasoning as to why they refused to forgive (as Jesus forgave) in each of their specific scenarios. I did not refute their excuses; I had just delivered a message, and it was not my responsibility to quarrel over the validity of God's Word. The discussion moved to another subject, and a few minutes passed. I was en-grossed in reading notes concerning other issues while simultaneously listen-ing to the meeting. As one man described an issue with the finances, the head overseer joked, "You need to *forgive!*" The room burst out with laughter – *and the joke was on me.*[378] I did not even look up as I realized the reason Jesus

---

[375] Proverbs 4:7
[376] Job 32:18
[377] Psalm 39:3
[378] Job 12:4

came to earth was to forgive sins, and in this room, **His act of love was reduced to a punchline**. At that instant, and just for an instant, the Lord took me back to the day He was crucified. I could not see, but I could hear the mocking laughter. He said: "**This is what it sounded like**"[379]

I was able to **feel His pain.** Once again, the feelings of being misunderstood and loneliness came flooding back. There was no escape; all I could do was endure the angst until it subsided.[380] *This is how He felt*, I thought, *understanding the gravity of the situation, yet rejected, ridiculed, and alone.* Instantly I was back in the room and realized they did not know what they were doing; they had no *understanding.* That was proven by the fact that the man who preached the message about forgiveness that changed my perspective did not comprehend the revelation of the Holy Spirit concerning *how to forgive. How can one man preach a message that changes another man's life, but he himself is not changed?* It is because the Word of God is powerful;[381] it does not matter who speaks His Word. It can change people. The speaker himself was not changed because he did not have an understanding. Understanding comes from the Lord; He reveals it to those who exhibit the fear of the Lord:

> **Proverbs 4:7** *Wisdom is the principal thing; therefore, get wisdom: and with all thy getting get understanding.*

> **Proverbs 9:10** *The fear of the LORD is the beginning of wisdom: and the knowledge of the holy is understanding.*

> **Proverbs 2:6** *For the LORD giveth wisdom: out of his mouth cometh knowledge and understanding.*

Obedience is the key to all wisdom, knowledge, and understanding. I had come to understand the truth from God's perspective; knowing *about God* is not valued. Jesus spoke this to the Pharisees in John chapter five; He said life is not found in the scriptures. *It is found in Him.*

> **John 5:39-40** *Search the scriptures; for in them ye think ye have eternal life: and they are they which testify of me. And ye will not come to me, that ye might have life.*

Paul warns Timothy of those who seems to be saved through knowledge, but do not have the power that comes from Jesus living in them:

---

[379] Luke 18:32
[380] Psalm 119:134
[381] Hebrews 4:12

149

2 Timothy 3:5 *Having a form of godliness, but denying the power thereof: from such turn away.*

2 Timothy 3:7 *Ever learning, and never able to come to the knowledge of the truth.*

In the corporate world, there is an adage often quoted by those who are passed over for promotions: "It is not what you know; it is who you know." That adage is very close to the instructions given for operating in the spiritual world: *It is not what you know or how long you have known it; it is whom you know and what you do with what He tells you. The key to the kingdom of God is obedience!*

> **In the kingdom of God, it is not what you know; it is who you know and what you do because of it. When the "who you know" is God, obedience will create action,[382] fulfilling the first commandment. When the "who you know" is your neighbor, the actions which fulfill the second commandment prove discipleship.[383] Both are required.**

A Whisper of Encouragement

During the financial meeting, a fellow board member gave me the name of a book on forgiveness; I bought it to understand his perspective on what I had shared with the board. I began to read, and my heart sank. The book did not describe forgiveness the way the Lord had told me. I was beginning to feel disappointed because I thought there was at least one person who may have agreed with what I had spoken at God's behest. The next morning, I awoke to a whisper: **"Scott, horse."**

I thought my wife spoke the words, but she was still asleep. I had no idea what it meant, but the first verse in my reading was Exodus 15:1:

Exodus 15:1 *Then sang Moses and the children of Israel this song unto the LORD, and spake, saying, I will sing unto the LORD, for he hath triumphed gloriously: the horse and his rider hath he thrown into the sea.*

I immediately looked up a *horse* in Hebrew, and it means *to skip (properly for joy);* in the Ancient Hebrew Lexicon of the Bible, it means *Rejoice: As a dancing around in circles.* God told me He danced in circles_just as he described in Zephaniah 3:17 because I obeyed his Word. He told me by using just two words, **"Scott, horse."** Seven years earlier, He showed me the second word,

[382] John 14:15
[383] John 13:35

joy (***gheel*** in Hebrew) in Zephaniah 3:17, means *to spin around (under the influence of violent emotion)*

Zephaniah 3:17 *The LORD thy God in the midst of thee is mighty; he will save, he will rejoice over thee with joy; he will rest in his love, he will joy over thee with singing.*

God connected the meaning of a word (***joy***) from seven years earlier to a completely different word (***horse***) with the same meaning to convey to me. He was well pleased with my obedience in the meeting the night before. That is all I needed, a confirmation that even though I was all alone in my understanding, the Living God was on my side.[384]

Severed

I knew the next board meeting would inevitably contain the notes for the previous meeting, and I was interested in how the meeting minutes would read concerning forgiveness and the finances. As I perused the paperwork in front of me, I realized there were no meeting minutes from the previous month. Customarily, as in any board meeting, minutes must be read and accepted by a vote of the board. I patiently waited, and eventually, my leader spoke the words: last month's meeting was "off the record." *It was fitting,* I surmised, *I would receive understanding, one of the most important attributes of the kingdom of God on a night that man refused to acknowledge, effectively marking my spiritual journey with a milestone on "The Night That Never Was."*

Two days later, my leader summoned me to his office. I was not privy to the reason, but considering the past, I knew it would most likely not be pleasant. I prayed in tongues and asked the Lord to speak through me, as I had no idea what I was walking into.[385] The result was my leader asked me to step down from the church board; in effect, I was relieved of duty. My leader said I had embarrassed him as well as the overseers in the financial meeting regarding the revelation of leadership's unforgiveness. He made me aware of his disappointment and that he had "run out of patience," so I must be removed from the board. This was a Tuesday, and in just five days was the church business meeting. I still had a year to go on my three-year board term, so I expected my leader would most likely publicly denounce me at the meeting. Nonetheless, as I left his office, I had already decided to go to the business meeting. How they decided to notify the members, I was determined to accept. The Lord, my Redeemer, was with me. What could they do?[386]

---

[384] Romans 8:31
[385] Proverbs 16:1
[386] Romans 8:31

The morning after the meeting in my leader's office, I read in God's Word:

> **Leviticus 20:26** *And ye shall be holy unto me: for I the LORD am holy, and have severed you from other people, that ye should be mine.*[387]

As my Bible reading goes, I read the Bible straight through from Genesis to Revelation while taking notes. I read for at least one-half hour per day, six days a week. During these times, I may read one verse or multiple chapters. Following that plan, it took two and a half years to complete the entire Bible. The importance of that time frame is in the morning after I was asked to step down from the board; the verse that I read was **Leviticus 20:26**. Considering my reading practices, the chances of reading that particular verse on that particular day are approximately one in 27 million. The Lord orchestrated this reading on that day to show me He had used this rejection to release me from three and a half years of perseverance I had endured at that church. He had indeed severed me from other people.

As for the business meeting, I never made it. Three days after I was asked to step down from the board, my wife and I received a formal letter from my leader telling us we needed to find another spiritual home; my leader had effectively excommunicated us from the church. It was a convoluted form letter; the meaning was difficult to ascertain. If not read carefully, the message could have been missed. However, the next day I received a call from one of the other board members asking me what had happened; he read to me a much more scathing email sent to the board regarding all my shortcomings from the perspective of my leader. That certainly helped define the true meaning of the "form" letter I had received in the mail. I understood the feeling of being rejected and set free simultaneously. I then understood the reason God made me aware of the email that assassinated my character. He allowed me to be blessed:

> **Matthew 5:11** *Blessed are ye, when men shall revile you, and persecute you, and shall say all manner of evil against you falsely, for my sake.*

> **Matthew 5:10** *Blessed are they which are persecuted for righteousness' sake: for theirs is the kingdom of heaven.*

> **1 Peter 4:16** *Yet if any man suffer as a Christian, let him not be ashamed; but let him glorify God on this behalf.*

---

[387] Psalm 4:3

I took care not to be offended but to focus on the joy[388] of being set free.[389] Knowing the Word, I knew I must enact Romans 12:14:

Romans 12:14 *Bless them which persecute you: bless, and curse not.*

This was my third encounter similar to the story of Joseph as I was set free from the prison. I had learned all that I could in that place, and for the journey to continue, I needed to depart to commence the next part of my spiritual journey, much like Jones in the Travelers allegory.

A few days after I received the phone call from my fellow board member, I was in prayer and said to the Lord, "They disparaged my reputation." He quickly replied:

"It won't be the last time."

The Lord wanted to be sure I was not discouraged by this experience; it just comes with the territory. This was the Lord reiterating His Word:

Luke 6:26 *Woe unto you, when all men shall speak well of you! for so did their fathers to the false prophets.*

God had placed me in this church to understand perseverance and obedience regardless of the circumstances around me; by standing still, I had success-fully passed the test to completion. The day I was excommunicated from the church was almost exactly seven years to the day I had begun the journey when I asked the Lord, "Who are you? Tell me what to do, and I will do it." I had learned in order to worship God; I had to obey Him[390] through a sur-rendered life. Webster's 1828 dictionary defines **worship** as *extreme submis-sion.* Extreme submission, from God's perspective, is to lose our life com-pletely. In fact, Jesus said we must lose our life in order to find it.

When my journey began, I had no idea what "losing my life" actually meant, but I had come a long way; I had come to understand losing my life was exactly that – losing *my* life. The desires I had formulated for the plans in my life had nothing to do with the plan for which He created me. However, I now conversed daily with Him.[391] In order to progress on the spiritual path

---

[388] Isaiah 55:12
[389] Psalm 142:7
[390] John 4:23-24
[391] Luke 9:23

He predestined[392] for me, I continually listened very closely[393] to determine each step along the journey in order to precisely become who He had originally intended. However, I had not listened only but also obeyed His commands completely, not according to my understanding, but according to His Truth. Through practicing this behavior, God granted me the benefits of those who fear the Lord, receiving grace to overcome and the ability to perform levels of obedience I previously had not imagined possible. I understood the concept of grace; not only was it by grace through faith, I was saved,[394] but another facet of grace is the empowerment to overcome and achieve objectives that could never be accomplished in my own ability. These objectives are fulfilled by first trusting I heard His voice, then following His commands to completion. This is how to advance on the spiritual journey because He knows what must be done when to walk and when to stand still to progress spiritually on the path of life. God is a Spirit[395] , and by joining my spirit with His,[396] I could hear His voice[397] and perceive His plan for my life. That knowledge produces joy from within[398] and according to His Word - the joy of the Lord is my strength.[399] That strength, coupled with the power of grace, provides the ability to obey His commands, which brings extraordinary success to the journey. That means each act of obedience grows more faith to obey His next command. This is how faith is built by dutifully obeying each command regardless of the situation. The resulting spiritual growth confirms He performs His Word for those who believe.[400]

---

[392] Romans 8:29-30
[393] Mark 4:24
[394] Ephesians 2:8
[395] John 4:24
[396] 1 Corinthians 6:17
[397] John 10:27
[398] Proverbs 3:13
[399] Nehemiah 8:10
[400] Luke 1:45

CHAPTER 14

It is A Matter of Trust

Psalm 37:5 *Commit thy way unto the LORD; trust also in him; and he shall bring it to pass.*

It was about three weeks after I was excommunicated from my church that the Lord led my wife and me to a new church. One of the first sermons that struck me was how Satan uses shame to paralyze God's people; after all, according to the enemy, and ineffective follower of Christ is the next best thing to one who does not believe at all. As the sermon progressed, the Pastor showed how many attend churches with a mask and do not reveal their true selves. However, if a brave soul should remove their mask to reveal their true flaws, leaders become uncomfortable and quickly instruct that the mask be put back on at all costs. This is the behavior that shapes many in the church who seem to be in spiritual order but are, in fact, spiritually disheveled. I had taken off my mask at the board meeting and was subsequently shown the door. This is how the Lord revealed I had come to the right church at the right time; the sermon had described the last month of my journey, and I was now at the onset of the next segment of the path set before me.

Free from the constraints of my former church, I jumped at the chance to have a small home group so I could finally talk about God as He promised I could. But not yet. In my excitement, I had submitted my agenda, without inquiring of the Lord. He put a check in my spirit about it, and, even though I wanted to teach about Him with all that was in me, I withdrew the night before the deadline and immediately received peace with that decision. Instead, I told the Lord I wanted to know how to pray and joined the prayer team.

I spent a year on the prayer team, probably about 40 hours of classes concerning prayer as well as the etiquette of praying for others. The Lord had answered my prayer in a precise way, and my training was complete. The principal lesson I learned concerning prayer was to pray God's Word back to Him; any prayer warrior will proclaim this to be true. Then one day, as I was reading God's Word, He proved it; it is revealed in Psalm 119:99:

Psalm 119:99 *I have more understanding than all my teachers: for thy testimonies are my meditation.*

Webster's 1828 Dictionary defines **testimonies** as *the Word of God; the scriptures,* and Strong's Concordance defines **meditation** (*sîychâh* in Hebrew) as *prayer.* Therefore, Psalm 119:99 can be understood as:

"I have more understanding than all of my teachers: for thy scriptures are my prayer."

The Lord highly values understanding,[401] and He grants it to those who pray His Word!

Once the Lord equipped me with the power of a prayer warrior, He directed me to my next destination: the greeting team. I had come across another difficult leader and was determined to protect myself by "going silent." As the Lord had told me not to speak in the previous church, I was determined to follow that path again. However, as I was thinking the thought, He said: **"You cannot wait to be rescued; you must engage and be exalted."**

I was not sure exactly what that meant, but I was about to find out.

Watering the Cement
Meanwhile, I got a call from a friend who said she had a dream and needed to talk to me about it. The dream began as she and her sister were coming to my house in a blizzard and staying overnight in a shed outside the house. The shed was not insulated, so it was cold, but they settled in for the night. The next morning, it was springtime, and as they came out of the shed, I was watering around it. She asked, "Why are you watering the cement?" I gently replied, "Trust the process." That evening, it was winter, and again they went to bed shivering. The next morning it was warm again; as they opened the door, all they could see was beautiful pink flowers. Thus, the dream ended.

A few weeks later, I signed up for a web-driven course by a prominent evangelist and received an e-book: "Stuck in the Middle." I opened it to chapter

---

[401] Proverbs 4:7

one entitled: "Trust the Process." Later, I came to realize time and water strengthen cement; it is 50% stronger when it is kept wet while curing. The flowers? A sign of fruitful harvest.

This dream was a confirmation and encouragement of what I had been experiencing with publishing this book: Seeing hope, only to be dashed back to winter. Continually seeing hope in seemingly hopeless situations, watering what seemed like cement. I was trusting God[402] regardless of the circumstances and how hopeless they appeared.

I had been enjoying greeting, and I read a devotion one morning that confirmed it:

"Joy, not grit, is the hallmark of holy obedience."

~ Richard J. Foster

This was the obedience the Lord had instilled within me – an obedience that produces joy!

Dodging a Bullet

Feeling compelled, I decided: I needed to *do something* regarding getting this book published. I knew God could do it, but how would that happen if I had never submitted the manuscript to a publisher? As I was still thinking the thought, I got followed on Twitter by a published author who was the registrar of a writer's conference. That got me to thinking perhaps what I needed was to attend a writer's conference and the Lord would bring someone that would be interested in publishing it. So, I began looking for writing conferences across the country and settled on one by a published author who mentored just fifteen students over the course of a week. *Perfect*, I thought, *someone who could teach me about not only how to submit to publishers, but also how to market the book itself.* The location was in the exact town where my boss lived in Texas. I had worked for him for 17 years, and this was the perfect opportunity for him to meet my wife for the first time. My boss' grandkids attended school at the same church where the conference was held. All the pieces were falling together, and that usually means God is in it. However, by now, I knew God well enough to know making decisions like that warranted inquiring of Him first.[403]

---

[402] Psalm 37:5
[403] 2 Samuel 5:19

157

Many pray and trust God with what they cannot control; true discipleship is trusting Him with what you can.

Therefore, I set out on a four day fast to confirm all was well. I fully expected to receive a confirmed "yes, it is Me" from the Lord, and I had peace about it for the first three days; I even made tentative plans with my boss and researched flights and hotels.

Meanwhile, I got an email from a prominent evangelist asking for feedback on his book "God, Where are You?!" It was sitting on my desk, and I had not yet opened it. His email forced me to read his book during my fast so that I could give him timely feedback. By the time I finished, there was no doubt the Lord spoke a resounding "Don't do it! Wait for Me!" through the author's experiences; some of my experiences were almost identical. The next morning, The Lord directed me to this verse:

Isaiah 42:6 *I the LORD have called thee in righteousness, and will hold thine hand, and will keep thee, and give thee for a covenant of the people, for a light of the Gentiles;*

Later, as I got into the car, the radio played the Tom Petty Song "The Waiting" from 1981:

The waiting is the hardest part,
Every day gets one more yard;
You take it on faith; you take it to heart,
The waiting is the hardest part…

I had asked the Lord if I should go to this conference, and He answered "No!" and then confirmed it. The book I read during the fast confirmed it with statements such as: "If you are feeling you have been waiting too long and you need to do something to receive the promise, *whatever you do, don't do it!* Also, I read if you fulfill the promise through your own effort, the promise must be sustained by your effort; if you allow God to fulfill the promise, He will sustain it beyond what you can imagine.[404]

I had almost jumped ahead of God and suffered the consequences by not inquiring of Him first. It was an important lesson I would not forget: no matter how good it looks, inquire of the Lord to determine the path to take. I had learned fasting is how to inquire of the Lord. Thus, a fast is highly valuable to the overall understanding of scriptures themselves as well as the

---

[404] "God, Where are You?!" by John Bevere

proper path to take when presented with a quandary.

Many resolve to travel a good path, but inquiring of the Lord yields perfect results.[405]

One of the few who had never connected to Facebook or Twitter, I was living in the Stone Age as far as some were concerned. Then, one day the Lord impressed upon me to create Facebook and Twitter accounts. I added them both and began connecting with others, probably about ten years behind everyone else. I had about 283 "friends" as Facebook called them, but more like connections. Then one day, I connected with a Christian who had 5000 "friends," and people from that group began to be "suggested friends" to me from Facebook. Within two weeks, I also had 5000 connections, including Evangelists, Pastors, Prayer Warriors, Radio Hosts, Speakers, Writers, and many others from Africa, Pakistan, India, England, Scotland, Australia, and of course, the United States. Suddenly, I was awash in Christians all around me, able to inspire and be inspired. Then one day, I received a message from one of my newfound connections who said, "I know a publisher who would be interested in your work." I had to laugh; when justifying my decision to "go out and do something" to get this book published, I had said multiple times, "No one is going to knock on my door and say, "I want to publish your book." Yet here it was, virtually the same scenario happening on social media. This happened while my wife and I were away on a short winter vacation of solitude. I told her when I got back; I would fast for four days and inquire of the Lord as to whether I should send this manuscript to the publisher recommended from one of my connections on Facebook. Upon returning from vacation, I decided to commence the fast on Sunday at sunset and was sitting in church that same Sunday morning. The Pastor's wife approached the pulpit and stated that she had a word from the Lord; He had been dealing with her about sharing it with the congregation. She announced:

The Lord says,
The work I am doing behind the scenes is a setup. Do not be discouraged by what you do not see. The details are being worked out and may feel hidden at times, for that will be revealed soon. New purpose opportunities will be revealed soon to launch you into your destiny. Just like a bow and arrow, it seems I have had to pull you back to set up more power to propel you forward. You have not been withheld from this new season in your life. You are being prepared and set up for a greater purpose."
She said, "I had a strong impression, and I had a picture of an arrow, so I did

---

[405] 2 Chronicles 16:9

what everybody did in 2019, I googled "arrow," and I looked at a diagram of an arrow and, what does rest have to do with an arrow? I learned that before an arrow can be released, it is held back in the structure in what is called an arrow rest."

"Don't confuse the rest as being stagnant or lazy. It is the rest that is necessary to release you. The rest, or what feels like a pause, is necessary for the rapid release that is about to occur. What feels like a pause is actually preparation to propel you into your purpose."

"He has prepared you for a time like this. Everything, every part of our lives, is not wasted, every pain is not wasted. Every unexpected circumstance is not wasted.

I sat in tears because I knew it was personal. Two months earlier, my wife had signed up for an archery course to commence the following week; only the Lord could orchestrate a personal word corresponding to a life event like that. I knew this was His answer to my fast I had not yet begun. Nonetheless, I fasted the next four days to honor my word to Him.

I received another message from a Facebook friend; she knew of people in the publishing industry in the United States and South Africa, and to let her know when I was ready, she would introduce me. In the meantime, I had continually connected to pastors and radio show hosts and commentators across the country as well as a television show host in Australia.

However, I was concerned about my general lack of love for people, so one day, I mentioned it to the Lord.[406]

True Transformation

I have taken personality tests many times throughout my life, and I always scored the same – in the "D" quadrant – a direct communicator. Only three percent of the world scores in that category, and I understood why. While direct communicators do have redeeming qualities, communication is not one of them. Generally, I experienced problems communicating with the other ninety-seven percent of the population; I was misunderstood, and as a result, often mistreated. It was something I had come to accept in life, but I hoped perhaps someday I would break through the haze of complications surrounding my ability to relate to people and somehow experience the joy of friendship easily available to others. I had been unable to ascertain precisely how to emerge from the fog, but soon I would receive understanding through obedience that would change my life forever. However, there were questions to be answered, which would reveal exactly how much change would be needed.

---

[406] Psalm 138:8

As a precaution, before accepting my marriage proposal, my wife requested I undergo a personality test by a psychotherapist to determine if we were compatible. As I pored over the questions, I decided to reveal my true character rather than rely on what I determined to be my best qualities to answer what I had deemed an "interrogation." After all, I wanted to be honest, even to my own detriment, to avoid any semblance of deceit, which would eventually be revealed as the relationship progressed. The questions seemed to drive at the core of my shortcoming repeatedly:

"Do you have any friends?" "No"
"Do you want any friends?" "No"
"Do you care about people?" "No"

And so, the examination continued for 66 questions or so. I figured by the fifth question, the marriage proposal was probably moot but decided I would cross that bridge when necessary. A week later, I returned to the psychotherapist's office to receive the results. Apparently, I had a score like his; and to my surprise, he recommended to my fiancé that we were compatible. I consequently forgot about the examination into my character, and more importantly, the answers I did not know how to solve.

My work as a software engineer allowed me to circumvent relationships with others; I frequently found when I did interact for any length of time, I would eventually offend them somehow. Looking back, I realized I would often speak the truth without love, not understanding the ramifications. My mother affectionately referred to my brother and me as the "Sons of Thunder," the nickname Jesus gave to James and John when they desired to call fire down from heaven to incinerate a village that had rejected Jesus. But there was hope: after all, John had become the one who wrote all about love in the gospel of John as well as the books of first, second, and third John. I knew I was deficient in this area of loving others, and since it was the second commandment, I addressed it in my devotions. I spoke to the Lord: "I don't love people," I confessed, but there was no reply. So, I said, "If it is OK with You, then it is OK with me, but I think there is something wrong." Still, no answer; however, the Lord already had a plan in place. I just had to wait for Him to bring it to fruition. It would be two years before He addressed it, but one day I was in devotions, and He said to me:
"I want you to become more affable."
Then He brought me to 2 Timothy 2:24:

2 Timothy 2:24 *And the servant of the Lord must not strive; but be gentle unto all men, apt to teach, patient,*

161

Strong's defines **gentle** (**ēpios** in Hebrew) as *affable, admitting others to free conversation without reserve, complaisant, pleasing in manners; courteous; obliging; desirous to please.*

I thought about it; how could I possibly do that? Then it dawned on me: I would become a greeter at the church. After all, how much trouble could I get into by just saying, "good morning?" I realized the best way to become more affable would be to engage with people through greeting. So, in obedience to His Word, I joined the greeting team, which consisted of fifteen greeters at the time; but within two weeks, I was asked to become a leader, which meant I would be building relationships with others in the group. So, I accepted the position and trusted the Lord to protect me from myself, since I was in this position from obedience to His command. The church culture was for us to be connected to each other constantly, so the director of the greeters would contact me once weekly. After a month, I was asked to perform the duties of the liaison between the director and the team leaders. I was rapidly gaining responsibility because I obeyed the Lord when I joined this team. The reporting structure of this ministry was greeters, reporting to team leaders, who reported to the captain who reported to church staff. At the time, the captain slot was not filled and the Lord impressed on me: upon receiving the title "captain," it will be time for me to leave: all will have been grasped He had placed me here to learn.

> *When the Lord asks you to do something you know you cannot do; He is going to do it through you, creating spiritual growth within.*[407]

At this point, however, my concern was keeping the group intact and growing. It was a few months later I was walking through the church foyer thinking about how long it would be before His promise in my life would take shape. Just then, the Holy Spirit directed my attention to a leader (I knew to be harsh) about 40 feet ahead and said:

"If I cut you loose too early, you will be just like that"

I quickly replied, "I will stay here as long as You want; I don't want to be like that." I then became more relaxed in my current state; I knew during this time; He was working on molding me to fit the purpose for which He had created me. As the months passed, I continued to handle all aspects of the greeting team as it grew to twenty, then thirty greeters. One day, as I was

---

[407] 2 Corinthians 12:10

standing in the church hall overseeing the greeters, I suddenly felt a love for them; something I had never understood before. It was a love for people I had been missing my entire life, a compassion for others as if everything that concerned them concerned me. I truly felt as though these people were like family. It was a feeling of joy, love, and peace all mixed together: a warm feeling all was right with the world.[408] Just at that moment, I saw a vision of a quick flash of a vine growing from a corner within my heart. It was later I would find this verse in Psalm:

Psalm 57:7 *My heart is fixed, O God, my heart is fixed: I will sing and give praise.*

The word **fixed** (**kûn** in Hebrew) is defined by Strong's as *prepared, fixed, perfect.* However, the Ancient Hebrew Lexicon of the Bible defined **fixed** as *what I had seen in the vision:*

Stand *co:* **Root** *ab:* **Sure:** *The pictograph* k *is a picture of the open palm, the n is a picture of a seed.* **Combined these mean "opening of a seed". When the seed opens, the roots begin to form the base of the plant by going down into the soil. The plant rises out of the ground forming the stalk of the plant.** *A tall tree can only stand tall and firm because of the strong root system which supports it.*

The vision I saw was recorded in the Bible as the meaning to have *the heart fixed.* My heart had been fixed by the Creator, not because I was different than anyone else, but for one reason only: I had performed His Word. Seven years prior, the Lord had instructed me to fast in order to receive humility.[409] I believed it, so I did it; and because I did it, He performed His Word. But I did not know of the other benefits for those He considered humble:

Psalm 10:17 *LORD, thou hast heard the desire of the humble: thou wilt prepare their heart, thou wilt cause thine ear to hear:*

The word **prepare** is the exact same word (**kûn**) used in Psalm 57:7 for **fixed.** The Lord showed me with a vision that He had fixed (perfected), my heart because I had obeyed His Word through fasting. It took time to come to fruition, but He performed His Word, just as He said He would:

1 John 2:5 *But whoso keepeth his word, in him verily is the love of God perfected: hereby know we that we are in him.*

---

[408] 1 John 2:5
[409] Psalm 35:13

Once I knew I had received a new heart, I searched for the scripture that specifically described what happens when the Lord gives a new heart; I found it in Ezekiel 36:26-28:

> **Ezekiel 36:26-28** *A new heart also will I give you, and a new spirit will I put within you: and I will take away the stony heart out of your flesh, and I will give you an heart of flesh. And I will put my spirit within you, and cause you to walk in my statutes, and ye shall keep my judgments, and do them. And ye shall dwell in the land that I gave to your fathers; and ye shall be my people, and I will be your God.*

That was the verse I was looking for, but I was overwhelmed when I read the next two verses:

> **Ezekiel 36:29-30** *I will also save you from all your uncleannesses: and I will call for the corn, and will increase it, and lay no famine upon you. And I will multiply the fruit of the tree, and the increase of the field, that ye shall receive no more reproach of famine among the heathen.*

After giving me a new heart, the Lord said, "I will call for the corn." It was the final step to receiving the promise of the vision of the little white house in the cornfield from five years earlier. I needed a new heart for the vision to be accomplished, and He would soon confirm it again.

Meanwhile, I would soon learn while God directs a ministry leader to provide opportunities for people to grow; it is God who provides for the success of a ministry.[410]

> ### The world uses people to complete work; but God uses work to complete people.

The director of the greeters had left the church, and we were left in a conundrum: we lacked direction, so I began to perform the director's duties to keep the group intact. I was now leading 31 people by default: no doubt, the Lord's design. To maintain order, I sent an email to the group asking each greeter a question concerning the logistics of greeting schedules, and I received one reply that used the minimum words possible, just a direct straight answer with no softening – it almost seemed rude. Taken aback, I remarked aloud "That person is mean." Immediately the Holy Spirit said: **"That was you."**

I have learned upon hearing the Lord's voice, which He is altogether unlike

---

[410] 1 Corinthians 3:6

us: He does not say something and take it back, nor does He say things He does not mean. He used the past tense; He said that *was* me, but not anymore! He changed me on the inside. Because He said it, I believed; and because I believed it, I obeyed, and because I obeyed, He performed His Word. He had changed the very core of who I was in six months; ***something I had been unable to accomplish in 53 years***.

There were 15 greeters when the Lord placed me in that group; now six months later, there were 31; and within a month of the Lord saying "***that was you***," He had more than doubled the leaders in the group, and I had been asked to "lead the leaders." The Lord had placed me in a situation for spiritual growth, and because I obeyed, He anointed me and blessed me with love for others; and the church was also blessed in the process. I had come to realize through accepting new greeters into the group that some would have the personality for it, while others seemed to lack the necessary tact to be successful. However, I knew I was in the latter group; I had no business as a greeter due to the lack of compassion I had exhibited in the past, *and I knew it*, yet here I was, in charge of the entire group. That was how I came to understand the mantra of my group from God's perspective:

> ***Some people greet because they have what greeting needs; some people greet because greeting has what they need.***

I was able to understand it because I was the least of all the greeters in the group - I had no natural affection for people when I began to work in the ministry, yet *the Lord used the ministry to truly transform me* before my own eyes, something I had been told long ago was not possible. I was a new creature,[411] fitted for a plan He had set in place long before.[412] He needed my obedience to bring it to fruition, and once I fully submitted to every Word He spoke, He was able to perform a miracle in me, beyond what I ever knew could be. Amazed, I said to Him, "Lord, what you did to my heart!" His reply was a phrase I will never forget:

> **"Life is a song, and people are the individual notes. For the first time in your life, you were able to see the music."**

Leadership, Growth, and Rest

Every month at our church, each ministry leader stands before a group of new volunteers and gives a synopsis on the logistics of their ministry; the

[411] 2 Corinthians 5:17
[412] Jeremiah 29:11

need for the ministry, what is accomplished, and how serving is really a necessary part of spiritual growth. I was telling my wife how people were drawn to the greeting team: "When I pitch the greeting opportunity to the new volunteers," I said, "We always receive several new greeters." As I was speaking, I made a mental note: I would need to personally give that pitch every month, no matter how inconvenient, to make sure the greeting group had the best possible opportunity to grow. Just then, the Holy Spirit said: **"It's not you."**

Then He imparted the meaning: **"I am going to bless the presentation no matter who gives it -- *because* of you."**

True to His Word, God provides the increase; that is how leadership works. God gives rest through obedience; because I obey Him, He does the work of drawing people and blesses the organization, no matter who speaks the words.

Permission to Choose, Never a Rush
It was about a year prior to my involvement in the greeting team that one day the Holy Spirit said: **"You don't need to stay here."**

I knew it was probably because, concerning my difficult next-door neighbor, I thought to myself, "*I am going to stay here until I die to prove I can love my neighbor.*" Upon hearing that I did not need to stay there; my understanding of the Holy Spirit's statement was this book would be published, and I could move to wherever I chose. I was half right. It was not yet time for the book to be published, but I had been released from my caged thinking. I could move, but I could not yet see the provisions in place, so I continued watering the cement. It was about a year later I was walking into a store when I had an epiphany: I was done living in my current house. A complete peace swept over me; it was time to go. I explained it to my wife, and she asked me what time I had received that epiphany. We realized the Holy Spirit had imparted to her the same feeling at that very hour. Four days later, my leader at the church called and asked if I would consider being the captain of the greeting ministry, confirming what the Lord had spoken six months earlier: upon receiving the title "captain," it will be time for me to leave. I began to transition my work as the captain and pray for a replacement because I know God would not have me leave the greeter ministry in the lurch.

I had been researching where I wanted to retire someday and concluded I wanted to live in the Appalachian Mountains of western North Carolina. As a software engineer for a large company, I had been working from home for over ten years. My manager and director had just retired, and our workgroup had been moved to a new organization. I could now see God's provision, so I asked if I could move to North Carolina and keep my job. "No problem" was the answer, so I knew God was clearing a path for me to begin the next season of my life.

Given hope and a future,[413] my wife and I took a month-long vacation in North Carolina; we found choosing a house in the mountains must be carefully considered. The Lord put a few people in our lives He used to guide our decision. I had a house in mind and asked the Lord what I should do – I needed to know ASAP as I did not want it to be sold before I was ready. He replied: **"No rush, Scott."**

I have learned exactly that: God is never in a rush; He always has everything in hand. It is I that need to bridle the anxiety of what I can see and trust what I cannot. For some reason, even though I know Him, that is not always easy to do; selling our house was a lesson in patience and trust. Having heard God's voice and taken action in faith, it would seem as though everything would just "happen" with no fanfare, but as time passed, it was evident He was more interested in spiritual growth than physical comfort. Although it seemed like a long and sometimes painful process, God had His hand in it from the very conception: the actual decision to move was hinted at by Him over a year prior, and the final conclusion came after lessons learned in expectation, humility, trust, and understanding. I came to understand I needed to disconnect from my time leading the greeters emotionally; I was still engaged in fond memories of that perfect time when I led the greeting group even though I had relinquished my post. It was a time of fruitfulness, success, and joy like I had never experienced; the Lord had anointed me to lead the group, and I enjoyed every moment. But it was time to forget the things which are behind:

Philippians 3:13 *Brethren, I count not myself to have apprehended: but this one thing I do, forgetting those things which are behind, and reaching forth unto those things which are before,*

I understood for the first time Philippians 3:13 referred to forgetting successes as well as difficulties; I had to forget the past success so I could engage my heart to press on to the future. In this case, this verse is inextricably linked to 1 Corinthians 13:11:

1 Corinthians 13:11 *When I was a child, I spake as a child, I understood as a*

---

[413] Jeremiah 29:11

child, I thought as a child: but when I became a man, I put away childish things.

For the first time, I understood putting away childish things is to value the spiritual over the flesh. Decisions that feed fleshly desires are childish and must be put away and replaced with godly decisions which generate spiritual growth: this is spiritual maturity at work.

There was only one viable house for rent when we moved, and it had just become available five days before we signed the lease. It was all we could have hoped for and more; it was not by luck, but divine providence. Eight years prior to moving to North Carolina, the Lord told me to "***Prepare for Rain,***" and after receiving a new heart, He said, "***For the first time in your life you were able to see the music.***"

We are now living amid a rainforest, with an internationally known music school fifteen minutes away, where students attend from all over the world and performances are conducted by world-renowned music conductors. Then the Lord made it even more personal. When I lived in Massachusetts, I enhanced my backyard with rhododendrons and created a waterfall with a stream. As I was driving up the mountain where I now live in North Carolina, the Lord directed my attention to the indigenous plant all over the area: rhododendrons; on top of that, the town is in "The Land of the Waterfalls," the county with over 200 waterfalls, the most in the United States. It is above all I could ask or think.[414] That is knowing the Creator; He creates the desires within, then fulfills them for those who love Him.[415]

In the meantime, I wanted to determine if there was a market for this book I was writing. I had come to understand the Lord works through actions of faith, so I checked with Him to determine if I should put an ad on Facebook to research the market. He approved, so I posted a picture of the book cover and a short paragraph of how it came about – the picture itself and the meaning of it. I spent $100 and sent the ad across the United States over a ten-day period and waited. Meanwhile, I researched ads on Facebook; I was not looking for income, but to evaluate interest, so the ad return (number of clicks on the ad) was my primary measurement. According to the articles I read, a click rate of 1-2% was a good return.

I watched as the ad generated a click rate of 15% - 20% across the United States, United Kingdom, Canada, South Africa, South Korea, Australia, New York City and Texas. The last two were cities chosen to determine if the

---

[414] Ephesians 3:20
[415] 1 Corinthians 2:9

click rate would hold in a smaller demographic, and it did. By the time a month had passed, I had spent $1000 and reached 136,582 people; and 24,907 had engaged the ad (clicked or commented): an 18.2% click rate.

My wife told me she had a vision of the numbers rising as we were praying, so I said, "Let's pray now." Just as she began the Holy Spirit spoke to me: **"I am building the network."**

True to His Word, the Lord was going to sustain this book; all I had to do was stay out of His way; but as time an opportunity passed, frustration began to set in once again. I was attending a church where a much younger generation primarily staffed leadership. Over time, I saw I would have no influence in this church; I felt hidden and unimportant even though I believed I could have contributed in some way. Then on Father's Day, the pastor called a man (about my age) to the pulpit to honor him. Surprised, I watched him make his way to the stage, and the Holy Spirit immediately said: **"It is by design; you have been kept hidden because your time has not yet come."**

I received a final confirmation on December 19, 2019, from a Facebook friend in Australia who saw this post by Nate Johnston and sent it to me:

In a vision yesterday I saw an arrow being pulled back in a bowstring until it couldn't go back any further, then suddenly it was released, then I saw the same clock I have seen over and over this year and the hands started to spin around rapidly. We have been in a season of time where it feels like time itself has been slowed down, the brakes of delay have been in effect, and it's been hard to move forward in any area, but as we enter 2020 that bowstring is about to be released both globally and personally. We are entering an era where it will feel like time itself has sped up, and the wheels of motion will move forward rapidly. Kings and kingdoms will be affected; the destiny and future of nations will advance quickly. You will move from dealing with delay and hiddenness into having to steward your revealing and being launched into influence. It will not be a time to hide in the shadows or wallow in days past, but it will be a time to stand to be counted. You have said "Will I ever get there?" and the Lord says to you today that In a year's time, you will look back and be in awe of how far you have come in only one year. You will not smell like smoke anymore. You will not even be able to remember how deep the pain was anymore because the joy and fulfilment will be so deep. You will not be singing the dirge anymore, but the wedding song will be your soundtrack of a new day. And you will then say "I don't even know how I got here, but I know it's the GOODNESS of the Lord. I almost gave up, but now, here I am experiencing it!

This confirmed the message I had received on February 17, 2019, earlier in this chapter. Much like the Word of the Lord I received at the beginning of this journey, "*You have the feet of a priest*" was given at my local church, and then confirmed in Greece; this word was also given at my local church, and then confirmed in Australia.

A Hidden Obstacle

Many years ago, the Lord gave me a promise, and I would often wonder how He would bring it to fruition. At the time, my thoughts were the most logical prospect was to bring it about through an authority figure.

After being disappointed by my leader, the Lord said: **"You don't need a man."**

That was a liberating thought; my future was not connected to this man who did not value me. Years would pass as the sanctification process continued. Eventually, I moved to a different state in the U S. through the Lord's direction. A new location, a prepared heart, and a new church; I was sure I was now on the threshold of the promise. However, a situation developed with an offense at the new church and my reputation was damaged through no fault of my own. I was livid, seeing this as a threat to my future as my leader now had a false notion concerning my character.

I was in prayer and complained to the Lord, "I was faultless in this fiasco, yet I paid for the entire debacle with my reputation."

He replied:

"I was faultless, and I paid for the sins of the world."

"I hadn't thought of that," I replied.

Then He said:

"Are we done now?"

I immediately knew what he meant. I was again assessing the possibility of the promise based on a man's thoughts of my character. I had misunderstood what the Lord said years earlier: "*You don't need a man.*" I had miscalculated and thought He was speaking about the person in front of me at the time; however, when He speaks, His words are forever. Joseph made the same miscalculation when asking the butler to remember him when released from the prison. God delayed Joseph's dream two additional years to ensure Joseph understood: it would be the Lord Himself who granted the promise, not a man.

The Lord had asked me: **Are we done now?** I quickly answered: "Yes, we are done." From that moment forward, I would no longer tie the fulfillment of His promise to the action or inaction of any man. I had spent the better part of the previous ten years carefully obeying the Lord to be sure not to delay His Promise in my life. Although this incident was painful, He exposed another more subtle obstacle to my progress. It was a *belief* hidden deep within, a thought that had become an imagination, then an idea which permeated and compromised the faith so vital to my progress. This belief was the Lord would use a man to bring about His Promise. But it was skewed. When Joseph was finally promoted from prison to second in command, it was through a dream given to the king; the butler, who had not thought of Joseph in two years, suddenly remembered him. This was God's provision, a dream and a memory, not by man's plan, but by God's divine intervention. That is where I had misjudged just as Joseph had; I believed the correct process, but it was how that process would come to fruition that stymied the promise. I believed I had to find the right person at the right time to make it happen, and that was the very reason the promise was delayed. The Lord brought it to my attention to correct my thinking, my very *belief*, that however the Promise would be granted; it would be the Lord Himself who orchestrated the pieces to accomplish it, not the pieces themselves.

Two months later, I had a dream that I was in a room with a printing press talking to a publisher interested in my book, and he paid me $50 just for the privilege of reading it. Once I handed him the manuscript, he gave me a receipt with just one word written on it: ***Promises***.

171

CHAPTER 15

Navigating the Lighted Path

Psalm 16:11 *Thou wilt shew me the path of life: in thy presence is fulness of joy; at thy right hand there are pleasures for evermore.*

The Lord gave me yet another allegory; this time Jones and Smith are in the jungle and directed to find the path to the wedding feast. This allegory underscores the importance of *the journey* rather than the destination. How *the journey unfolds is the true goal;* and is of more importance than what most see as the destination itself.

The Path to the Wedding Feast

Smith and Jones are standing in the jungle, and the Lord hands them swords.[416]

"I want you to study the sword closely. [417,418] There is a wedding feast 500 miles due north."[419,420]

Smith takes a quick look at the sword and sees it is extremely sharp.[421] Noting that 500 miles of the jungle is a long way, he decides to waste no time and begins hacking a path through the jungle.

Jones studies the sword and looks ahead. He knows he cannot perform this task, so he drops to his knees and says:

"I cannot do this, Lord; I don't know what to do. I do not have the ability or stamina to do this. I need your help."

---

[416] Hebrews 4:12
[417] 1 Timothy 4:13
[418] 2 Timothy 2:15
[419] Matthew 22:2
[420] Psalm 75:6 (north)
[421] Hebrews 4:12

The Lord tells Jones to stay put and study the sword. He does just that,[422] although he hears Smith making progress through the jungle while he has not even yet begun. Days turn into weeks and weeks into months. He can no longer hear Smith cutting through the jungle – Smith is so far advanced. Yet he continues to stay put until one day the Lord tells him:[423] **"It is time for you to move; begin making a path due west."**

Jones does not understand[424] but believes this is the Lord's voice as he has been studying the sword for months. So, he begins cutting a path due west.

Meanwhile, Smith has determined if he progresses one mile each month, he will reach the goal in less than 42 years. He now works to achieve at least one mile a month and attempts to achieve more, because he knows as time passes, he will be older and not able to advance as efficiently.

One day as Jones is progressing west, the Lord tells him to stop and wait,[425] and to continue to study the sword. He stays put and comforts himself by telling the Lord of his fears, hopes, and desires. One day as he opens his eyes, he sees a mile marker – he is at the 100-mile mark. He is greatly encouraged by this just as the Lord tells him:

Make a path due south for 10 miles; there is someone there I want you to talk to.

Jones immediately begins going south[426] and eventually comes to a clearing where a woman is waiting, completely worn out and discouraged. Jones explains to her[427] what he knows about the Lord and how he has invested time knowing His voice and building a relationship with Him.[428] The woman is greatly encouraged as she has been on this journey alone until this time, and is determined to follow Jones' advice. As they part ways, Jones turns and sees he is at the 200-mile marker.

Smith meanwhile, has run into some major obstacles – deep thick brush has

---

[422] 1 Timothy 4:15
[423] John 10:27
[424] Isaiah 55:8
[425] Psalm 46:10
[426] John 15:14
[427] Hebrews 3:13
[428] Jeremiah 9:24

impeded his progress, and he has had to reassess his one mile per month goal, hoping there will be some easy going ahead so he can catch up to the schedule he has set.

Days, months and years pass, and finally one day Smith breaks through to the wedding feast he has been searching for and is relieved that he has finally reached it. He is quite worn out, but it was worth all the toil, as this has been his goal since the Lord spoke to him at the beginning of the journey.

At the same time, Jones arrives, not appearing tired,[429] and not surprised, but rather delighted.[430]

Smith enters the wedding gate, takes a right, and climbs the stairs[431] to find an open seat just in time for the feast to begin. Jones walks in and pulls up a chair close to those who are sitting near the gate[432] and they begin to exchange stories about their journey through the jungle. Jones soon realizes, though, these people do not have stories like his own, but of turmoil, fear and pain.

Smith meanwhile is overlooking the feast from where he is seated when someone approaches him and says, "Sir, how did you get in here? You do not have the proper clothes."[433]
Smith has no reply. He is escorted to the gate and removed from the feast.

Suddenly, Jones hears his name being called and is escorted to the seat where Smith was sitting.[434] As he is assessing his new position, Jesus approaches and says:
"Well done Jones. You heard my voice and obeyed it.[435] That was the one reason my Father created you – to worship Him and fellowship with us here. Do you have any questions?"

Jones looks around and asks where Smith is sitting.
"Smith was escorted out.[436] He did not study the sword. If you re-member, while you took the time to study the sword carefully, Smith

---

[429] Matthew 11:30
[430] Psalm 1:2
[431] Luke 14:8
[432] Ibid
[433] Matthew 22:12-13
[434] Luke 14:10
[435] John 10:27
[436] Matthew 22:12-13

immediately began cutting a path to this destination. His entire goal was just to get here. He spent his entire life doing the work,[437] but he never heard My voice. Therefore, he spent most of the time doing things I did not tell him to do. To man, it appeared as though he was making great progress, but I do not look at the outside. I test the heart and the mind.[438] Smith was so preoccupied with getting here; he never took time to study the sword. The first and great commandment is to love Me with all your heart, soul, mind, and strength.[439] Smith never knew Me because he ignored this principle,[440] and therefore he failed at many of the other commandments.

The first commandment is so important because once you know Me; I am able to guide you through the proper path you must take to get here.[441] Each person is different, and the hidden path is only revealed through Me – I am the door.[442] One person cannot follow the path of another person to get here. Unfortunately, many attempts to follow paths set up by men, ignoring the very path I put in the sword itself. No one can possibly know their specific path to get here – that is the mystery.[443] They must build a relationship with Me; that is part of the path. So, although Smith did a lot of work and arrived at the destination, his goal was flawed because he did not know Me.[444]

The people sitting at the table where you first came in the gate did not make it here as Smith did, but they took some time to know Me. They were limited by fear, sickness, and disobedience - all limits of their faith. So, although they invested some time with Me, most of their life they were primarily waiting to be rescued.[445] I had pity on them because although they had the same goal as Smith, they did understand the first commandment and tried to obey Me; they just did not have the faith to progress the way I had planned for them.[446] Others were given tests and failed to pass. They were put on a lesser path where

---

[437] Romans 4:4
[438] Romans 8:27
[439] Mark 12:30
[440] Matthew 7:23
[441] Psalm 73:24
[442] John 10:9
[443] Colossians 2:2-3
[444] Matthew 7:23
[445] 1 Corinthians 3:15
[446] Revelation 3:8

they obeyed the remainder of My commands, but they failed to acquire the fear of the Lord so notably described in the sword.[447] Therefore, they were allowed into the Kingdom, but not as rulers. You will see some of them living in your region.

You chose to follow my commands and continued to obey Me – this brought you to a true relationship with Me. I know some of the things I wanted you to do did not always seem to make sense, but they were designed to remove any remainder of your sinful nature so you would be sanctified and perfected. You prioritized your relationship with Me, so I knew you could be trusted.[448]

Now, since you were proven on earth, you can be trusted here in the Kingdom. There are vast provinces here – far and wide.[449] Because you chose Me over everything during your life on earth, you will be greatly rewarded here in heaven.[450] You will be a ruler over an entire region, which consists of many provinces.[451]

My Father, the Holy Spirit and I will fellowship with you each day or anytime you want to talk, or if you have any questions. After this feast, we will take you for an orientation of the provinces so you can see your residence and the people living in your region.

You will learn how the physical laws we set up on earth do not exist here, so travel is instantaneous.[452] You already know how we communicate, as you were communicating with us daily when you lived on earth. We are so excited to have you here!"

And Jones, one more thing. This is just the beginning. You will remain here for eternity, and we will never be separated.[453] You are a part of our family, and we will always be together.[454]
Forever.[455]

This allegory is all about knowing God through relationship versus attempting to know God through works. When building a relationship with the

---

447 Proverbs 19:23
448 Matthew 6:33
449 Revelation 21:16
450 Matthew 16:27
451 Revelation 2:26
452 Hebrews 11:5
453 1 John 2:25
454 Revelation 21:7
455 John 10:27,28

Lord, *the journey is the destination.*

Knowing God is the High Calling

Philippians 3:14 *I press toward the mark for the prize of the high calling of God in Christ Jesus.*

Knowing God is not **what** you know or how long you have known it; it is **who** you know and how well you know Him. Knowing God is to love Him, and loving Him is our true destiny; it is *why* we were created; it is not the most important thing in life; it is the only thing. He created us to live with His presence *within* us; that we may know and understand Him and commune with Him; and **through that relationship,** we would show others that knowing Him is the ultimate goal[456] of our very brief lives on earth.[457] The end of our lives on earth is the beginning of our eternity, and our eternity depends entirely upon the depth of our relationship with the Creator at the very moment this life is completed. God will not judge us on what we have accomplished in His name, but rather **why** we chose to accomplish it. He will examine our motives to determine whether our actions were driven by self-notoriety or by obedience to His voice. We cannot begin to hope to know God through our own devices; He teaches us about Himself.[458] While God may use man to reveal details of His character, it is the Spirit of God that provides the revelation of the mysteries He has hidden; to be given only to those who know Him **intimately.**

Our eternal destination will be determined by whether or not **He knows us.**[459, 460] The depth of our intimacy with Him on earth will drive the level of obedience to His Word, and that level of obedience will, in turn, drive us to a deeper intimacy with Him. That intimacy will ultimately determine the level of rewards received while in His presence.[461] It is important to understand the rewards from God's perspective.[462] He holds understanding, knowledge, and wisdom above rubies, silver, and gold.[463,464] We know this is true because

---

[456] Jeremiah 9:24
[457] James 4:14
[458] Psalm 25:12
[459] Galatians 4:9
[460] Matthew 7:23
[461] Hebrews 11:6
[462] Genesis 15:1
[463] Job 28:12-17
[464] Proverbs 8:10

these three: wisdom, knowledge, and understanding can be acquired while here on earth.

Praying for wisdom must be done without wavering, but there is a more excellent way to acquire it:

Proverbs 9:10 *The fear of the LORD is the beginning of wisdom: and the knowledge of the holy is understanding.*

These attributes are highly esteemed by God and are ***only available to those who obey His voice.*** How deeply we know Him is determined by how quickly and completely we obey His commands, and ***He rewards obedience with intimacy.***[465]

Heaven is not the goal; it is the place prepared for those who have achieved it; an intimate relationship with God, resulting in life transformation.

This is the definition of one of the facets of ***grace*** (***charis*** in Greek): ***the divine influence upon the heart, and its reflection in the life.*** The goal is not a place to reside; rather, the goal is to be perfect in Him.[466] Perfection is accomplished through obedience and patience,[467] which drive intimacy, which, in turn, drives us to our anointed calling, viewed as a success by God. Our anointed calling is a specific purpose God called us to do in this life. He reveals our purpose ***only when we so deeply invested in our relationship with Him that we will forsake all to accomplish it. It is then that we have utterly lost our life in order to save it.***[468]

This is the abundant life Jesus came to give.[469] We receive it through a deep intimate relationship with God and doing His Word. Through this relationship, He reveals our purpose that He has already anointed us to accomplish. He already guarantees our success; our only task is to find our purpose and remain deeply committed to the Lord. It is then we receive physical blessings on earth and spiritual rewards in heaven as we live according to what He called us to do. He anointed us for this specific purpose, so we cannot fail

---

[465] Proverbs 9:10
[466] Matthew 5:48
[467] James 1:4
[468] Mark 8:35
[469] John 10:10

as long as we walk in the light, as He is in the light.[470] This is also known as abundant life; acquired through investing in a relationship with the Creator.

Building a Relationship: Works vs Dedication and Devotion

We cannot work for salvation.[471] However, oftentimes work is confused with the investment when we are building a relationship with the Lord.[472] The Bible refers to "works" as the fruit of the tree;[473] the fruit cannot produce itself; it is a result of healthy roots. Building a relationship with the Lord is all about *investing in the roots of our tree through dedication and devotion*. The commitment with which we invest in the roots is solely responsible for the quality and quantity of the fruit. This is where many misunderstand the order of Jesus' commands in Mark 12:

> **Mark 12:30-31** *And thou shalt love the Lord thy God with all thy heart, and with all thy soul, and with all thy mind, and with all thy strength: this is the first commandment. And the second is like, namely this, Thou shalt love thy neighbour as thyself. There is none other commandment greater than these.*

Not understanding how to build a deep relationship with the Lord, many immediately begin loving their neighbor by doing good works; they love their neighbor, in order to know the Lord. However, it is possible to love your neighbor without knowing the Lord as Jesus reveals in Matthew:

> **Matthew 7:21-23** *Not everyone that saith unto me, Lord, Lord, shall enter into the kingdom of heaven; but he that doeth the will of my Father which is in heaven. Many will say to me in that day, Lord, Lord, have we not prophesied in thy name? and in thy name have cast out devils? and in thy name done many wonderful works? And then will I profess unto them, I never knew you: depart from me, ye that work iniquity.*

Our relationship with the Lord is the source of all good fruit. Trying to generate fruit in and of ourselves may look good on the outside, but good fruit must be produced from roots that have been carefully developed. Webster's 1828 definition of root:

> ***ROOT***, verb transitive
> *To plant deeply; to impress deeply and durably. Let the leading truths of the gospel be deeply rooted in mind; let holy affections be well rooted in the heart.*

---

[470] 1 John 1:7
[471] Ephesians 2:8
[472] Philippians 2:12
[473] Luke 6:44-45

In Scripture, to be rooted and grounded in Christ is to be firmly united to him by faith and love, and well established in the belief of his character and doctrines. Ephesians 3:17.

Ephesians 3:17 *That Christ may dwell in your hearts by faith; that ye, being rooted and grounded in love,*

Many become frustrated by lack of good fruit, but the condition of the roots determines the quality of the fruit.

When we refer to work, we are referring to the fruit of the tree. We in ourselves cannot produce fruit, just as a tree branch cannot produce fruit on its own; it must be connected to the tree. The health of the tree is known by observing the fruit[474] , and the tree can only be healthy if the roots have been properly developed. Healthy roots will produce a healthy tree, which brings forth good fruit.[475, 476] The quantity of fruit produced is determined by the time we invest in preparing the soil and developing the roots, and the diligence with which we care for the tree determines the quality of the fruit. We make our tree good by first preparing the ground;[477] the ground is prepared by seeking the Lord.[478] We invest in our roots by joining them with His;[479,480] once we join with Him, our tree has the capability to produce good fruit;[481,482] and He provides the growth.[483]

The increase is directly proportional to our investment[484] in connecting our roots with His by the relationship we have built with Him. The increase is of *measures of faith*[485] *and grace.*[486,487]

---

[474] Luke 6:44
[475] Matthew 7:17
[476] Matthew 12:33
[477] Hosea 10:12
[478] Matthew 6:33
[479] Revelation 22:16
[480] 1 Corinthians 6:17
[481] John 15:5
[482] Jeremiah 17:7-8
[483] 1 Corinthians 3:7
[484] 2 Corinthians 9:6
[485] Romans 12:3
[486] Ephesians 4:7
[487] John 1:16

Observation shows curiosity, but action reveals commitment which begets wisdom:

Psalm 119:105-106 NUN. *Thy word is a lamp unto my feet, and a light unto my path. I have sworn, and I will perform it, that I will keep thy righteous judgments.*

Matthew 7:24 *Therefore whosoever heareth these sayings of mine, and doeth them, I will liken him unto a wise man, which built his house upon a rock:*

Through building our relationship with Christ, we receive priceless attributes of wisdom, understanding, and knowledge,[488] and as our relationship with Him develops, we also receive the fruit of the spirit.[489]

The investment we make in a relationship with the Lord produces the works tested at Judgment;[490] those that will abide are produced from intimacy with Him. All other works contrived by actions outside that relationship will be burned, resulting in a loss. It is important to note our relationship with the Lord is determined by Him, not us. As mentioned in chapter one, many will believe they know the Lord personally because they know about Him. However, like any relationship, our intimacy with the Lord takes devotion to maintain. That investment is outlined in the Bible, and the Lord taught it to me over the course of seven years: The Seven Pillars: Devotions, Tongues, Tithe & Offering, Speaking God's Word, Fasting, Obedience, and Perseverance.

The Seven Pillars
Many times, I have heard preachers say, "You can have as much of God as you want." I found that to be unequivocally true. The level of our relationship with Him is solely our responsibility; He is always available;[491] the time He spends with us is determined upon our availability to Him. Prioritizing faithfulness through deep fellowship with the Lord, and exercising the courage to be set apart through constant communication with Him, prepares us to be ready to do His will.[492] The Lord taught me the seven pillars are *the foundation* for a perfect relationship with Christ. It is a question of intimacy; many who have a relationship with the Lord are not where they could or should be; that is the prerogative of each person. Knowing Him personally by performing that which He instructed us to do for devotions to know Him,

---

[488] Proverbs 2:6
[489] Galatians 5:22-23
[490] 1 Corinthians 3:11-15
[491] Matthew 28:20
[492] Philippians 2:13

is *how* He sets us apart.[493] That is, detaching the affections from the world and exalting affections to the supreme love of God Almighty through obedience to His Word.

The seven pillars are how to have an optimal relationship with Him. They are *not all required for salvation*, but *they are all required to receive abundant life.*

The impact of God on your life is directly proportional to your devotion to His.

How we enter heaven will be dependent upon the depth of our relationship with the Lord; those without understanding will have their work burned up and will enter heaven *as by fire:*

> **1 Corinthians 3:15** *If any man's work shall be burned, he shall suffer loss: but he himself shall be saved; yet so as by fire.*

However, God will reward those who lose their lives in order to find them.[494] They will enter heaven abundantly:

> **1 Corinthians 3:14** *If any man's work abide which he hath built thereupon, he shall receive a reward.*

> **2 Peter 1:10-11** *Wherefore the rather, brethren, give diligence to make your calling and election sure: for if ye do these things, ye shall never fall: For so an entrance shall be ministered unto you abundantly into the everlasting kingdom of our Lord and Saviour Jesus Christ.*

The next ark will be our relationship with the Lord; the only thing upon which the Lord will judge believers is how close (or far) our life has been lived as compared to the original blueprint He created for us to accomplish. The only way to understand His original plan is to know and obey Him; the seven pillars are the map to finding that design to assure success in Him. Everyone has the same opportunity for success from God's perspective. Whether rich or poor, educated or illiterate, privileged or unprivileged, God sees everyone the same;[495] He searches for those with a friendly heart towards Him and "He shows Himself strong on their behalf."

---

[493] Leviticus 20:8
[494] Matthew 16:25
[495] Acts 10:34

2 Chronicles 16:9 *For the eyes of the LORD run to and fro throughout the whole earth, to shew himself strong in the behalf of them whose heart is perfect toward him…*

The word perfect in this verse means *especially to be friendly.*
The entire objective of this book is to reveal that anyone can achieve a friendly and perfect heart through a perfect relationship with Jesus by exercising the seven pillars, the seven physical actions that generate spiritual results.

These seven Biblical actions are the map to an intimate relationship with God. The **details** of each action (pillar) are **different for each reader** as they are personal to the relationship each of us has with the Creator. The Lord determines the details of each physical activity for each person. Paul said God inspired the scriptures that the man of God may be perfect.[496] Oswald Chambers describes Christian perfection in *My Utmost for His Highest®:*

"Christian perfection is not, and never can be, human perfection. Christian perfection is the perfection of a relationship with God that shows itself to be true even amid the seemingly unimportant aspects of human life."[497]
~ **Oswald Chambers** *My Utmost For His Highest®*

Webster's 1828 definition of **perfection** reveals it is not the same for everyone:

PERFECTION, *noun* [Latin perfectio.] The state of being perfect or complete, so that nothing requisite is wanting; as *perfection* in an art or science; *perfection* in a system of morals.

"Moral *perfection* is the complete possession of all moral excellence, as in the Supreme Being; **or the possession of such moral qualities and virtues as a thing is capable of."**
~ **Webster's 1828 Dictionary**

This means each person has different capabilities of perfection. Often others' perception of perfection, or even our own understanding of perfection

---

[496] 2 Timothy 3:16-17
[497] Taken from *My Utmost for His Highest®* by Oswald Chambers, © 1935 by Dodd Mead & Co., renewed © 1963 by the Oswald Chambers Publications Assn., Ltd., and is used by permission of Our Daily Bread Publishing, Grand Rapids MI 49501. All rights reserved.

stymies our growth; this happens when we attempt to live by others' or even our own self-perceived standards. However, the Lord is the definer of our spiritual capabilities of being perfect in Him:

Hebrews 12:23 *To the general assembly and church of the firstborn, which are written in heaven, and to God the Judge of all, and to the spirits of just men made perfect,*

The Holy Spirit determines what action each of us takes to join our spirit with the Lord. One person may spend an hour in prayer while another prays throughout the day. Someone may fast twice a year while another may fast regularly, as determined by the Lord. It is a spiritual battle, and the Lord has need of different kinds of warriors for different purposes to reach different people. One may feel unimportant when their task is to procure the ammunition; however, without them, the soldiers on the front line can do nothing. Never underestimate what God has called you to do; He anointed you for this time[498] for a specific reason. When you understand and walk in your anointing, to Him, that is true perfection. That is why He highly values understanding. The path is personal, efficient, restful, and will garner abundant life and eternal rewards, as we become the exact representation He created us to be. It is important to note the *physical actions generate spiritual fruits,* so although spiritual fruits are not part of the seven physical actions, they (love, joy, peace, patience, gentleness, kindness, faith, humility, and self-control)[499] *are the results.* For instance, obedience is one of the seven pillars of the foundation of an intimate relationship with God, and love perfected is one of the results of obedience (keeping His Word):

1 John 2:5 *But whoso keepeth his word, in him verily is the love of God perfected: hereby know we that we are in him.*

It is not what you accomplish in Him that counts; the final measurement of success will be what He accomplishes in you.

The seven pillars are necessary to fulfill a perfect relationship with Jesus; however, *the details of each pillar must be found through investing time with the Lord.* It is important to note that more time invested in doing each pillar will not necessarily garner a closer relationship with the Lord because the *time invested is defined by Him, not us.* I made a conscious decision to engage my heart; that was the only requirement to set the relationship in motion. That conscious decision drew Him near, and He began to reveal the path. At that point, the

---

[498] Esther 4:14
[499] Galatians 5:22-23

journey had begun; I committed to obeying His voice. It was not always easy because growth never is, but *when this life is over, and the only thing I bring to the Judgment Hall is my relationship with Him, I will be glad I chose to know Him more intimately.*

The Premonition
The Lord imparted the understanding of Final Judgment to me through an experience in District Court. I had been speeding on a major highway and subsequently received a speeding ticket. Of course, my first thought was to deny I deserved it. *After all, others were going faster than I was,* I thought. I was hoping it was a warning, but when the officer handed me the ticket, I saw there was a $300 fine. *Great,* I thought, *that translates to probably an additional $1000 in insurance surcharges over the next several years.* Later that day, I decided to appeal the ticket on the off chance that I could get it removed from my record. When I arrived at the District Court about four weeks later, the Lord sent a young man who asked me if I was going to see the magistrate regarding a speeding ticket. "Yes," I replied.

He offered: "Let me tell you what to do. No matter what, keep your mouth shut and tell them you want to see the judge. No matter what they say, do not argue with them; just tell them you want to appeal to the judge. I have had so many tickets I cannot count them, every one of them dismissed. Just do what I am telling you, and you will be found not guilty."

I entered the room, and an officer representing the state police was present as well as the magistrate. Remembering the advice I received in the hallway, I declared that I wanted to appeal to the judge. The police officer set a date for the hearing and told me it would cost $50; I paid the fee, and the hearing date was set for about a month away.

When I arrived at the courthouse, I took note of the several state police officers present – the officer who pulled me over was not in the room. Rumor has it if the actual police officer who issued the citation does not show up, you are found not guilty. I thought this was a good sign; however, the courtroom was full of people and backed up with cases, so I figured I was not out of the woods yet; he could show up at any time. I watched each plaintiff lose case after case as the judge found him or her 'responsible.' The court officer would announce each case number, the name of the plaintiff, then the infraction in detail. No matter how prepared the plaintiff – some brought pictures, others presented detailed arguments, etc. The judge determined every one of them to be responsible, and they were forced to pay the fine associated with the infraction. I thought this was a bad sign as I sat uncomfortably in a full

185

courtroom. After about two hours passed, I suddenly heard my name announced, and I nervously rose to my feet and waited for further instruction. As I walked toward the front of the court, I was preoccupied, mulling over exactly how I was going to push the words from my mouth that I did, in fact, commit the infraction but was here to throw myself on the mercy of the court. However, the next words I heard were, "You were found not responsible; come and get your paperwork." There was no mention of a violation, and the court officer never called the name of the police officer who pulled me over to determine if he was present. The judge determined I was not responsible before I ever showed up. What were the determining factors? After all, I had committed the infraction. The only facts that determined the outcome were my past record and my attitude at the different levels as I advanced through the court system to the final hearing date. Humility, respect, and my past record were the main factors, I realized, as I recounted my treatment of the police officer, as well as the police representative and the magistrate in the first hearing. These factors were all the information the court had to determine whether to find me responsible.

This is exactly how it will be on the final day as we stand before God's Judgment. Some will be unprepared, others will think they are prepared, and God will only pardon those who know Him.[500] We will not be able to change our destiny at Final Judgment; all we will have is the past, and whether or not He knows us will seal our fate.

Do not miscalculate your relationship with the Heavenly Father. Many bask in His love and mercy, ignorant of His conditions regarding obedience. His throne is based upon righteousness and judgment:

Psalm 97:2 *Clouds and darkness are round about him: righteousness and judgment are the habitation of his throne.*

Commit to devotions with Him daily and join your spirit with His;[501] then He will lead and give you an understanding of righteousness and judgment.

Psalm 23:3 *He restoreth my soul: he leadeth me in the paths of righteousness for his name's sake.*

---

[500] Matthew 7:23
[501] 1 Corinthians 6:17

Proverbs 8:20 *I lead in the way of righteousness, in the midst of the paths of judgment:*

Proverbs 2:8-9 *He keepeth the paths of judgment, and preserveth the way of his saints. Then shalt thou understand righteousness, and judgment, and equity; yea, every good path.*

Proverbs 12:28 *In the way of righteousness is life; and in the pathway thereof there is no death*

Conclusion

There is nothing special about me; I am just an ordinary man with a relentless desire to please the extraordinary God living within. God is looking for those who are willing to have their hearts perfected by Him. Through this ten-year journey, I found out that knowing God is not knowing **about** Him, nor attempting to do the good works outlined in His Word *through my own decisions*. Rather, I discovered *loving the Lord God with all my heart, mind, soul, and strength* is the *true purpose* of life, and knowing Him is accomplished through physical acts of obedience.[502,503,504] These acts caused me to draw near to Him, and in turn, He drew near to me.[505] It is then I heard His voice and was able to choose a deeper relationship by obeying the commands I heard. It is through obedience He sanctifies and imparts wisdom, knowledge, and understanding; *this is how to build the spiritual house described in His Word and how to establish it permanently.*[506] Abundant life is available to any and all who wish to attain it; there is no circumstance, education, or income level that makes one person more special to God; He values obedience to His Word[507] and *searches the earth*[508] for any who are willing to diligently seek Him.[509] Everyone has the exact same opportunity to know God, and obedience is the key to all understanding.[510] Obeying the first commandment is the beginning of the journey.

> *Our one true purpose is to know Him, and doing His Word is the genuine path to accomplish it.*

---

[502] Psalm 111:10
[503] Proverbs 1:7
[504] Proverbs 9:10
[505] James 4:8
[506] Proverbs 24:3
[507] Hebrews 5:9
[508] 2 Chronicles 16:9
[509] Hebrews 11:6
[510] Psalm 111:10

It is also the fundamental element to avoid the pitfall of those who think they know God but will be told to depart from Him at the final judgment.[511] He created us for one purpose: *to have fellowship with Him.*

I now understood Paul's statement in Philippians:

> **Philippians 3:9-16** *And be found in him, not having mine own righteousness, which is of the law, but that which is through the faith of Christ, the righteousness which is of God by faith: That I may know him, and the power of his resurrection, and the fellowship of his sufferings, being made conformable unto his death; If by any means I might attain unto the resurrection of the dead. Not as though I had already attained, either were already perfect: but I follow after, if that I may apprehend that for which also I am apprehended of Christ Jesus. Brethren, I count not myself to have apprehended: but this one thing I do, forgetting those things which are behind, and reaching forth unto those things which are before, I press toward the mark for the prize of the high calling of God in Christ Jesus.*

I now recognized the importance of finding God's perfect will for my life, the meaning of abundant life,[512] and how to receive it. The most important task I ever completed is finding the path to know God intimately. Knowing Him, or rather, *being known by Him*, is of the utmost importance because this life is just a vapor;[513] decisions made during this infinitesimally brief time will forever affect whether we receive eternal life. Actions during this life will not just determine our eternal destination, but also *the quality of our eternal life as well.* Understanding these things, I adjusted my value system to match His, so I could please the One who created me:

> **Jeremiah 9:23-24** *Thus saith the LORD, Let not the wise man glory in his wisdom, neither let the mighty man glory in his might, let not the rich man glory in his riches: But let him that glorieth glory in this, that he understandeth and knoweth me, that I am the LORD which exercise lovingkindness, judgment, and righteousness, in the earth: for in these things I delight, saith the LORD.*

Choosing obedience became the basis for all my life decisions, and through that obedience, God rewarded me with *the revelation of the unveiled truth to set others free and enter into His kingdom on earth as it is in heaven.*

He designed a specific plan for me before I was born; my purpose was to

---

[511] Matthew 7:21-23
[512] John 10:10
[513] James 4:14

find and follow it. When I obeyed Him, He illuminated the path for me to follow. When that path is perceived and followed through relentless obedience, abundant life is given, and rewards are accounted in heaven. All knowledge, wisdom, and understanding come from Him; everything *that exists is His.*[514] That is why the Lord highly values our obedience; it is a result of surrendering our free will to Him; the one thing He does not possess.[515]

Throughout His Word, the Lord provides many signs through stories, historical accounts, and direct quotes about the importance of a personal relationship with Him. The following two verses illustrate the high value of knowing Him:

John 17:3 *And this is life eternal, that they might know thee the only true God, and Jesus Christ, whom thou hast sent.*

Ecclesiastes 12:13 *Let us hear the conclusion of the whole matter: Fear God, and keep his commandments: for this is the whole duty of man.*

May God bless your journey with revelation and power as you draw ever closer to the Lord Jesus Christ in your quest to know Him intimately.

"The difference between who you are and who you want to be is **what you do."**

Be the one without shoes!
In Him,
Scott A. Harris
P.S.
> *You can have as much of God as you want.*
> *Do not shortchange yourself,*
> **Your future depends on it.**

---

[514] Psalm 24:1
[515] Deuteronomy 6:2

A Personal Note

Writing this book was a journey into the recent past that fulfilled the dream the Lord placed in my heart – to speak about God. When the Lord told me, I could receive anything I wanted from Him, I determined what gave me the most joy was talking about Him. He revealed who He is, then granted the gift of communication: speaking and writing. The course of the journey took me through difficult times in preparation to step into His promise. It took patience and perseverance as I suffered through disappointment and rejection. I would come to understand disappointment often comes from dashed expectation, so I learned to put my hope in God:

> **Philippians 1:20** *According to my earnest expectation and my hope, that in nothing I shall be ashamed, but that with all boldness, as always, so now also Christ shall be magnified in my body, whether it be by life, or by death.*

I persevered to the end because, although I did not know the timing of His plan, I always knew it was better than mine.

What's Next?

Wherever the Lord directs, nonetheless, my hope is to glorify God wherever He takes me. It has been an absolute pleasure writing this book; I had a chance to relive some of those astonishing moments as the Creator manifested Himself in my life in many ways. More has happened since, and I have been trying to keep up the journal while writing this book, a challenge, to say the least. He is continuously teaching, and I am constantly learning; it is not always easy, but in the end, it is always rewarding.

Afterword

If you are reading this book and you do not know the Lord Jesus Christ, all you need to do is tell Him you want to be saved from the sinful nature you were born into. God's Word says *now* is always the time:

2 Corinthians 6:2 *For he saith, I have heard thee in a time accepted, and in the day of salvation have I succoured thee: behold, now is the accepted time; behold, now is the day of salvation.*

Confess with your mouth aloud that you need forgiveness and believe in your heart Jesus was raised from the dead to save you.[516] At that exact moment, your old life will pass away, and all things will become new.[517] Then tell someone! Find a church that preaches Jesus is the Son of God, and He died and rose again to save us. Attend it regularly. Then get a Bible and read it regularly **and do what it says**; this is God's love letter to us – it is alive, and He speaks to us through it. After confessing, Jesus is Lord and believe He rose from the dead to save your sins; here are several suggestions to help you progress on the path:

- Find a Spirit-led church
  Be sure to find a church that believes:
  The Bible is the Word of God
  Jesus is the Son of God, and He rose from the dead
  To be saved, you must be born again
  Believers can be Spirit-filled and Spirit-led
  Then get involved in the church by helping others

- Read the Bible regularly
  Suggestions:
  Read the Bible *aloud* to avoid distractions and mind wandering (this

---

[516] Romans 10:9,10
[517] 2 Corinthians 5:17

193

also fulfills the "Speaking God's Word" pillar)
Read the Bible by "time." Read at least 15 or 30 minutes per day
rather than by chapter. This will eliminate "rushing through" to
reach the end of a chapter. Do not worry how far you get in the
timeframe – sometimes, it may only be one verse!

Read first thing in the morning and the last thing at night.
- Journal while reading the Bible
  Write anything the Lord speaks to you. This book is a testament of
  journaling; it is a culmination of ten years of life events correlated to
  God's Word.

- Ask God for the Baptism in the Holy Spirit[518]
  Some believers do not believe in speaking in tongues. I had a friend
  who attended two different churches: one believed in tongues, and
  the other did not. He was confused, so he knelt next to his bed and
  asked the Lord, "Is this real?" He began speaking in tongues immediately. Tongues are a fundamental ingredient of knowing God intimately.[519]

- The Seven Pillars
  Invest in implementing the seven pillars of your life. These pillars
  are what God created to draw us closer to Him, so He will draw
  closer to us.[520] Note the pillars are necessary for abundant life; however, the resources you invest in implementing each one is entirely
  between you and the Lord: that is your personal relationship with
  Him. For instance, how much time you spend in devotions is *strictly
  between you and the Lord.* The seven pillars are *not a formula for knowing
  God*; they are the *foundation[521] (the physical actions) of a relationship with
  Him that generates the spiritual results, which, in turn, build the house.*

- Remember, Spiritual growth comes from obedience!
  Obey what you hear from the Lord, no matter how you feel. The
  Bible clearly tells us not to forsake the gathering together of our-
  selves.[522] Attending church is a requirement of obedience to God's

---

[518] Luke 11:13
[519] 1 Corinthians 6:17
[520] James 4:8
[521] 1 Timothy 6:19
[522] Hebrews 10:25

Word. If able, attend an actual physical church; an integral part of growth comes from interacting with others.[523] God often speaks through the pastor to impart knowledge, comfort, or correction.

Do not discount the value of physically attending church. The sermon is 5% of growth, and the other 95% comes from applying it to over-coming offense, forgiving, and loving others. It is how to flourish.[524]

- However, to grow spiritually, you must also have a close relationship with the Creator. Through that relationship, He reveals your spiritual gifts, your one true purpose, and your individual specific path. He created each of us with a specific purpose in mind.[525] Knowing that purpose or how to achieve it is inherently found in knowing *Him*. It is not what you know or how long you have known it;[526] it is whom you know (God) and what you do with what He tells you. One of the most important lessons I learned through this journey is knowing God is not accomplished through head knowledge, but by engaging the heart. That is because all we have comes from Him;[527] the only thing we can offer Him is *our will to obey.*

Do not settle for a temporary one-sided relationship; invest in a personal and eternal one.

---

[523] Proverbs 27:17
[524] Psalm 92:13
[525] Jeremiah 29:11
[526] 2 Timothy 3:7
[527] 1 Chronicles 29:14

About the Author

Scott Harris grew up in the church, and although he became an elected official in multiple churches, he had a crisis of faith and came to understand he did not value what God valued. In desperation, Scott looked at the sky and asked, "Who are you? Tell me what to do, and I will do it." What followed was the most extraordinary journey of spiritual revelation and understanding directly correlated to God's Word. The Lord imparted revelation knowledge on *how to* know Him through the key to the kingdom of God: ***Relentless Obedience***

ABOUT
KHARIS PUBLISHING

KHARIS PUBLISHING is an independent, traditional publishing house with a core mission to publish impactful books, and channel proceeds into establishing mini-libraries or resource centers for orphanages in developing countries, so these kids will learn to read, dream, and grow. Every time you purchase a book from Kharis Publishing or partner as an author, you are helping give these kids an amazing opportunity to read, dream, and grow. Kharis Publishing is an imprint of Kharis Media LLC. Learn more at https://www.kharispublishing.com.

www.ingramcontent.com/pod-product-compliance
Lightning Source LLC
Chambersburg PA
CBHW062100080426
42734CB00012B/2703